FRONT
AND CENTER

Other AUSA Books

Bussey   FIREFIGHT AT YECHON: COURAGE & RACISM IN THE
    KOREAN WAR

Galvin   THE MINUTE MEN: THE FIRST FIGHT–MYTHS &
    REALITIES OF THE AMERICAN REVOLUTION

Hilsman   AMERICAN GUERRILLA: MY WAR BEHIND
    JAPANESE LINES

Kelly   THE GREEN BERETS IN VIETNAM, 1961–71

Kinnard   IKE 1890–1990: A PICTORIAL HISTORY

Kinnard   THE CERTAIN TRUMPET: MAXWELL TAYLOR & THE
    AMERICAN EXPERIENCE IN VIETNAM

Matthews & Brown   ASSESSING THE VIETNAM WAR

Matthews & Brown   THE PARAMETERS OF WAR

Matthews & Brown   THE PARAMETERS OF MILITARY ETHICS

Matthews & Brown   THE CHALLENGE OF MILITARY
    LEADERSHIP

Sajer   THE FORGOTTEN SOLDIER: THE CLASSIC WWII
    AUTOBIOGRAPHY

Related Journals*

Armed Forces Journal International
Defense Analysis
Survival

*Sample copies available upon request

An AUSA Book

FRONT AND CENTER

Heroes, War Stories, & Army Life

Edited by L. James Binder

PUBLISHED WITH
the Institute of Land Warfare
Association of the U.S. Army

BRASSEY'S (US), Inc.
A Division of Maxwell Macmillan, Inc.

Washington · New York · London · Oxford
Beijing · Frankfurt · São Paulo · Sydney · Tokyo · Toronto

U.S.A. (Editorial)	Brassey's (US), Inc. 8000 Westpark Drive, 1st Floor, McLean, Virginia 22102, U.S.A.
(Orders)	Attn: Brassey's Order Dept., Macmillan Publishing Co., 100 Front Street, Box 500, Riverside, New Jersey 08075
U.K. (Editorial)	Brassey's (UK) Ltd. 50 Fetter Lane, London EC4A 1AA, England
(Orders)	Brassey's (UK) Ltd. Headington Hill Hall, Oxford OX3 0BW, England
PEOPLE'S REPUBLIC OF CHINA	Pergamon Press, Room 4037, Qianmen Hotel, Beijing, People's Republic of China
FEDERAL REPUBLIC OF GERMANY	Pergamon Press GmbH, Hammerweg 6, D-6242 Kronberg, Federal Republic of Germany
BRAZIL	Pergamon Editora Ltda, Rua Eça de Queiros, 346, CEP 04011, Paraiso, São Paulo, Brazil
AUSTRALIA	Brassey's Australia, P.O. Box 544, Potts Point, N.S.W. 2011, Australia
JAPAN	Pergamon Press, 5th Floor, Matsuoka Central Building, 1-7-1 Nishishinjuku, Shinjuku-ku, Tokyo 160, Japan
CANADA	Pergamon Press Canada, Suite No. 271 253 College Street, Toronto, Ontario, Canada M5T 1R5

Brassey's (US), Inc., books are available at special discounts for bulk purchases for sales promotions, premiums, fund-raising, or educational use through the Special Sales Director, Macmillan Publishing Company, 866 Third Avenue, New York, NY 10022.

Library of Congress Cataloging-in-Publication Data

Front & center : heroes, war stories & army life / edited by L. James Binder.
    p.   cm. — (An AUSA book)
    "Published with the Institute of Land Warfare Association of the U.S. Army."
    ISBN 0-08-040586-X. — ISBN 0-08-041063-4 (pbk.)
    1. United States. Army—Military life. I. Binder, L. James. II. Title: Front and center. III. Series: AUSA Institute of Land Warfare book.
U766.F76   1991
355.1'0973—dc20   91-7476
                                                           CIP

British Library Cataloguing in Publication Data

Front & center : heroes, war stories & army life.
    1. Armies. Military life
    I. Binder, L. James II. United States Army III. Army magazine
    355.10973
    ISBN 0-08-040586-X

PRINTED IN THE UNITED STATES OF AMERICA

10 9 8 7 6 5 4 3 2 1

An AUSA Book

The Association of the United States Army, or AUSA, was founded in 1950 as a not-for-profit organization dedicated to education concerning the role of the U.S. Army, to providing material for military professional development, and to the promotion of proper recognition and appreciation of the profession of arms. Its constituencies include those who serve in the Army today, including Army National Guard, Army Reserve, and Army civilians, and the retirees and veterans who have served in the past, and all their families. A large number of public-minded citizens and business leaders are also an important constituency. The Association seeks to educate the public, elected and appointed officials, and leaders of defense industry on crucial issues involving the adequacy of our national defense, particularly those issues affecting land warfare.

In 1988 AUSA established within its existing organization a new entity known as the Institute of Land Warfare. Its purpose is to extend the educational work of AUSA by sponsoring scholarly publications, to include books, monographs, and essays on key defense issues, as well as workshops and symposia. Among the volumes chosen for designation as "An AUSA Institute of Land Warfare Book" are both new texts and reprints of titles of enduring value that are no longer in print. Topics include history, policy issues, strategy, and tactics. Publication as an AUSA book does not indicate that the Association of the United States Army and the publisher agree with everything in the book, but does suggest that the AUSA and the publisher believe this book will stimulate the thinking of AUSA members and others concerned about important issues.

v

Contents

CONTENTS

Preface

Besides a sublime gift for expressing mankind's most profound thoughts about itself, its world and its Maker, what else did Cervantes, Tolstoy, Dante, Jonson, Goethe and Spenser have in common? Along with many other literary immortals whose creative genius will awe as long as there is civilization, at one time in their lives they were soldiers.

That those who wear the sword have also been some of the world's mightiest wielders of the pen has an incongruity about it that might seem to fly in the face of the fact that the soldier's ultimate purpose, in the eyes of many, is to destroy while the writer's is to create. All kinds of correlations present themselves as possibilities when one considers these contrasting goals. Often the making of a writer-soldier was that in many early societies all male citizens were expected to participate in the nation's defense. Cervantes, Tolstoy and Jonson, to name a few, apparently were able to reconcile these contradictions, for they took to the warrior's life with zest and recalled their war experiences with pride. It is conceivable that battle contributed to their greatness, for few calamities that befall mankind can equal war in its capacity to test the limits of mind and body, and show man at his best and worst.

To be sure, these giants of literature achieved their fame after they had returned from the wars, although it seems probable that whatever drives such men to express themselves was sown long before they were old enough to take up arms. The desire, even compulsion, that persons in uniform have to write has always been a source of wonder to me. Soldiering is hard work and so is writing, and yet practically any article that was authored by an active-duty officer or enlisted person for *ARMY* was written after the military day was over or whenever the writer could find some spare time. This is remarkable dedication in a profession in which there are no time clocks and seven-day weeks are routine.

Whatever spurs the modern soldier to write may be the same spark that has been glimmering in the minds of comrades-in-arms for many years, for the military journal is a very old tradition. Back into the last century and perhaps beyond, a prime factor undoubtedly has had to be an urge to communicate in a profession in which rapport between arms and units is vital in battle. It is the way of professionals in all fields to strive for ways to improve on the "state of the art" by sharing ideas, teaching and stimulating discussion. Too, a soldier's life often is more exciting than the average citizen's: wars, historic events and even just being in far-off places most people never see, can generate first-rate stories that burn to be told.

Or, as in the case of Ulysses S. Grant and his superb memoirs, the motive simply was to make money, at least when he first undertook to write what has become a literary classic. Others, like Liddell-Hart, Mahan and Clausewitz, won fame and left enduring marks on their profession, surely one of the most coveted rewards to which a member of any field of endeavor can aspire.

The range of topics in the manuscripts that find their way to *ARMY* is very broad, but so is the Army. Leadership is a favorite theme, as are tactics, strategy and "this is how we do it in our unit" pieces which can cover everything from keeping a company roster to simulating a firefight. During the war in Vietnam and after, the magazine published a steady stream of after-action reports, often written at a firebase or tactical operations center in forward combat areas. History is perhaps the most popular subject from the standpoints of both the freelance contributors and our readers. Where there are soldiers, there is humor, and so it is in *ARMY* where it is emphasized enough that it has become a hallmark in an area of publishing which, by and large, is too serious.

While perhaps 80 percent of *ARMY*'s outside contributors wear the uniform, are retired career professionals or belong to reserve components, many of the best articles that have appeared over the years have come from civilians. Some of them are fulltime freelancers and many, like their military colleagues in wordsmithing, write when they can find the time.

The editor of a magazine like *ARMY* reads thousands of manuscripts in the course of his or her duties. Despite the considerable respect I have for anyone who undertakes something as difficult as writing an article for publication, unfortunately the vast majority have to be returned to their authors, the casualties of a winnowing process in which the reasons for eschewal may range from space limitations to any of a multitude of disqualifiers. A few, perhaps one in 20, are kept for publication. Out of those that make it to the printed page, maybe one in 100 has something about it that makes an editor remember it with special fondness. The gem could be a 150-word anecdote or a 7,500-word cover story. The number of words doesn't count; it's what they say and, when orchestrated with verve, they can make an editor's heart sing.

The idea of putting some of these pieces into a book originated with the publisher, Brassey's (US), Inc. General Jack N. Merritt, U.S. Army retired, president of the Association of the U.S. Army (AUSA) liked the concept, and so did Lieutenant General Richard L. West, U.S. Army retired, director of AUSA's education arm, the Institute of Land Warfare. Work began on *FRONT AND CENTER*. There was a precedent for the volume we had in mind. Fifty years ago or so the *Infantry Journal*, *ARMY* magazine's predecessor, published a similar book. Named the *Infantry Journal Reader*, it was immensely popular for its time and is today regarded as a collector's item.

The *Infantry Journal* was a remarkable publication. Staffed by uniformed active-duty personnel, it was an official Army publication which was given an extraordinary amount of leeway to let its contributors express themselves freely. Most of the names that were to become famous in World War II—Marshall, Eisenhower, Patton, Bradley, MacArthur—had appeared in its pages as authors at one time or another. They and their fellow contributors expressed themselves as they saw fit, whether it was taking on a sacred cow or outlining a more effective way of training a regiment. It was a tradition that *ARMY* has worked hard to emulate.

One way in which *ARMY*, the professional magazine of the Association of the U.S. Army, is not like its illustrious forebearer is that it is not an official publication. Its charter, as carried on its masthead, is simple and broad: "*ARMY* is a professional journal devoted to the advancement of the military arts and sciences and representing the interests of the U.S. Army."

The standards for inclusion in our new book were just as broad, although if any of the "judges" had ever been called upon to explain precisely what we were looking for I doubt if any of us could have given an answer that would have satisfied even us. The criterion settled upon was "readability," which upon first glance might seem to be fraught with all kinds of frustrations for a group trying to reach a concensus. As it turned out, there was a remarkable degree of agreement on which articles measured up to this seemingly hopelessly subjective term.

Quite simple, "readability" to the judges meant that the article had to be something anybody, soldier or not, would pick up to read for enjoyment at the end of the day. It could absorb, inspire, instruct, amuse, sadden or any of hundred other things the printed word holds for the reader.

We have been careful not to label our collection the "best of *ARMY*," for there are many articles and essays which had to be passed over because of other criteria: we wanted to offer the reader as broad a sampling as possible which meant that lengthy articles of great merit could not be used; subject matter had to be varied; no author's work could appear more than once; and dated material was ruled out.

The "jury" was a hard-working board of volunteers from AUSA's staff and the *ARMY* magazine staff under the project coordinator, Colonel James D. Blundell, U.S. Army retired, assistant director of the Institute of Land Warfare. They reviewed articles from *ARMY* magazines dating back to when it was founded, and from their choices a working list of well over 300 articles and essays was compiled. This was passed around for votes and what was left (about 100) went to the final judges. From the deliberations came the bits and pieces that make up *Front and Center.*

L. James Binder
Editor in Chief
ARMY Magazine

FRONT
AND CENTER

PART ONE

THE WARRIOR SPIRIT

CHAPTER ONE

OMAK

by Edmund G. Love

I n the 30 years or more since I served as a combat historian in World War II, the question most frequently asked of me is, "Who was the best soldier you ever knew?" The answer is easy: Artie Klein.

I first met Artie Klein at the battle for Eniwetok. He was then 33 years old, a veteran of 18½ years' service in the U.S. Army. He stood five feet 11 inches tall and was squarely built with narrow shoulders and narrow hips. The beginnings of a beer belly bulged out over the top of his pants. He had wide, soft brown eyes, almost doe eyes. He had a slightly hooked nose and a skeptical smile that he bestowed on very rare occasions.

He walked with small, mincing steps and wore his overseas cap perched just over the right eyebrow, the way a tough would wear it. And make no mistake about it, Artie Klein *was* a tough in spite of that innocent pair of eyes. There was something of the clown about

3

him. He had a sardonic sense of humor and was prone to making wisecracks which displayed the worldly wisdom he had picked up in the old regular Army.

Artie Klein was a Jew. He was born in the Williamsburg section of Brooklyn, the son of an immigrant father and mother. Shortly before World War I, Artie's father joined the New York National Guard and served in France with the 106th Infantry, a Brooklyn regiment. During his overseas service, the older Klein was promoted to sergeant, an honor of such magnitude for an immigrant Jew that it could not be ignored.

He was proud of those stripes and grateful to the country that bestowed them upon him. He reenlisted after the war and stayed in the Army for 20 years. He moved about from Army post to Army post, spending his furloughs with his wife and son in the little flat that nestled under the Williamsburg bridge.

The result of his long absences from home was a son who was largely undisciplined. Artie ran loose in the Brooklyn streets. He was a leader of street gangs, a brawler and devoted to petty crime. He quit school as soon as it was legally permissible. When it became apparent that he was going to be sent to reform school, he took the only step he could think of: he lied about his age and joined the U.S. Army. He was just 14 years old.

Artie Klein's regular-Army career was undistinguished by any standards. He served on the China station, in the Philippines, Hawaii and Panama. He knew the address of every bar, whorehouse and gambling dive from Shanghai to Governor's Island. He never rose above the rank of private. Strangely enough, his father was disappointed that his son never achieved the rank of sergeant, yet he was proud that Artie had become a career soldier and, after the old man's retirement in 1937, he bragged to everyone in Brooklyn about the chip off the old block.

At the time of Pearl Harbor, Artie Klein was stationed at Ft. Benning. A few days after war was declared, in one of those blanket orders the Army sometimes issued, Artie was promoted to sergeant and put to work drilling recruits.

He was not enchanted. The three stripes cramped his style, but the news of his promotion pleased his father so much—a fact which amused Artie—that he decided to go along with the gag, as he put it. After 16 years in the Army he had absorbed enough knowledge to hold his rank instinctively.

Two things became apparent at once. He was an expert on every infantry weapon and he had a flair for teaching, although his favorite

4

phrase was, "Now youse men listen to me." These two factors brought him to the attention of his officers and he was soon promoted to technical sergeant as an armorer.

In the summer of 1942, desperate for officers, the Army issued another blanket order sending all top three graders at Benning to Officer's Candidate School. He was graduated in the fall, was commissioned a second lieutenant, and assigned as a tactical officer in charge of weapons instruction at the Infantry School.

This rapid rise from private to second lieutenant was almost too much for Artie Klein's father. The news came shortly before the old man died of cancer and he got out of bed and marched down to Governor's Island to ask one last favor of an old friend there.

He was from the old country and he remembered that in Germany service in the famous old regiments was an established tradition among the great families who passed rank and honor from generation to generation. He asked that Artie serve in *his* old regiment, the 106th Infantry, which was then a part of the 27th Division, stationed in the Hawaiian Islands.

Artie Klein was not pleased to find himself assigned to the 106th Infantry. The colonel was a West Pointer who had had long dealings with soldiers of Artie's type. To him, Artie was a bum. He was more at home in a sleazy bar than he was in an officers' club, and his table manners were not calculated to win him friends in the officers' mess.

He was an outsider and remained so for some time. But there was one good thing. Most of the enlisted men in the 1st Battalion, to which Artie was assigned, came from the Williamsburg section of Brooklyn. They murdered the English language with the same aplomb.

They were tough. Some of them had even belonged to street gangs. Artie knew how to handle them. It was rumored that he fought most of his men out behind the latrine at some time or another in the first six months. It was also rumored that Artie lost every fight. He was a brawler, not a good fighter. It made no difference. He was dead game and there was something indomitable about him that soon won the respect and devotion of every man in the battalion. The men sensed that he was still an enlisted man at heart, and that he was one of them.

Artie certainly did nothing to endear himself to the other officers in the regiment. In the officers' club he might have passed as the bouncer, but never as a member. His very entrance was hostile. He would push his little potbelly in the door and take up a stance just inside with his hands on his hips and his hat cocked over one eye.

His whole attitude suggested that he was ready to fight his way inside, if necessary. It was the women, more than anything else, that got Artie into trouble in the officers' clubs. It was one of his basic principles never to have anything to do with a beautiful woman. He liked the fat ones, the ugly ones, the old ones.

"They're pleased when I say something nice to them," he said once. "After that they're afraid I'm gonna go away. I never struck out with one in my life."

From time to time Artie would escort one of his 200-pounders into one of the clubs. She might have three teeth missing, or be barefoot. He would wave her to the bar with the deference most men give a duchess. As long as the woman stayed, Artie's eyes would wander the room, his ears cocked for the inevitable insult. As often as not it came and, as often as not, Artie would lose another fight.

Artie's closest friend was Lt. Max Renner. Renner was a member of the New York Police Force in civilian life, and a former Golden Gloves champion who had also done a hitch in the regular Army. Rumor had it that Klein looked upon Renner as a kind of bodyguard, a man who would take his part in some of those losing fights.

Renner never did, of course. He was a peaceful man and spent a lot of his time calming Artie down, a fact that also made Artie mad. Sometimes he would end up fighting Renner. Still, they remained more or less inseparable.

Klein also had other friends as time passed, and he always made them in the most peculiar ways. One such friend was Lawrence J. O'Brien, the son of former New York Mayor John O'Brien.

O'Brien was a company commander in the 165th Infantry, another regiment of the 27th Division, and one night he happened to end up standing next to Klein at the bar where Artie was pounding his fist for service.

"When you became an officer, Klein," O'Brien said to him, "you were also expected to become a gentleman. Why don't you act like one?"

Artie backed away from the bar and began to roll up his sleeves. O'Brien simply reached out, grabbed Klein by the seat of the britches and by his collar, waltzed him over to the door, and threw him out. When O'Brien got back to the bar, Renner was making angry noises so O'Brien grabbed him and dragged him across the floor and threw *him* out the door.

Klein was just getting up from the ground when Renner landed beside him. Artie looked first at Renner and then at O'Brien, then walked to the door and looked up.

"Youse mean you're not afraid of him?"he asked O'Brien, jerking his thumb at Renner. O'Brien shook his head.

"Then youse must be one hell of a man," Artie said, and stuck out his hand. O'Brien was to become one of Klein's staunchest friends and admirers.

The 106th Infantry received its baptism of fire at Eniwetok on 19 February, 1944. Baker Co., of which Klein was weapons platoon commander, landed in the first wave. The Japanese contested the landings at the waterline with artillery and heavy automatic-weapons fire. Almost half of the American landing craft were sunk before they reached the beach.

Some of the 1st Battalion companies were decimated before they ever set foot on dry land. Platoons and companies were separated and disorganized. Key officers were killed and wounded. Radio communication was disrupted and almost nonexistent. In the swirling, smoke-filled, fiery melee, the first waves dissolved into little islands of beleaguered men who were stalled a few feet from the water's edge.

Landing with his platoon in a trailing wave, Klein immediately took charge. He walked or crept from one end of the beach to the other, through the heavy enemy fire, putting squads and platoons and companies back together again, finding the leaders and then leading the reorganized groups in attacks that wiped out the nearest and most menacing enemy positions.

In the first two hours, Klein's platoon sergeant, his radio operator and his runner were killed within inches of him, but he kept moving about without regard to what was liable to happen to him. He brought order out of chaos on that beach, but more important, his calmness and courage marked his men. From that morning on, the 1st Battalion, 106th Infantry, was molded in Artie Klein's image. It soon became known as one of the finest infantry units in the Pacific.

The battle for Eniwetok lasted for three days and to the men who were there it has been known as Artie Klein's war ever since. They tell a lot of stories about him. On that first day, for instance, the attack had pushed inland and by noon had reached a clearing which was crossed by a dirt road behind which the enemy had erected a series of bunkers from which poured a steady stream of machine-gun fire.

The advance was held up here while weapons were brought up. While the men were waiting, huddled in ditches along the road, Klein suddenly appeared out of the jungle to the right. He came walking down the middle of the road, his helmet perched jauntily on the back of his head, his carbine slung over his shoulder. One of the infantrymen shouted a warning to him. "For Christ's sake, Artie, get down."

Klein stopped and looked around, a shadow of annoyance on his face. "Now, youse men listen to me," he bellowed, loud enough to be heard all along the road. "I been giving youse lectures for seven months about what to do in a case like this and youse have forgotten them already."

He yanked a hand grenade from his shoulder strap and held it up. "I want to call your attention to this little object. It is known as a hand grenade, M1. In order to operate it, you pull this little loop, otherwise known as the safety pin, being careful to hold the handle down so that it will not explode too quick."

He pulled the pin and held the grenade for all to see. "Now all that youse have to do is put it where it will do the most good. This can be done by throwing it. Personally, I prefer to plant it, just to be absolutely sure."

He calmly walked over to the nearest pillbox and dropped the grenade through the gun slit, then dropped to the ground. "And don't forget to duck," he shouted.

About an hour after this incident, the Japanese launched a counterattack. It was a massive, screaming, all-out rush of several hundred men which hit the front of the 1st Battalion just at the moment when the companies were in the process of regrouping and waiting for a resupply of ammunition.

These were still relatively green troops and the shortage of small-arms ammunition made their situation worse than it otherwise might have been. Slowly, at first, and then in increasing numbers, the riflemen began to give up their positions and move back toward the beach.

Klein had gone back with a party of ammunition carriers when the counterattack broke out. He heard the heavy fire and the screaming and rushed forward. About 50 yards in from the beach he began meeting American soldiers coming the other way. He knew exactly what was happening, looked around for something and found a small hillock and climbed onto it.

He could be seen quite plainly by virtually everyone within his area, including the enemy. He began waving his carbine at first one American and then another.

"I'll shoot the first son of a bitch that takes another step backwards," he yelled. "Youse bastards are supposed to be all-American soldiers. Now let's see youse show a little guts."

The soldiers stopped where they were, looked up at Klein, and turned around. The counterattack ended a few minutes later.

No one at Eniwetok could help but know the things that Artie Klein accomplished in those three days. On the first night after the landing, the battalion had gone into a perimeter near one end of the island into which several hundred Japanese soldiers had been pushed. For the first hours of darkness the perimeter was attacked by enemy suicide parties who threw grenades, launched mortar shells and periodically strafed the foxholes with machine-gun fire.

At about one o'clock in the morning, Klein raised his head out of his foxhole and yelled at the top of his voice. "Now youse Japs listen to me. We're tired and we want to get some sleep. Knock off all this stuff and go to bed."

It was quiet on the Eniwetok front for the rest of the night.

After the battle was over, the 106th Infantry returned to the Hawaiian Islands to prepare for its next operation. Soon after the regiment got home, *Yank* magazine published an article about Klein's exploits under the title of "The One-Man Army—Klein." As a result Klein was stuck with the nickname "Omak," which he bore for the rest of the war.

Klein's battalion commander, Winslow Cornett, a former regular-Army sergeant, like Klein, was well aware of what Klein had done at Eniwetok and he meticulously collected 52 affidavits from the men who had served at Eniwetok and submitted a recommendation for the Medal of Honor.

Late in May, 1944, at a regimental ceremony, Klein was awarded the Bronze Star.

All of the officers who had passed on Col. Cornett's recommendation had been the same ones who had run into Klein at one time or another in one of the officers' clubs and they had turned it down. Even some of those at Central Pacific headquarters vetoed it.

Then, shortly after the Bronze Star was awarded, I was asked by Col. Cornett if I could do something about the whole business. I had, by that time, collected a complete account of everything Klein had done at Eniwetok and I knew that he richly deserved the Medal of Honor. I went around to see Klein to find out his reaction.

"What the hell difference does it make?" he asked me. "Some day, after I'm dead, somebody will plant a tree for me on the Staten Island Ferry. Then everybody will put cigarette butts in it. It don't mean nothing."

Nothing would have come of all this if Artie Klein had not happened to drive down to Aiea Naval Base just before embarkation for Saipan a few days after he was awarded the Bronze Star. His jeep rounded a curve on a narrow mountain road and almost ran over a plank that had fallen off a truck. It was studded with big spikes and it lay across both traffic lanes.

Artie motioned his driver to pull off to one side and he went back, picked up the plank, and carried it off to the side, out of the way. He was just getting back in his jeep when a staff car came skidding to a stop beside him. A door opened and a three-star general got out. It was Lt. Gen. Robert C. Richardson Jr., commanding general of the Army in the Central Pacific.

"For your information, lieutenant," the general said, "that plank fell off a truck a half-hour ago. I've been parked up there on the hill ever since. Seventy-four vehicles have passed by. Every single one of them slowed down, but until you came along not one of them had the gumption to get out and move it from the road. Lieutenant, I am personally recommending you for the Legion of Merit. I would be honored if you would have lunch with me on the day of the presentation."

I heard about this and it so happened that I had lunch with the general before Artie did. I took along the *Yank* article and my notes on Artie's performance at Eniwetok, plus the original citation for the Medal of Honor with its 52 affidavits.

The general immediately reinstated the recommendation and sent it off to Washington. Two days later the 27th Division sailed for Saipan, Artie Klein with it. He was now executive officer of Baker Co., 106th Infantry.

The last paragraph of the *Yank* article on Artie Klein said, "If One-Man-Army Klein ever goes into combat again, he probably will not live for more than ten minutes." Artie Klein knew that this had been written. All his men knew it as well.

Ironically, at almost the same time Gen. Richardson forwarded his citation to Washington, the War Department issued a new regulation which automatically removed any recipient of the Medal of Honor from further combat duty. No one who had ever received this high honor would ever be placed in jeopardy of his life again. It was too late to do Artie any good, even if he'd received the medal.

Klein lasted 30 minutes at Saipan. On a Sunday afternoon just above ChaCha Village, while leading his company in an assault on a fortified position, he was cut down by Japanese machine-gun fire after deliberately exposing himself so that his men could advance. He was evacuated to Tripler General Hospital in Honolulu where he was hospitalized for four months.

It was said that he would never walk again and on three different occasions he was ordered back to the states. On all three occasions he successfully fought these orders. While he was hospitalized, President Roosevelt came and personally pinned the Distinguished Service Cross on his pajamas for the action at Eniwetok.

I visited Klein in the early fall of 1944 on the occasion of the award of the Silver Star and the Purple Heart. I found him to be a changed man. He'd been reading a book about American history. I told him he ought to accept the orders back to the states. It would get him out of the war. He held up his right hand.

"Youse see that hand? You know who shook it? The President of the United States, that's who. What the hell do you think my old man would say if he knew that?"

He shook his head. "I'll stay out here as long as there's anything going on. Just think, the President shook hands with a no-good bum like me."

Artie Klein reported back to duty with Baker Co. late in October, 1944. He limped off the plane at Espiritu Santo just three days after his discharge from the hospital. Since he had been wounded, the command of Baker Co. had passed to his best friend, Max Renner.

Like Klein, Renner had distinguished himself in combat. By a strange coincidence, the date of promotion for both Renner and Klein to first lieutenant had been the same and Klein's return to duty resulted in one of those rare moments of comedy which could not have been foreseen by the U.S. Army. Renner insisted that Klein was the rightful company commander and Klein insisted that Renner was.

On the day of Klein's return to duty, the two men sat up all night arguing about who was in command. When reveille blew the next morning they both rushed out to the executive officer's spot in the formation and stood there arguing, jaw to jaw, their helmet liners bobbing up and down, each trying to get the other to take the company commander's spot.

Renner finally assumed command, but only on condition that Klein would take command the next day. For six weeks they went through this same performance each morning and on one day Klein would command and on the next Renner would command. Neither one would go near the battalion commander with the problem because he was afraid the decision would be in his favor.

One morning, the battalion commander noticed that the morning reports were being signed by a different man each day and he finally called them in and ascertained the truth. As a result, he transferred

Renner to Dog Co.—as company commander—and Klein took over Baker Co. all by himself. Shortly thereafter, both were promoted to captain.

This was the last act in the long relationship between these two old friends. At some time that fall, Max Renner contracted an infection in the wounds he had suffered at Saipan. He was hospitalized and was eventually sent back to the states for treatment. On the day before he left Espiritu Santo, Klein went to see him at the hospital and gave him a handkerchief to take back to his mother in Brooklyn.

Wrapped in the handkerchief were the medals he had won and a set of his captain's bars. "I think maybe she ought to take them down to the cemetery and show them to my old man," Artie said. "I think he'd like to know."

"That's when I knew I'd never see Omak again," Renner said later.

The 27th Division went into the attack on Okinawa on the morning of 19 April, 1945. The division's objective was to capture a ridge line known as the Machinato Escarpment, the northern anchor of the main Japanese defensive position of the island. In a complicated maneuver designed to take the escarpment from the flank, it was necessary to send a rifle company along the face of a sheer cliff to clear out a network of cave and pillbox positions so that the rest of the division would have room to deploy.

It was an action that would have to be accomplished without any heavy support. All the men would have to work with were rifles, grenades and bayonets and a few satchel charges. Baker Co., 106th Infantry, was chosen for the task.

On the day before the attack, I went up to a forward observation post to look over the situation and found Klein there with two of his sergeants. I sensed at once that he was a different man. His little potbelly was gone and the cocky belligerence was no longer there. He was all business and I didn't hear him say "youse men" once.

When I turned to leave he came over and shook my hand and thanked me. When I asked him what he was thanking me for, he just shrugged and said, "Well, for being a friend, I guess."

Beginning at dawn the next morning, Baker Co., with Klein in the lead, began moving along the cliff face. For two days, sometimes clinging to rocks or bushes, at other times moving hand over hand, they scrambled along. In the end they had wiped out a whole Japanese battalion. Gen. Simon B. Buckner Jr., the Tenth Army commander, later characterized this movement along the escarpment as the most masterful infantry action he had every seen.

During that long and arduous attack down the cliff, virtually the whole attention of the 27th Division was focused on Klein and his men—not only because the attack's success depended upon them, but because by this time Klein's reputation was well known, and so were the dire predictions that had been made concerning his future.

There was, therefore, a general sense of relief when, on the evening of 20 April, Artie himself picked up his radio. "Sir," he said to his regimental commander, "Baker Co. is on its objective as of this hour."

He was ordered to dig in for the night and hold his ground. Baker Co. would be relieved at ten the next morning.

"Quite frankly," the colonel told me afterwards, "I was relieved that Artie had gotten out of it again safely. I'd already talked it over with Gen. Hodge, the corps commander, and I intended to recommend Artie for the Medal of Honor and to relieve him of his command and get him out of there to where he'd be safe."

The capture of Machinato Escarpment had endangered the Japanese Shuri defensive line. During the night of 20–21 April, the enemy committed a fresh battalion with the express mission of driving Baker Co. back over the cliffs. Counterattack followed counterattack all night long. Baker Co. held, strewing the ground in front of it with Japanese dead.

At about quarter of ten in the morning, regiment called Artie Klein to tell him that his relief would be a little late.

"That's all right with me," Artie said, "we need a little more time anyway. These jokers have been running at us all night and some of them have got into the caves and rocks around here and they've got us pretty well pinned down. We know the terrain pretty well by now and we know where these clowns are. In about an hour we should have the place cleaned up."

It was not that easy. Not long after his report to regiment, Klein called Oscar Vigan, his executive officer, over to him and pointed at a high pinnacle rock 50 yards to the front. "They've got good observation on us and I figure that's where the suckers have to be," Klein said. "What we have to do is get them busy watching something while the rest of us go get him. Somebody's going to have to go after that rock."

"Artie," Vigan said, "anybody who goes after that rock is a dead man."

Vigan said that Klein smiled and nodded. "I'll take the rock. You get everybody ready and move in on whoever is up there when I give the signal." And then he stuck out his hand. "Thanks."

"What for?"

13

"For taking good care of the company."

Klein borrowed an automatic rifle and six grenades. He talked briefly with his sergeants, telling them what he wanted them to do. Klein was no blessed martyr. He moved forward from rock to rock, never giving the enemy a good target. Every few feet he would stop and throw a grenade off to one side or the other and then squeeze off a burst of fire from his BAR.

Somehow or other he got within five yards of the base of the pinnacle rock and he was in a position from which he could toss a grenade up into the opening he had discovered. By then the only way the Japanese could get at him was to expose themselves in the opening and fire straight down at him. He pulled the pin on the grenade and straightened up and threw it.

The Japanese were ready for him. Four or five of them showed themselves in the opening and fired straight down at him. And every man in Baker Co. was ready for them, too. The Japanese soldiers were cut to pieces. In the few seconds that it took them to tumble down the face of the rock, Baker Co. let out a small cheer and then they looked for Artie Klein.

He was sitting there at the base of the rock. Twice he tried to get up and then he sank back and slowly rolled over on his side and was still. Ten minutes later Oscar Vigan called regiment on his radio.

"You can move the 3rd Battalion in now," he said. "There isn't a live Jap within 200 yards of us. By the way, colonel, Artie Klein is dead. He died at five minutes of 11 this morning. He was a good man, colonel. So help me, I never saw a better one."

They brought Artie Klein's body out two days later. They found 24 bullet wounds in it. He must have suffered most of those wounds before he tried to throw that one last grenade.

Artie Klein was buried in the 27th Division cemetery on Okinawa with full military honors. When I last visited his grave his battered old helmet still hung from a prong of the Star of David. After the Okinawa fight was over, Artie Klein was again recommended for the Medal of Honor, the only man I ever knew who was recommended twice for it. There was no one to follow up on it and Artie was presented posthumously with something less.

Artie Klein is long forgotten now. Some years later I went to the Williamsburg section of Brooklyn and made a few inquiries. I found no one who had known him, but I did find his father's grave in a cemetery. Inscribed above it were the words, "Anything is possible in this country." One set of sergeant's stripes was painted on either side of the inscription.

CHAPTER
TWO

Patton: 'You Might as Well Die a Hero'

by Gen. James H. Polk, USA (Ret.)

(This intimate view of Gen. George S. Patton Jr. in peace and war, by a subordinate who himself later rose into the Army's highest ranks, was published on the 30th anniversary of the great commander's death, 21 December, 1945, the result of a motor accident in Germany.)

Mid-morning on 23 April, 1945, my radio operator–gunner came running over to me and said, "Lucky Six is calling on your radio net and wants to talk to you."

I hotfooted it over to my jeep and reported in, "This is Cowhand Six," I said.

The reply came quickly, "This is Lucky Six. Jimmy, are you going to get that bridge over the Danube at Regensberg intact for me to-day? Over."

"We will give it a good try, sir. Over," I said.

And back came the clincher, "Try hell, you get it and I'll make you a brigadier general; you fail and I'll sack your——. Out."

That was Gen. George S. Patton Jr., our army commander, doing what was known as motivating me and my troops. However, from long association in the earlier peacetime cavalry and from almost a year's service in his renowned Third Army, we both knew that he didn't really mean what he said about discharging me, although he did want that bridge—and badly. And we both knew that any spare radios in the 3rd Mechanized Cavalry would be tuned to the regimental command channel to stay abreast of the situation.

As expected, the troops got the message and we did give it a good try, but when the bridge was blown up at the last instant, a number of my men expressed regret that I would be leaving soon. Things were sometimes done differently under G. S. Patton Jr., and it took experience to become accustomed to them.

I never heard George Patton tell a dirty story or even utter an off-color remark, but his profanity was, to say the least, quite effective. Once in a pick-up polo game at Fort Riley, Kan., I was playing No. 2 and he was No. 3. When he laid the ball up very nicely in front of the goal, I missed the shot for a score and let out a pretty fair oath. He rode up and said, "Lt. Polk, you will not use profanity on this polo field, but it's a goddamned shame you can't hit the ball."

He was a great student of military history with a splendid library and a keen knowledge of details and terrain, from both study and on-site visits to famous battlefields. One day in a little village under the guns of Fort Driant near Metz, he jolted me by observing what a great privilege it was for us to participate in this, the third battle of Gravelotte. On seeing my blank look, he told me with some disgust that in 1870 there was a very decisive battle fought here with the Germans facing north and the French south, while in 1914 the French attacked to the north while the Germans faced south. Now, he observed, we will kick hell out of the Germans while for the first time fighting an east-west battle on this hallowed ground.

Lt. Col. Patton taught us tactics at the Cavalry School in the mid-1930s, mainly about how armor might possibly operate alone, a somewhat unpopular subject with the horse cavalrymen of that era. I cannot recall his ever suggesting any tactical readings or study, perhaps because he thought we were beyond redemption. We regarded him as a wealthy and somewhat eccentric sportsman who had rather novel, but still interesting, ideas about modern warfare.

He was always beautifully turned out, rode fine, blooded horses and was very active in polo, drag hunting and horse shows—as was his whole family. They were very popular and everyone loved Mrs. Patton, a charming woman and very gracious hostess. War was far from our minds in those days and soldiering was somewhat of a game, but certainly none of my young lieutenant contemporaries thought of George Patton as the great wartime leader he was to become in a few short years. We junior officers admired him and tried to emulate his dress and bearing, were a little afraid of him because of his sudden outbursts of temper and wished we could afford the fine horses he rode.

In that same vein, one hot summer day at Fort Myer, Va., he asked me to help him train a young thoroughbred hunter that was "sticky over the big fences." Of course, I was honored to be asked to help my colonel and showed up at the horse show jumping pen at the appointed hour in our summer uniform of that day: a wool shirt, khaki breeches, boots, spurs and a crop. After warming up the hunter, putting him over a few low jumps and working up a good sweat myself, my regimental commander suggested that his horse was now ready for more serious training.

At that point, his orderly brought out an electric shocking pole consisting of a long bamboo stick wrapped with two bare wires and hooked to a hand-cranked static electricity generator. With the orderly on the crank, Patton stationed himself at a big oxer fence and instructed me to bring the horse in hard. If the hunter began to prop, I was to put the spurs to him, hit him with the crop and if that didn't work, my mentor would touch him up with a shock on the rump—or so was the plan.

The scenario was not exactly to my liking, but I was already committed, so I did as instructed and the horse started to slow and refuse, as expected. I hit him with the crop and the next thing I experienced was a terrific electric shock across my shoulder blades, then down we went, the horse and me and the jump, in a welter of logs and brush. I am reported to have said, "Damn you, I'll never ride your horses again," while George S. Patton Jr. exploded in gales of laughter.

He did have the grace to apologize for bouncing that pole off the horse's rump onto my sweaty wool shirt and observed that we had really given his hunter a great lesson.

. . .

This is not to imply that in 1939–40 at Fort Myer, the 3rd Cavalry was not serious about getting ready for war because indeed we were, under the leadership of our colorful colonel. The idea was that we worked hard and played hard, we led by example and took pride in the fact that we were equally as good at official Washington parades and funerals as we were on maneuvers and exercises. Also, our ideas changed a bit about our CO. He drove us through training while we expanded and furnished cadres for new units and faced all the problems incident to the sudden growth of a small and rather intimate army into a huge fighting machine.

The first big step for me was to be given command of a new "G" troop, all mine to nurture and train into what would surely become the best troop of horse cavalry in the Army.

One incident of that period etched in my memory began innocently enough as a live ammunition attack problem for my "G" troop on the Fort Belvoir, Va., reservation. We advanced to contact in approved mounted formation, scouts in front; then the command group followed by the deployed platoons. We moved to within sight of the targets, dismounted and walked forward to a well-defined firing position, then placed each soldier carefully on line at intervals of about five yards, issued ball ammunition and prepared to engage the enemy targets with live fire. Col. Patton had been following us throughout and I thought with some pride that we had done extremely well and were in for praise. Some things you never learn.

His first remark was "What the hell is going on here?" I attempted to explain the problem and was cut short when he asked why we had not opened fire when we first saw the enemy instead of permitting an unconscionable delay in opening the fire fight. When I explained that it was against peacetime safety regulations to issue ammunition or open fire earlier, he said, "I helped write those very same stupid regulations for damn fools like you. Now let's have a real exercise."

So, we went back, loaded our rifles and had a realistic, exciting, hell-roaring battle that violated every regulation in the book. And we both realized that some soreheaded soldier could have creased our respective skulls, without a chance of getting caught. By this and other very realistic exercises, it was obvious to all of us that our colonel was preparing us for the real thing.

Another incident during this period gives some insight into Patton's little-known attitude towards military justice and punishment. The garrison's general court met every Wednesday at 1300, ordinarily to try deserters who, for some unknown reason, thought it was better to turn in at Washington than elsewhere in the United States. Most were long-term absentees. There was no question about their guilt once their identity was established and they were, without exception, found guilty and given the absolute maximum penalty. As the trial judge advocate, I could try, and the court process, two or three cases an afternoon.

Naturally, the frighteningly stiff sentence was without exception reduced or suspended by the court's reviewing authority—then Col. Patton—but this type of speedy justice caused the War Department to write our colonel a letter which censured him, ordered that he reprimand the president and the judge advocate of the court, and suggested that we change our ways. The resultant calling to account was a Patton classic.

First, he told us to consider ourselves reprimanded as ordered. Then he explained how the War Department was all wrong as they reduced the court's authority to be tough, so necessary in order to make the culprit appear as a horrible example for the whole command. But far more important from his view, it put him in a bad light as it made it much more difficult for him to exercise the quality of mercy so essential in a good commander. We were then dismissed with the admonition that from now on, the sentence should be only half the limit prescribed by the court-martial manual.

The pressures and responsibilities felt by Gen. Patton for the administration of equitable military justice were demonstrated once again some years later, this time at the height of the Battle of the Bulge. Orders came down late one night for me to report to the Army commander the next morning at his headquarters in Luxembourg City. This sounded like bad news in the making. Surely he was going to put his old regiment in a real hard place and I had forebodings of imminent and violent combat.

Oddly enough, I was ushered right into his office on arrival, and Gen. Patton first showed me a picture of a very good-looking thoroughbred that Mrs. Patton had just purchased. While we admired the set of his withers and his fine head, I was in a cold sweat because I knew this was not the purpose of my visit. Finally, he passed over a blue-covered legal document, explained that it was the court-martial record of a lieutenant colonel who had worked for me and asked me to sit over in the corner, read it and give him my recommendations.

While I sat over to one side of his office in the Luxembourg Palace,

19

he reverted to running the battle, with staff officers and aides bringing in messages, telephones ringing and orders issued, all at the fast-paced tempo of very active operations.

After reading the proceedings, I waited for a break in the action and then handed the document back to him. Gen. Patton then explained that he was the reviewing authority in the case, that the officer was unquestionably guilty of keeping a French girl friend and transporting her, along with the outfit, in an ambulance during combat operations, and that he could approve the sentence of dismissal from the service or reduce it as he saw fit. He next asked if the culprit was a competent combat battalion commander, to which I replied that he was.

Gen. Patton then stated that he proposed to reduce this officer's sentence to a severe reprimand and put him in command of a front-line infantry battalion, as we were then rather short of fighting commanders. When I agreed, Patton thanked me for my time and advice, then directed that I report to the chief of staff's billets in the palace, where I would find awaiting me a hot bath, a change of long underwear and a martini. Naturally, I returned to my then-quiet sector a very happy man.

Early in the war, the 3rd Cavalry was mechanized with light tanks and armored cars, given an armored reconnaissance role and re-trained for a combat mission in Europe. Gen. Patton asked for the outfit to be assigned to his army, regarded it as his regiment and it seemed to us at least that he visited us far more than he did any other similar unit of his command. He stopped in unannounced at our command post in Luxembourg in October, 1944, wearing one of his more outrageous outfits: an off-green, double-breasted jacket, green jodhpurs and jodhpur boots and, of course, his general's belt, with two ivory-handled pistols. With his ribbons and gleaming stars, he looked somewhat like a wild West cowboy ready to go fox hunting.

After briefing him on the situation, I complimented him on his uniform of that day. He laughed delightedly and said that he was on his way to visit the British and had put on his outfit especially to infuriate "Monty." He surely must have succeeded.

Gen. Patton's next visit was in November when our XX Corps was preparing to make an assault crossing of the Moselle River. I picked him up at an adjoining division headquarters and heard him deliver to a big assembly of soldiers one of his famous fighting speeches, full of profanity and graphic descriptions of bloody heroism. On the way up to the 3rd Cavalry, he seemed very pleased with himself and I was fearful that we would be treated to this same lurid set piece that we had already heard more than once.

As the regiment was in the front line at the time, we could only assemble a rather modest group of men, seated on a hillside in a natural amphitheater. We rode up to the center of the group in his jeep and Gen. Patton stood up before the men, looked around with his piercing eyes, spoke to several NCOs he recognized and then told us to be seated. He drew himself up to full height, hit his boots with a crop he was carrying and in his rather high-pitched voice said: "This is my old regiment and you SOBs know what to do, now go do it!"

With that, he saluted and drove off. We were far too respectful to applaud, but we loved him for it.

To go back in time a bit, there have been several accounts of the dialogue that took place when Gen. Patton gave me command of the 3rd Cavalry and it was quite an event. First, he told me that the former CO had just been wounded and captured in front of Metz and that I was to take command immediately. He then asked me how old I was and when I said that I was 32, he remarked that I seemed awfully young for the job. I felt rather bold at that point and said that if memory served correctly, he had been the same age when he commanded a tank brigade in World War I. He laughed and replied that he had been only 31, but that he had looked a good deal older.

He then got serious again and gave me some stern command guidance that I have never forgotten. The sense of it was that if the regiment ever got overrun or badly beaten because of my poor decisions, I was relieved of my command and he never wanted to see me again. On the other hand, if some stupid orders from higher headquarters caused us to be severely mauled, I would still be relieved, as a beaten commander was of no value to him, but he would get me a nice job on some higher staff.

Finally, he remarked that Gen. Bernard Montgomery should have been relieved after Caen because after that battle he was unquestionably a beaten commander and his troops no longer had confidence in him. On leaving his presence, after a handshake and a salute, I was a very serious young man, for I knew he meant every word he had said.

During the Battle of the Bulge, the German guerrilla fighter Skorzeny and his "werewolves" were supposed to be prowling our rear areas in American uniforms, and we were under instructions to ask questions of strangers to verify correct identity since the passwords were considered compromised. As an amusing aside and in obedience to this order, one of my young sentries stopped Gen. Patton's jeep—

which was being followed by a jeepload of MPs at a rear area cross-road—despite the very obvious occupant and asked the general for the password.

When he got the proper reply, this grimy youth announced that per instructions he would have to ask several questions. The conversation went like this:

"Sir, does Bing Crosby have any sons and if so, how many?"

Gen. Patton: "My God, son, I don't know."

Sentry: "Well, who won the Army-Navy game?"

Gen. Patton: "Son, I don't know that either."

Sentry: "Well, you should know, because you are a West Pointer, aren't you?"

Upon receiving an affirmative reply, the sentry informed our commander that he knew him all the time, that for his information Army had won the game and that the general could pass, but that he'd better be more careful in our rear area as some less intelligent sentry might shoot him. The aide, Maj. Codman, called me up that night and, roaring with laughter, said it was one of the few times he ever saw a young soldier really embarrass the "old man."

Shortly after the end of the war in Europe, the 3rd Cavalry was assigned responsibility for an occupation area around Gmunden and Seewalchen, Austria, in the beautiful mountain lake country. We decided to celebrate the 99th anniversary of our activation as the 3rd Regiment of Mounted Rifles with a review, luncheon and assorted activities, and invited Gen. Patton, along with all former officers of the regiment we could locate. It was a gala occasion in beautiful weather, and Gen. Patton delivered the principal address, full of compliments for our distinguished combat accomplishments over almost a century's span.

At the end, he indicated that he would soon be on his way to fight the Japanese and that he had asked the War Department for only one particular outfit to accompany him, his own 3rd Cavalry. I understand that he said this to several units, but in my own experience it was the only occasion that I ever heard a large group of soldiers give forth with a collective groan.

At the luncheon—largely GI rations—that followed, served on a beautiful terrace overlooking the Attersee, our guest of honor was utterly charming, entertaining my officers and our other guests with reminiscences and stories of his encounters with famous personages. Toward the end of the meal, however, he became quite serious and expounded on the theme that the Russians were undoubtedly our mortal enemies and that we should, at a minimum, throw them back to their old prewar boundaries in order to insure the eventual freedom of the countries they had overrun and occupied.

Most of us were very naive and at that point regarded the Russians as our gallant allies, so naturally we were quite dismayed at these highly controversial views.

It soon became obvious that Gen. Patton had devoted considerable thought to the details of such an operation. He outlined the Third Army's first and second objectives for us to capture and, to our horror, put the 3rd Cavalry back to leading our XX Corps' attack and indicated a rough time schedule for the imaginative scenario. In addition, he indicated that we could use the just-conquered German soldiers in such support tasks as transport, engineer and supply operations, as well as restoration of the rail system to operable condition.

We soon realized he was in deadly earnest and since that memorable occasion I have often thought how far ahead of his time were his penetrating perceptions of future events.

Some of the things he said to us on such occasions undoubtedly reflected his philosophy of how subordinate commanders and units should operate. A few of his favorites were: "You only die once, so you might as well die a hero"; "Hold the enemy by the nose and kick him in the——"; "Once you get an enemy retreating, go after him like the hounds of hell"; "In a crisis, be seen going towards it, never away"; "Look like a commander, your soldiers expect it of you." And that favorite which was useful to me on a number of occasions: "I helped write that stupid regulation for damn fools like you."

He once remarked that none of my soldiers was wearing a shoulder patch and asked why we had none. I was quite apprehensive about giving him the answer, but finally admitted that we were entitled to wear his Third Army patch; his army, however, was just too big and diversified a unit for us to enjoy any real sense of affiliation or of belonging to it. He was pretty quick and noted that, except for the cavalry regiments, all others wearing his patch were support and rear area troops like truck companies and such.

He then asked if we had any solution and I suggested that we be allowed to develop our own patch of green with the well-known "gold bug." He authorized it on the spot and we wore it proudly, probably the first regimental-size unit to have its own patch. In later years, I was quite often asked if my shoulder patch was regulation and the reply that it was personally authorized by Gen. Patton always ended the challenge.

23

Some 25 years later it was finally authorized for official wear by Army regulations.

I had returned to the United States when we heard the news of Gen. Patton's unfortunate accident and tragic death, so unnecessary and strange in view of all the real risks he had taken in a lifetime of active soldiering. My letter of sympathy to Mrs. Patton was answered in due time and in it she asked me if I would like to have some of his uniforms or boots for my personal use or any other object of his that I might desire as a remembrance.

When I replied that his uniforms would not fit, but that some little keepsake would greatly be appreciated, a small box addressed to Col. Polk arrived in the mail. In it was a calling card and a pair of single brigadier general's stars. The card was engraved, "Mrs. George Smith Patton Jr." and written on it was the following message: "I gave these to Georgie who wore them. You will want to wear them, too, and (on the other side of the card) I know you will be worthy of them. B.A.P. Look on the back."

These stars are surely unique, for on the reverse and above the clasp is engraved "Patton" and below the clasp is stamped "14K." They are of 14-karat gold, but silver plated. I did indeed want to wear them and was mighty proud the day they were pinned on my shoulders.

CHAPTER
THREE

Stalking Peace

by Gerald Weland

T he arm hurt like hell. It gave him more agony now, ten years
    after he lost it, than it ever did attached to his body. Such a
    phenomenon was not unusual, but that did nothing to ease
the pain. Still, he thrust the pain from his mind. Nothing else mat-
tered except the mission.

He surveyed the gray-green vastness spread out before him: the
Dragoon Mountains, early-day cavalry had dubbed them. He had no
idea what the denizens called them, except home.

They would be watching, of course, those lean, emotionless men
wearing headbands, leather britches and perhaps a buckskin vest or
ragged shirt. Some were on the distant ramparts. Some would be
closer, skulking among the sandy, scrub-covered hills to his front,
swift as striking rattlesnakes but more silent and twice as deadly.
Stealth, raiding, pillage, bloodshed—these were not part of their heritage, but rather its entirety. In nearly 40 years of constant strife, they

had managed to make their very name a synonym for terror in the Southwest. Apache! But then, they, too, were a part of the mission.

Everybody in any position of authority in the Arizona Territory had warned him against this trek. There was no guarantee of his safety. The two Indian scouts, Ponce and Chee, were not expected to turn on him, but neither were they likely to die defending him. The other man, Tom Jeffords, was the key.

Nobody knew much about Tom Jeffords. He claimed to have been a part of Col. James H. Carleton's California column, which had marched east to join the Civil War in 1862, only to end up blasting its way through Cochise's minions at Apache Pass and staying on to garrison the territory. Tom Jeffords said he had served with their artillery, now famous in Apache lore as "The Wagon Guns," but nobody, himself included, had offered much proof.

There were rumors about Tom Jeffords, some more than just whisperings. That he knew Cochise and had entré to his legendary Stronghold was never denied. It was why that bothered many people. Some suspected he had made his fortune selling ammunition to the dreaded raiders in exchange for stolen livestock, but he genuinely sought peace on behalf of his Indian friend. That made him, too, a part of the mission.

Slowly, the blue-clad figure took the reins in his teeth and reached his left arm back to feel for his most comforting possession. It was still secure in his knapsack, square and bulky. He ignored his gun completely. Then he rode sedately on.

The mission moved steadfastly ahead of him. . . .

Oliver Otis Howard had been born in Maine in 1830, spawned by people as dour and rock hard as the soil they tilled. His religious fundamentalism had been part of his psyche throughout life. Since the Civil War, it had become predominant.

He had graduated from the U.S. Military Academy in 1854, fourth in a class of 46. His early service was mainly in eastern arsenals and as a math instructor at West Point. In June, 1861, he took command of the 3rd Maine Regiment in the War of the Rebellion. By 1862, he was commander of the 1st Brigade in Maj. Gen. Edwin V. Sumner's division. It was then, at Fair Oaks during Maj. Gen. George B. McClellan's abortive Peninsula campaign, that he had been seriously wounded, not once but twice.

He should never have survived. A shattered arm had to be rudely hacked off to give him any chance at all. But Col. Howard was made of stern stuff. He lived to fight again, but also to serve a different cause. The living owed good works to God, as well as faith. He would serve the Union faithfully from 1863 on—but something over and beyond that as well.

He still saw plenty of combat, first at Chancellorsville as commander of the XI Corps and then with Brig. Gen. George G. Meade at Gettysburg. Shortly thereafter, he was transferred to the Army of the Cumberland, becoming one of Maj. Gen. William T. Sherman's most trusted aides during the Atlanta campaign and earning promotion to brigadier general in December, 1864. Both men truly believed that war was hell. Gen. Howard, however, did all in his power to spare even the enemy the worst examples of it.

When the hostilities ceased, he had a promising career open to him. Indeed, he never formally resigned from the Army. When he finally retired in 1894 as a major general commanding the entire Division of the East, he was one of the most senior men in the American military.

Yet a different brand of service, possibly even his true niche in life, irresistibly beckoned. That he had been one of just 15 men officially voted the Thanks of Congress after Gettysburg barely registered on him. The Medal of Honor awarded for his action at Fair Oaks was never more than a piece of metal and a ribbon.

By that time, he had long since put the war behind him, choosing instead to clutch its cause to his bosom with equal ardor. On 12 May, 1865, he became commissioner of the Freedman's Bureau. Although the employment was an all-consuming passion, it soon became evident that his administrative ability and zeal could not overcome the inefficiency and outright corruption of his underlings. Trouble and investigations wracked the agency through 1872, although none of it ever attached to him. By then, of course, he had already founded and was serving as president of the nation's first Negro university in Washington, D.C. To this day, it bears his name.

In fact, as he slowly wound his way towards the Stronghold of the famed, fabled and feared Cochise that blistering autumn day in 1872, he still was president of Howard University. His days were filled with a different mission, however. A new group of belabored, battered Americans awaited his efforts as government representative.

The administration of President Ulysses S. Grant, repelled by the possibility of endless frontier strife, had sincerely opted for a policy of peaceful coexistence with the western plains Indians. Gen. Howard set forth as a government plenipotentiary to pursue mankind's most merciful goal.

With precious little thanks.

So far, the efforts of "The Christian General" had been greeted with decidedly mixed opinions. Nobody, it seemed, was terribly interested in peace except him.

The citizenry of Arizona had derisively dubbed compassionate Vincent T. Colyer, territorial Indian commissioner, "Vincent the Good." Their opinion of a man who they regarded as "a one-armed, eastern evangelist" who proposed to offer Cochise peace with honor need hardly be spelled out.

Lt. Col. George Crook, who had already earned the nickname "Gray Fox" for his Indian fighting exploits, saw little chance of success. A year older than Gen. Howard and vastly more experienced in chastising such deadly warriors, he viewed any attempt to generate a feeling of amity in the territory as little short of "a humbug."

Officially, relations between the two men were "harmonious" when peacemaker Howard reached Ft. Apache with President Grant's edict. There is little doubt that when Gen. Howard left to pursue peace, Col. Crook was certain he would never see his colleague again, although he did his best to make the mission a success.

It seemed that the Apache were not particularly interested in giving up the struggle either. Gen. Howard's first trip west had culminated in a meeting with some of their leaders, including the aged Arivaipa Eskiminzin, at Camp Grant in May, 1872.

Cochise had led those who stayed away in droves. One can hardly blame them. Exactly a year earlier, a group of drunken Pima Indians and Mexicans under a seedy Tucson rancher named Oury had massacred 150 peaceful Apache in the same location, carrying 29 children off into slavery as trophies. As a result, there were no longer any peaceful Apache in Arizona.

Disappointed at the turnout, Gen. Howard had grandiloquently asked if it were not possible to visit Cochise in his lair. Arivaipa Eskiminzin, who nurtured a surly disposition at the best of times, was in no mood to cooperate. "Not unless," the old warrior snarled, "you are ready to die!"

Nobody knows if Gen. Howard sought such martyrdom or not. The two books he wrote about his life are filled with Biblical quotations and religious reflections which less-sensitive critics have scoffed at ever since. He rarely speaks of death, and it seems unlikely that it was a part of what he conceived his mission to be. On the other hand, he was not a man to be daunted by such a venomous response.

Now on this dark, dry, dangerous, final dawn in the fall of 1872, the general who preferred reason to rifles as a shield had come to meet the man who would make that mission a success. His small party entered the western, or San Pedro, entrance to the Stronghold.

They saw no Apache, which was precisely what one could expect to see when being watched by them.

Without pause, they rode on, along the nearly six-mile route that wound its way through rocky outcroppings and scrub-shrouded hillocks into the heart of the "impregnable" bastion of Cochise.

To this day nobody knows precisely how many Indians were there at the time. Sporadic water sources always prevented great numbers for any length of time, and the Stronghold was always more refuge than fortress. Still, should Cochise give the order, there were more than enough hostile Indians willing to terminate the mission of Gen. Howard forever.

Little is known of Cochise today. Physically, he stood six, ramrod-straight feet tall and possessed a large nose and melancholy demeanor. He was a Chiricahua—and a warrior of no small repute.

Today, Cochise is the quintessential expression of the noble savage concept, even in Arizona where his ravages were best known. No other Indian leader has his own town and county named after him. Yet he owes much of that image to the one-armed soldier-chief he was about to confront.

It is often tossed about by "revisionist" historians that Cochise was driven to war in January, 1861, by a "blundering officer" named Lt. George Bascom during a dispute over some hostages and stolen livestock. There is, however, no evidence that he was quite that pristine. He was already a war chief among the Apache, and such a rank was not achieved through enlightened, philosophical oratory. His mentor was Mangas Colorado, whose hatred for the white man remained undying even years after his flogging by miners at Pinos Altos, N.M.

It is almost certain Cochise was part, if not the actual leader, of the Chiricahua raid which nearly obliterated the mining town of Patagonia, Ariz., as early as 1859. His most famous stand had been at Apache Pass against Col. Carleton. The resultant death of Mangas Colorado allowed him to assume the mantle of leadership throughout Apacheria. For a decade since then, Cochise rampaged through Arizona and Mexico.

For whatever reasons, Geronimo remains the symbol of wily ruthlessness throughout the Southwest. But he must have learned his lessons someplace. Cochise may not have led every raid or overseen every atrocity. Neither was he noted for committing atrocities personally. Yet throughout history, soldiery has always reflected the character of its leadership.

In just the last few weeks, his warriors had slaughtered 13 Mexicans in Sonoita Valley. Shortly before that, they had raided as far west as Prescott, Ariz., stealing 2,000 head of livestock and engaging in numerous skirmishes with troops from Ft. Whipple, in which at least a dozen Apaches and several soldiers had perished.

Cochise's followers had staged their most recent coup in Davidson Canyon near Camp Crittenden. They killed an officer and captured an Army corporal. The latter was tied to a tree and slowly burned alive before his comrades discovered what was going on and could ride to the rescue.

The tree had scarcely stopped smoldering when Gen. Howard departed for Ft. Apache for his rendezvous with destiny.

As many of his detractors have pointed out, we know only Gen. Howard's version of what transpired in the Stronghold. But then, since he was the only man courageous enough to go there, we can extend him the courtesy of assuming he did not fabricate anything.

The initial meeting, Gen. Howard admitted, was brief. He barely had time to mention his purpose before being cut off.

"No one," the Apache leader gruffly assured him, "wants peace more than I do."

If so, Cochise displayed no alarming alacrity to rush into its arms.

"Ten days," Cochise informed Gen. Howard. "I must call in my chief warriors. I cannot make peace without their advice."

And so the man with the mission waited. He waited through endless days of sand-swept, enervating heat that even the shadowy recesses of rocks in the Stronghold did little to dissipate. He waited through endless nights in which the mountain wind turned the hideout from a frying pan to a freezer. For nearly a fortnight he waited. The alien environment, the mixture of hatred and contempt so obvious on every Apache face—nothing discouraged him. The cause which had brought him was company enough.

Perhaps Cochise really wanted peace. He could be moved by blood lust, honor, compassion or common sense, depending on his mood. Possibly the specter of endless conflict with the ever-increasing and persistent blue columns opposing him merely made it expedient.

Any leader worthy of the name could calculate that to accept peace via a paper was vastly preferable to having it imposed by a club. Cochise was generally unpredictable, occasionally bloodthirsty and always an Apache. Nobody, however, has ever described him as a fool.

This became apparent when the negotiations began in earnest, the participants sitting around a council fire in the Stronghold. Cochise declined to speak in English, forcing Tom Jeffords to translate from Spanish. His first question as to just why "the graybeard" was bothering them left Gen. Howard under no illusions as to the task ahead of him.

"The Great Father, President Grant," Gen. Howard patiently explained, "sent me to make peace between you and the whites."

Cochise again stated that nobody wanted peace more than he did.

Gen. Howard then proved that he could maneuver at a peace conference as well as on a battlefield. "Then," he replied quickly, backing Cochise into a corner, "we can surely have peace."

The particulars of the negotiation were sticky, but peace was had at last.

Gen. Howard assigned the credit not to himself but to the righteousness of the cause itself. Cochise probably thought it was the best deal available. For both of them, it probably was. The Apache were to have the homeland they desired, encompassing the Dragoon and Huachuca Mountains, even including Apache Pass, which Cochise swore to keep secure for the white man's use. Whatever faults he may have evidenced elsewhere, he proved a man of his word in that regard.

Gen. Howard returned in triumph. The mission had succeeded.

Unfortunately, he had not thought of everything. For that he has ever since received the condemnation of the citizenry, a phenomenon modern military personnel may not be totally unfamiliar with.

Gen. Howard had been unable to resolve the issue of Apache raiding into Mexico, an activity so engrained in their behavior as to be impossible to exorcise. Thus, it became inevitable that some bands of "broncos," uncontrolled by Cochise, would devolve into old habits, with Americans supplanting Mexicans in their attentions.

By November, 1872, Col. Crook had been forced to unleash nine separate columns to corral these renegades before peace could become reality. Though handicapped by a deadly plague among his horses, dubbed "Epizootic" for lack of a better moniker, he still put together the most brilliantly successful antiguerilla campaign in frontier history. His mule train supply system was still employed during jungle operations in World War II.

It was all made easier, if not actually possible, by the fact that the Chiricahuas, the backbone of Apacheria, remained quiet throughout.

When peace finally came, most believed it would not last a month. Yet it might never have been broken had not fate betrayed The Christian General who brought it to fruition.

In July, 1874, Cochise, who had suffered for years from a digestive disorder, died in his Stronghold, attended at the last by the faithful

Tom Jeffords. Within months, George Crook, by then a brigadier general, was detached from Arizona to help pursue the Sioux to the north. The policy of temperate behavior departed with both men.

The results were predictable. It was only after more than a decade of brutality that Geronimo surrendered for good. The tens of thousands of lives on both sides that Gen. Howard thought he had saved were squandered anyway.

Today, Howard University remains the only tangible memorial to Oliver Otis Howard. Otherwise, he is either completely forgotten or written off as an egotistical eccentric. Somehow, such a glib dismissal fails to give him his due.

Given the prevailing circumstances, Gen. Howard's penetration of Cochise's Stronghold must rate as one of the most awesome feats of valor in nineteenth-century Americana. He was the standard bearer for a brief era of governmental enlightenment which, had the policy succeeded, could have fundamentally altered the history of the American West.

However, neither side really gave it a chance. So the bloody denouement—from the lava beds of the Modocs through the northern plains of the Sioux to the arid wilderness of Apacheria and all points in between—became unavoidable.

The mission of The Christian General possibly did fail in Arizona. If so, that failure is the truest measure of his stature.

For in his time and place, men like Oliver Otis Howard could do nothing else.

CHAPTER
FOUR

Dean of the Dustoffers

by L. James Binder

E very few years, the government publishes a new volume up-
dating the nation's roster of Medal of Honor winners. There
is seldom anything deliberately lyrical or dramatic about the
wording of the citations which make up the bulk of these publications, but there is no more fascinating reading anywhere.

As the eye takes in the terse accounts of incredible acts of bravery
and sacrifice in battle, the mind instinctively gropes for pictures of
the kind of man who singlehandedly fights off wave after wave of
enemy attacks in force or who dashes repeatedly into hostile fire to
rescue wounded comrades. Being human—and American—we tend
to think of such a superman as being 10 feet tall, brawny and young
in years, and as fierce as a jungle tiger.

Relatively few of us are ever privileged to meet a Medal of Honor
holder, and so it is apt to come as a shock of sorts when this unconsciously held image is found to have been false. There *is* something

very special about a man who wears the Medal of Honor but it is not necessarily physical mass, youth or meanness.

No better living proof is CWO Michael J. Novosel, a recent recipient who is old enough to be the grandfather of most of the men who have fought in Vietnam. At 48 (he will be 49 next month), he is the Army's oldest Medal of Honor winner of the war. The soft-spoken Mr. Novosel is no giant: he is 5 feet 4 inches tall and weighs less than 150 pounds. As for meanness, he wasn't even carrying a weapon during those 2½ desperate hours on 2 October, 1969, when his repeated bravery in the face of heavy Viet Cong gunfire brought him an award of the Medal in ceremonies at the White House this summer.

The account of what he did in snatching 29 wounded South Vietnamese soldiers from under the blazing guns of an encircling enemy force is one of the most stirring stories of heroism of the war. But even if there had been no Medal of Honor, Michael Novosel would have been a remarkable man. How else could you describe a person who enlisted in the Army nearly a year before Pearl Harbor, ended World War II flying B-29s over Japan, gave up an airline pilot's job and an Air Force lieutenant colonel's commission to serve in the Vietnam war, and who the year before the action that resulted in the Medal was found to be suffering from glaucoma? These and other highlights of his life bespeak of qualities which make considerations like mere size insignificant in comparison.

Mr. Novosel won his Medal as a "dustoff" pilot, that almost legendary breed of helicopter flier whose record in rescuing wounded men during battle is one of the proudest chapters of this or any other war. When the word went out for him to pick up the injured during intense fighting in the Plain of Reeds, Kien Tuong Province, near Cambodia's enemy-dominated Parrot's Beak, he was on his second tour of Vietnam as a member of the 82nd Medical Detachment, 45th Medical Co., of the 68th Medical Group.

Three companies of crack South Vietnamese Special Forces had attacked a large enemy bunker system hidden in six-foot elephant grass within rifle distance of Cambodia. The site of a huge training center, complete with a full-size model of a triangular South Vietnamese fire base, the bunker was occupied by a large Viet Cong force armed with mortars, rockets, heavy automatic weapons and small arms. In the heavy combat that followed, the well-entrenched VC inflicted severe casualties on the South Vietnamese attackers, pinning down two companies for six hours and damaging several helicopter gunships and Air Force fighters which were sent in to cover their withdrawal. Many wounded men were still scattered throughout the three-kilometer area, and at 4:00 p.m. Capt. Harry L. Purdy, who was circling above in his command and control (C&C) helicopter, radioed for a dustoff ship.

Mr. Novosel had already been in the air for seven hours on other missions that day when he and his three-man crew were dispatched to evacuate the wounded. Flying through heavy thunderstorms and rain, he reached the battle area in clear weather and began looking for injured soldiers.

The most cogent account of what happened in the next 2½ hours is in the citation accompanying Mr. Novosel's Medal. It reads in part: "He unhesitatingly maneuvered his helicopter into a heavily fortified and defended enemy training area where a group of wounded Vietnamese soldiers were pinned down by a large enemy force. Flying without gunship or other cover and exposed to intense machine gun fire, Warrant Officer Novosel was able to locate and rescue a wounded soldier. Since all communications with the beleaguered troops had been lost, he repeatedly circled the battle area, flying at low level under continuous heavy fire to attract the attention of the scattered friendly troops. This display of courage visibly raised their morale, as they recognized this as a signal to assemble for evacuation. On six occasions, he and his crew were forced out of the battle area by the intense enemy fire, only to circle and return from another direction to land and extract additional troops. Near the end of the mission, a wounded soldier was spotted close to an enemy bunker. Fully realizing that he would attract a hail of enemy fire, Warrant Officer Novosel nevertheless attempted the extraction by hovering the helicopter backward. As the man was pulled on board, enemy automatic weapons opened fire at close range, damaged the aircraft and wounded Warrant Officer Novosel. He momentarily lost control of the aircraft, but quickly recovered and departed under withering enemy fire. In all, 15 extremely hazardous extractions were performed in order to remove wounded personnel. As a direct result of his selfless conduct, the lives of 29 soldiers were saved."

But citations cannot tell the whole story, any more than can any of the men who took part in the action on 2 October, 1969. All can agree on a chronological set of highlights, but few after-action reports describe how it feels to dive time and again into the very muzzles of blazing hostile weapons, or what is on the mind of a crew member

35

as his helicopter sits on the ground in a hail of bullets while a soldier with his intestines hanging out drags himself slowly toward you through the grass.

Sp. 4 Joseph Horvath, crew chief on Mr. Novosel's Huey, recalls receiving heavy automatic weapons fire "from all sides" as the ship first made its way along the fiery gantlet. "I never heard so much enemy fire before," the veteran dustoffer recalled. "We made several passes . . . and I see many gun flashes from bunkers which are all around us. These bunkers are all over the place." The rest of Horvath's account tells of repeated landings, of being driven away only to return again by another route, and of such feats as hanging out of the hovering craft on a litter strap to scoop up a wounded soldier from the elephant grass below. And around the ship the shooting, always the shooting.

CW2 Tyron Chamberlain, the co-pilot, tells the same story of passes, landings and near-landings, and adds that during the entire 2½ hours "we could hear the enemy machine guns firing at us." When the crew returned to base that night, he notes at the end of his report, it had flown "a total of 11 hours this day."

Said Sp. 4 Herbert Heinold, the craft's medical aid man: "As soon as we touched down we started receiving fire [but] we stayed till we got the wounded aboard. Numerous times, we tried to get down to pick up survivors but the intensity of the fire is too great; it's coming from all sides, so we try again. . . . The VC know what we are trying to do and open up on us every time we come close for pickups. At one time, I saw gun flashes coming from at least a half-dozen bunkers. . . ."

Capt. Purdy adds a note not covered in the citation: Mr. Novosel was instrumental in the successful withdrawal of the main South Vietnamese force because, between runs to pick up wounded, he guided the troops around the high-water areas which dot the marshy Plain of Reeds and to waiting U.S. Navy boats.

One of the things that stands out in Mr. Novosel's recollection of the rescues was of his first attempts to find a wounded soldier that the C&C ship had seen from high above. "Then we spotted him and all of a sudden we started seeing others all over. It happens that way all the time, but then you don't know if they're friendly troops or VC."

Another time, he recalls, he was taking especially heavy fire during one of his passes and he radioed up to Capt. Purdy that "They're most unfriendly down here." Capt. Purdy replied that he had strayed across the border into Cambodia, at that time forbidden to U.S. or

South Vietnamese incursion despite the enemy's huge concentrations of troops and weapons there.

He even picked up two unwounded South Vietnamese soldiers who apparently had thrown their weapons away during the action and, despite their protests, flew them back to their units.

The part of the action he remembers most vividly was the last rescue, made just as impending darkness was forcing a return to base. The bullet-scarred ship was filled with wounded soldiers when crew chief Horvath saw a South Vietnamese soldier lying near one of the bunkers from where enemy soldiers had been firing at them. Mr. Novosel warned the crew to stay low because he expected heavy fire, brought the helicopter around and low, and began backing it toward the wounded man. Backing is a ticklish maneuver which is supposed to protect the crew from gunfire from the rear. Horvath seized the injured soldier by the hand and was pulling him aboard when a VC opened up from pointblank range with an AK-47, spraying the plexiglas windows in front and below Mr. Novosel, and hitting the door and the rotor.

Plexiglas and copper-bullet fragments tore into his right calf and thigh (they are still there), something struck the control stick, injuring his hand, and another bullet hit the bottom of his shoe. Shock and the impact of the bullets made him lose control of the helicopter.

"I can remember saying 'Aw, hell, I'm hit.' I was disgusted, but I think the main reason was to warn the co-pilot, because you can be hit one second and unconscious the next," he said.

He recovered instantly, however, and climbed the ship quickly out of the elephant grass. Meanwhile, the wounded man had slipped from the ship but was seized by the hand by Horvath as he fell and finally was pulled inside about 60 feet in the air.

Mr. Novosel, who was back flying the next day, thinks often about the VC soldier who wounded him. "He must have been scared out of his wits, coming that close to take on something like a helicopter. I can just imagine his leader in that bunker telling him to 'get outside and get that bastard; he's been around long enough'."

But mixed with the wonder about the pluckiness of the man who tried to kill him is anger at himself "because I was outmaneuvered by the enemy. I try to outwit him when I go in and most times I think I'm smarter than he is, but he outfoxed me that afternoon."

What was he thinking as he dove repeatedly into the gunfire? What kept him going as the odds kept falling?

"The simple fact is that I was absolutely sure that I was not going to be hit. I felt that I was invulnerable. I know that it was a false sense of security but it kept me going."

Conversely, "I knew when I headed into that bunker backwards that I was going to be hit. Don't ask me how, but I knew it."

(The rest of the crew also escaped injury from enemy action, but Horvath suffered cuts when he fell while pulling a wounded man aboard. The helicopter, which was struck repeatedly by gunfire, had its VHF radio and air-speed indicator knocked out.)

"People ask me questions like, was I thinking of my family when I went in there and, if I was, how could I risk my life that way," Mr. Novosel said. "I suppose if I was thinking hard about them I probably wouldn't have done it but if everyone who ever went to war kept worrying about his family there wouldn't be anybody left to fight— kind of like the saying, 'suppose they had a war and nobody showed up'."

"You keep going because that is what you are supposed to do and because there are people down there who need you. I knew that those Vietnamese soldiers were in a bad way and I felt that I could at least *try* to get them out. Actually, I had a few things going for me—like the elephant grass. I just did not pose a very good target.

"You always tell yourself, too, that the enemy might actually *let* you come right in and pick up the wounded without firing a shot. That has happened to me before. I'd know they were there and could have blasted me if they wanted. But this time they opened up."

Because the enemy rarely respects the large red crosses on the sides and front of dustoff ships, at least enough to hold his fire, some of the rescue craft carry door guns. But not Mr. Novosel's chopper, nor does he carry any sidearms himself. "Guns are a hindrance on a mission like ours," he said. "They take up weight and space that could be used for patients."

One of the techniques Mr. Novosel used that day brings whistles of wonder from his oldest son, Michael Jr., a husky 21-year-old who is also a dustoff pilot with one full tour of Vietnam already on his record. It is called a "running landing" and consists of bringing the helicopter down and then skidding it along the ground to present a more difficult target to the enemy while crewmen reach out and scoop up the wounded. It is a tricky maneuver at best, even when the pilot does not have to contend with high elephant grass and soft, marshy ground. It is also supposed to be against regulations—but then so is flying a dustoff ship into heavy gunfire.

The veteran flier admits that he broke several rules that day but asserts that regulations sometimes have to be ignored when there are wounded who need prompt attention. Both Novosels, for example, say they have carried as many as 26 Vietnamese or 18 Americans at one time. Dustoff ships are supposed to hold seven Americans and a few more of the smaller Vietnamese.

Mr. Novosel has "extracted" more than 5,500 wounded soldiers and Vietnamese civilians during his two tours, more often than not from areas where the enemy was still shooting. "Sure, we take a lot of fire," he said, "because usually when we are called it means that people are in a bind."

One indication of how busy a dustoffer's life is was Mr. Novosel's log for the last year he was in Vietnam. He accumulated 1,407 hours in the air which averages out to about four hours of flying time, seven days a week. Another gauge is the 60 Oak Leaf Clusters he has for his Air Medal; basically, to be eligible for one medal it takes 25 combat assault hours on at least 25 missions, or 50 support missions for at least 50 hours.

(He also has three awards of the Distinguished Flying Cross, the Bronze Star, the Purple Heart and the Vietnamese Cross of Gallantry, the latter for the action in Kien Tuong Province.)

In conversation with him about his war record, he talks easily and modestly about his own exploits but reserves his superlatives for all of those who man Vietnam's medical evacuation ships.

"I don't know of any dustoff pilot who wouldn't have done the same thing if he had been in my shoes," he said.

A dustoff (or medevac) crewman is a proud and clannish kind of soldier whose performance in the war is given a large share of the credit for the high survival rate among the wounded. Flight in and out of dangerous places under heavy fire is routine, and the system has been so highly developed that medical care facilities are seldom more than an hour away by air.

"The kids I worked with are the most dedicated people in the world," said the Medal of Honor winner. "They keep going out into all kinds of tough situations, in all kinds of weather, day and night. The country owes a lot to the corps, much more than it has been given. On top of that, they have to fly into some of the most difficult and hardest places to find imaginable—and under life or death deadlines—with less navigational equipment than Lindbergh had."

Mr. Novosel's son, a chief warrant officer second class, served in his father's unit in Vietnam after graduating from flight training and was, in fact, qualified under the elder Novosel's supervision. He is credited with evacuating more than 2,200 wounded persons during his tour. Both he and his father are stationed at Fort Bragg, N.C., where the son flies helicopters and his father a C-47 as a member of the U.S. Army's parachute team, the "Golden Knights". Mr. Novosel and his wife, Ethel, are the parents of three other children: Patricia, a student at Georgia Southwestern College; Jean, 17; and John, 8.

A native of Etna, Pa., Mr. Novosel began his 16 years of active and 14 years of reserve service on 7 February, 1941, when he enlisted in the Regular Army. In those pre-Pearl Harbor days, he recalls, the chief impetus was his desire to become an aircraft mechanic, a skill he could make into a career when he became a civilian again. "We were just out of the Depression and the Army seemed like a good place to get an education," he said. "Besides, I'd wanted to fly all of my life."

If the Army had been scrupulous about using a measuring tape and scales, Mr. Novosel might never have got out of the repair hangars. At 5 feet 4 and about 125 pounds, he was considerably under the 5 feet 8 and 160 pounds which were the minimum for acceptance to flight training. Nevertheless, 13 months after enlisting he traded his staff sergeant's stripes for a flying cadet's uniform. He had simply told the Army he was considerably bigger than he was and in those times of rapid military build-up it chose to believe him.

After receiving his wings in December, 1942, at the Army Air Field at Lake Charles, La., he became an instructor and later a test pilot at Laredo, Tex.

"I flew every kind of bomber we had and three kinds of fighter planes besides," he says of those days.

But the urge to see action was great and he finally was assigned to the Pacific Theater where he piloted B-29s in a "few raids" over Japan before the war ended. He stayed in the Air Force after the war, and as a captain commanded the 99th Bombardment Squadron on Tinian, in the Marianas. In 1949, he left active duty and bought a restaurant in Fort Walton Beach, Fla.

He left his successful business to volunteer for service in the Korean War and, as a major, was in just long enough to complete a course at the Air Command and Staff School. Back off active duty, he spent several years managing a private club and a post exchange at Fort Walton Beach before going to work in 1959 for Southern Airways as an airliner pilot.

When the Vietnam conflict began to broaden in the early 1960s, Mr. Novosel was a lieutenant colonel in the Air Force Reserve. Feeling that he could be of help to the effort, he "made inquiries" about going back on active duty but soon learned that the Air Force was over-strength in its senior officer grades. So he obtained four years of military leave from Southern Airways and rejoined the Army on 29 June, 1964, as a warrant officer.

There is nothing complicated or especially high-sounding about Mr. Novosel's reply today when asked why he interrupted a good civilian career, took a sharp reduction in rank and volunteered to go back to war at an age when many military men are thinking about retirement. He answers, "Because I thought I could be of help." If pressed for a more easily understood explanation, he adds: "I felt that because of my military background I could do something to help the country [South Vietnam] out of its predicament."

His first medevac experience in an emergency situation was as a member of the Special Forces in 1965 when he carried wounded civilians to hospitals when the United States intervened in the Dominican Republic civil crisis. The next three years included a year's tour of dustoff duty in Vietnam where he evacuated his first 2,000 patients. Then in 1968, his leave from Southern Airways was up and he applied for discharge.

But his hopes of going back into a healthier branch of aviation were dashed during his discharge physical. Army physicians found that he had glaucoma, a serious eye disease which can result in progressive loss of vision. Doctors were able to check the affliction, but Southern physical requirements prevented him from resuming his job as a commercial pilot.

The Army let him go on flying on a waiver, however, and in 1969 Mr. Novosel—who is proud of the fact that he has never been grounded because of illness—was back in Vietnam. He still is required to apply medication to his eyes four times a day, although he has 20/20 vision and apparently has suffered no ill effects from the disease.

When the officer to whom he reported back in Vietnam saw his record, he assumed that Mr. Novosel would want a relatively safe assignment to fixed-wing duty. "I knew, though, that they needed dustoff pilots and I asked to go back to the helicopter," he recalls.

As a member of the Golden Knights, he flies on jumps and plays golf as often as he can. He has made three jumps since joining the team but gave it up after the third one "because I'm getting too old." His plans for the future are to retire in four years, probably back to Fort Walton Beach where he still owns a house.

He has been asked the inevitable question about his views of the war: "I have no quarrel with our being there" is as close as he will come to commenting on our commitment. Other remarks, though, indicate that he considers the question immaterial to a soldier with a duty to perform.

But he is more voluble about the quality of the American fighting man and the effect opposition to the war has had on him.

The subject came up when he was asked his reaction to the claim made by the most publicized of the five men who received the Medal of Honor with him in late June. The soldier, Sgt. Peter C. Lemon, boasted afterward that he had been smoking marijuana when he stood off the enemy attack that won him the Medal.

"I do wish he hadn't said that," Mr. Novosel said evenly. Then, asked if he thought the claim would cheapen the award, he added softly: "No; nothing could do that."

But he does not belong to that breed of old campaigner who feels that the Army is going to hell in a handbasket because it is letting soldiers wear their hair longer and making other compromises to accommodate youthful life styles:

"I don't care how long a man's hair is or whether he goes strictly by the book or not. What I want to know is, can he do his job. I look for little things, like a cook or a clerk going to the trouble of moving an oil drum out of the way because a helicopter might have to land where it's standing. That's the kind of man I want in my outfit."

He is an easy-going man but his eyes glint in anger when he talks about the public's attitude toward those fighting in Vietnam:

"Our soldiers keep going and have been doing a tremendous job in spite of all kinds of opposition at home. A soldier feels like he's hated and there isn't anything he can do about it—it isn't his fault he's in Vietnam. Afterward he goes back to an environment which at best merely tolerates him. It's a tribute to his toughness that he holds up."

Allegations that our troops are less than first-rate fighting men also get short shrift:

"In all my time in Vietnam, I never saw an American soldier do anything even approaching cowardice."

No accolade to courage ever came from a higher authority.

CHAPTER
FIVE

Adolphus Washington Greely, Renaissance Warrior

by George M. Hall

I t was the stuff of Walter Mitty's daydreams. Although underage, he fought for his country, was wounded three times, received a wartime commission and was later a hero of the American frontier and a renowned explorer of the Arctic. His promotion to brigadier general in the Regular Army came after only nine months in grade as a captain, in peacetime. He was a founder of the National Geographic Society and occupied an academic chair at George Washington University with only a high school education. He was on speaking terms with 12 presidents and an equal number of foreign

43

heads of state and principal ministers. He was easily one of the most famous men in the world of his time. His life culminated, at age 91, with the award of the Medal of Honor.

This remarkable record of Maj. Gen. Adolphus Washington Greely is documented beyond refute in official records. What is more, the account understates the character of the man. His active military service spanned 47 years—20 formative years, six years that tested his mettle in the Arctic wastelands and the bitter aftermath, and then 21 years as a general officer. To this must be added another 27 years of largely unremunerated public service after military retirement, yet he has become a forgotten man. Worse, the only widely disseminated official publication to make significant mention of Gen. Greely maligns his reputation by a misstatement of facts and by innuendos regarding his conduct during the Arctic expedition. Ironically, this experience was the crucible of his life and led within a few years to his remarkable promotion. His story is one that begs telling.

He was a direct descendant of the Mayflower settlers, and everything about a proper New England upbringing seems to have coalesced in this one individual. The attributes of hard work, respect for others, application to studies, good manners and prudent outspokenness developed during his childhood years of genteel poverty. When the Civil War broke out, Greely was still 17 years of age, a year younger than the Army would then tolerate. Nothing he did could persuade the recruiters to accept his enlistment until he wrote the number 18 inside his shoes and swore that he "was over 18." As far as can be determined from the records, it was his first and only prevarication.

The war years were spent on the battlefield except when convalescing from wounds. One of those wounds was received at Antietam when a Confederate round tore his jaw apart. The great bushy beard he wore thereafter was no affectation; it concealed the terribly disfiguring scar incurred on the bloodiest day of the Civil War. His capabilities, however, were easily recognized. His promotions to corporal and then to sergeant came rapidly, followed by his wartime commissioning at the age of 19. Subsequently, he was promoted to first lieutenant of Volunteers, then captain and finally received a brevet promotion to major before he was 21.

With the end of the war, however, the Army had little room for volunteer officers. In recognition of his unusual leadership abilities, Greely was retained on active duty for two more years, but then he had the choice of separation or a second lieutenant's commission in the Regular Army. Choosing the latter, he followed Horace Greeley's advice and, of course, that of his superiors and went West.

His many years of frontier duty yield a fascinating narrative. He combined the expertise of the signal corps, the engineers and the quartermaster as he almost singlehandedly established telegraph lines throughout the Southwest—in between uprisings of Indians for whom, unlike most Army professionals, he had great empathy.

Greely's motivation can only be construed as devotion to duty; it certainly was not promotion. His first chance for captain would not come until 1884, which meant serving a minimum of 17 years as a lieutenant, not counting his service in the Civil War. His assignments were rarely easy. After 11 years of frontier duty, he married Henrietta Nesmith and was promised a tour in Washington. The promise was kept—for four months—and then he was transferred back to the frontier. Nothing seemed to discourage him, however. From 1878 to 1881, he advocated an Arctic expedition and volunteered to lead it.

In 1881, the North Pole was inaccessible and would remain so for another 28 years. Nations settled for explorations and scientific studies of the surrounding polar regions and strove to place individuals in successive forays closer and closer to the goal. Such was the intent of the congressionally authorized and funded Lady Franklin Bay expedition.

The concept of that expedition was simple enough. The expedition party would be transported by ship to a point 81 degrees north latitude on Ellesmere Island during the summer of 1881. A supply ship would bring fresh provisions in 1882, and a relief ship would bring the party back to the United States in the summer of 1883. During the two-year period, they were to conduct numerous scientific experiments, make multitudinous observations and strive for "the farthest north."

The first year passed with outstanding results and an absence of any significant mishaps. A three-man party did set a new record for farthest north, and the effect of the universe (not just the moon) on the tides was discovered. The expedition had some hardships. For more than four months, no sunlight breached the dark of the base camp, and during that period, the *high* temperatures never exceeded minus 37 degrees Fahrenheit. The windchill factor as a concept had not yet been invented, but every member of the party learned a great deal about it. These difficulties notwithstanding, the morale remained higher than anticipated until the supply ship failed to show.

This contingency was anticipated. The original supplies, augmented by local hunting and fishing, were adequate for the second year, but the fear of the relief ship scheduled for 1883 also failing to make it through was on everyone's mind. That fear turned out to be more than justified. Greely's orders stated he was to start moving south as best he could if the relief ship did not appear by 1 September. What followed during the next ten months proved beyond all doubt that hell could freeze over. It is impossible in the space of a few paragraphs to describe accurately the experience of that period. A year later, Greely himself would write:

> No pen could ever convey to the world an adequate idea of the abject misery and extreme wretchedness to which we were reduced at Cape Sabine. Insufficiently clothed, for months without drinking water, destitute of warmth, our sleeping bags frozen to the ground, our walls, roof, and floor covered with frost and ice, subsisting on *one-fifth* of an Arctic ration—almost without clothing, light, heat, or food, yet we never were without courage, faith, and hope. The extraordinary spirit of loyalty, patience, charity, and self-denial—daily and almost universally exhibited by our famished and nearly maddened party—must be read between the lines in the account of our daily life penned under such desperate and untoward circumstances. Such words, written at such a time, I have not the heart to enlarge on.

Of the 25 members of the original party, 17 died of starvation, frostbite or complications arising from malnutrition. Another was shot. Of the seven survivors, one died within two weeks, and three were on the point of death. An extended review of the evidence and, more important, the outcome of the investigations that followed the rescue suggest that only Greely's rock-solid leadership, compassion, decisiveness and courage explain why there were any survivors at all.

The rescue, as the reader might well surmise, was dramatic and widely reported, but for Greely it only meant a change of venue—from the trials of the Arctic to those of Washington. He would face two years of unfounded allegations, criticism and reprobation until the President, Congress and the Army became convinced of his sterling character and abilities. Any lesser man might well have crumbled under the points of vexation foisted on Greely.

The most serious of the allegations was that he condoned, if not practiced cannibalism, on the deceased members of the expedition—at a time and place in history when cannibalism was regarded on a par with murder and treason. The widow of the expedition's contract surgeon—Dr. Octave Pavy—made this allegation. In time, a revelation of the facts indicated that a few members of the party had committed the offense but that they in turn died from the effects of it. Moreover, it was determined that no human being under the circumstances could have prevented this action from occurring among some members of the expedition.

The second point was Greely's order to execute Pvt. Charles B. Henry for disobeying orders. This was true, but Greely made no attempt to hide it. On the contrary, his first action upon his return was to request a court of inquiry, but the secretary of war, Robert Todd Lincoln (Abraham Lincoln's only surviving son) decided it was unnecessary. Pvt. Henry proved to have been a convicted forger and a deserter from the Army who reenlisted under an alias. On the expedition, he repeatedly stole and consumed large amounts of the meager rations available and jeopardized the lives of the survivors. He was given every opportunity to stop his intolerable behavior, but it only grew worse. In the end, Greely had no choice but to order Pvt. Henry's execution. Until this matter was cleared up, however, the public was led to believe Greely was a harsh and insensitive tyrant.

Another point of vexation for Greely was that he had been passed over for promotion to captain, not because of any lack of ability, but because it was presumed he would not survive the expedition. His promotion quota instead went to the direct commissioning of a civilian. Far more galling to him was his discovery of the lack of effort to ensure the expedition was relieved in 1883. As far as can be inferred from the records, only the personal plea of Mrs. Greely directly to Congress energized the successful attempt the following year.

The fourth point was the refusal of the Army to provide proper compensation to the survivors of his command. On the contrary, the Army tried to charge the survivors for loss of clothing and other equipment during the harrowing final ten months. Greely's compassion was tested to the full.

The Army was his career, the only professional life he knew; but at the time, it was questionable if he would ever see promotion to captain. Instead of protecting his own interests, he openly advised his men to employ a lobbyist to assist in obtaining passage of a private relief bill in Congress, which was successful.

Then, in striving to obtain a direct commission for one of the survivors, he took the President and Congress to task in his widely published account of the expedition:

> It is inevitable in most great undertakings that the subordinates should be relegated to secondary places, but I cannot believe that our great nation, which spent money so lavishly to save these men, will allow their heroic endurance and manly virtues to pass unrewarded. Lieutenant Lockwood and the Eskimo Christiansen have unhappily passed away, but Sergeant Brainard, who strove with them successfully to gain for the country the honors of the Farthest North, yet remains, after eight years of stainless and extraordinary service in the ranks, a sergeant. His manhood, courage, and self-sacrifice, displayed on the polar sea and at Sabine, would have gained him a commission at once in any other service of the world.

After two years, the nightmare showed signs of abating. His promotion to captain came through. Nine months later, when the chief signal officer, Brig. Gen. William B. Hazen, died, Greely was selected for the position. President Grover Cleveland forwarded it to Congress with the strongest recommendation. Dr. Pavy's widow tried once more to smear Greely's reputation, but her testimony no longer had any effect. Congress gave its consent, and on 3 March, 1887, Greely was promoted directly to brigadier general in the Regular Army. Shortly before, President Cleveland had commissioned Sgt. Brainard a second lieutenant, and he eventually rose to brigadier general.

Understandably, Greely's military career as a general officer was more physically comfortable than his days as a lieutenant, and his accomplishments had a greater influence by virtue of his rank and position. Notwithstanding more temptations than faced by most senior officers, nothing went to his head. He continued as a respectfully outspoken leader of men, of organizations and of ideas, and in time, he developed a wry sense of humor. His worse fault consisted of expressing his desire for promotion to major general (after 15 years in grade as brigadier general) and evincing some pride in a few of his accomplishments in the memoir he wrote at 83. His were not trivial accomplishments.

At a time when the Army—and Navy—advocated exploration, Gen. Greely was a principal founder of the National Geographic Society. This was not in itself a chore, but it led to some personal disappointments that further demonstrated the character of the man. On four occasions, he felt it necessary to decline the presidency of the society because of conflicting duties.

A more painful episode arose from Adm. Robert E. Peary's claim to have been the first person to reach the North Pole (in 1909). Adm. Peary had been Greely's most severe critic after the rescue, but the general maintained his silence and advised Adm. Peary, whenever asked, on conditions in the Arctic. Twenty-eight years later, when Adm. Peary reached the Pole, or so he believed, Gen. Greely was among the first to proffer congratulations and praise, although by rigorous study of Adm. Peary's documents he ascertained that Peary had missed the mark because of some technical errors in navigation. An article in the September 1988 issue of the *National Geographic* implies that Peary's navigation may have been faulty, that he missed the Pole and apparently was aware of that fact at the time. Greely maintained his silence on this until 1927, seven years after Adm. Peary died.

As a result, Adm. Peary went down in history, it is believed, incorrectly as the first man to reach the Pole. Notwithstanding Gen. Greely's silence, the admiral remained a bitter and outspoken critic of the general. When in 1919 the National Geographic Society awarded the Hubbard Trophy to Vilhjalmur Stefansson, another famed Arctic explorer, the society asked Gen. Greely to introduce the recipient. Adm. Peary presented the award itself. The next day, Dr. Gilbert Grosvenor, president of the society, said Mr. Stefansson's achievement of having the two explorers shake hands in public was greater than the achievements for which the Hubbard Trophy had been awarded.

Gen. Greely's most important scientific contribution, however, arose not from the Arctic but from his personal and technical leadership of the U.S. Weather Service until it was transferred from the Army to the Department of Agriculture in 1891. Although the Weather Service has vastly improved since that time, Gen. Greely laid the intellectual groundwork for that achievement. His major technical contribution to the Army itself was even more significant. At the time, most Army professionals were adamantly opposed to telegraphic communications on the battlefield. The cavalry, in particular, believed there never would be a substitute for the messenger on horseback.

The moment of truth came with the Battle of Santiago during the Spanish-American War. The senior commanders selected for the campaign made a point of refusing to take telegraph equipment, but Gen. Greely took the initiative and established an undersea cable from Key West to Cuba and laid tactical wire on land. The field commanders afterward begrudgingly admitted to the usefulness of the wire, but the more important consequence was the timely transmittal of then-Col. Theodore Roosevelt's famous round-robin letter.

The Battle of Santiago had not incurred particularly large numbers of battle casualties, but an epidemic of typhoid, yellow fever and malaria broke out in the camps. The War Department ordered the Army to remain in camp until the epidemic was over.

Col. Roosevelt immediately recognized that in this instance the climatic conditions would increase the number of deaths and wrote a letter to that effect, which he and eight general officers signed. It was transmitted over Gen. Greely's cable and caused the immediate reversal of the order and the evacuation of the troops from Cuba.

Depending on which estimate one reads, between several hundred and several thousand lives were saved. From that moment forward, the Army became a believer in electrically transmitted communications and kept Gen. Greely quite busy overseeing the establishment of telegraph lines in Alaska and the Philippines.

This growing record of accomplishments led Teddy Roosevelt, after he became President, to promote Greely to major general in 1906. He was assigned as commander, Western Department of the Army headquartered in San Francisco—a few days before the devastating earthquake. Gen. Greely's administration of martial law that followed became a model of prudent judgment, initiative and leadership in time of civil disaster. By the time civil authority was fully restored, however, Greely had little more than a year to serve before statutory retirement on his sixty-fourth birthday. For that one year, he led a relatively passive existence, except for an Indian uprising among the Utes that he personally settled before hostilities broke out.

Retirement came in April, 1908, although he was recalled in 1911 to represent the U.S. Army at the coronation of George V of Great Britain. In retirement, however, Greely followed an even busier schedule than he had as a general. He often lectured, but when he spoke on the subject of the Arctic expedition, out of respect to his fallen comrades, he would accept no fee. Annually on 22 June, as often as circumstances would permit, he would observe the anniversary of the Arctic rescue by dining with Gen. Brainard.

In all of his career after the rescue, the most remarkable aspects were not the achievements but his relationship with presidents and Congress. He absolutely refused to perform any political favor unless the individual for whom the favor was sought was the most deserving. In one case, after he had twice refused to honor a congressman's request, Gen. Greely inquired why he was not asked to do something for a very deserving man from the congressman's state. The latter replied that a deserving man could take care of himself and that congressmen had to plead for the low-down and shiftless. So consistent and unblemished was Gen. Greely's conduct that no congressman ever sought vengeance in private or in public, and it seems that Greely was on speaking terms with every president from Andrew Johnson to Herbert Hoover and was often invited to the White House.

As he approached his ninety-first birthday, seven months before he died, one of his former subordinates realized the country had not appropriately honored Gen. Greely for his many accomplishments. Billy Mitchell, whose father served as U.S. senator from Wisconsin, pleaded to Congress to make amends for that oversight. Congress agreed and voted to bestow the nation's highest recognition on him. Under ordinary circumstances, the award would have been presented with public ceremony, but since the general was no longer in the best of health, the secretary of war, George Dern, and other dignitaries went to Gen. Greely's home in Georgetown and there presented him with the Medal of Honor. The citation was the shortest in the history of that medal (to this day): "For a life of splendid public service." *The New York Times* suggested it was an understatement.

His posthumous honors include the Army post near Delta Junction in Alaska and the headquarters building at Ft. Huachuca, Ariz., being named for him. More than one officer, however, has thought the honored name referred to Horace Greeley. Why the memory of this remarkable man and his record have been forgotten is speculation. Perhaps it is because Greely was not a senior general in time of war or that he was not colorful and lacked amiableness.

Justice Oliver Wendell Holmes Jr., who served in the Civil War with Greely's sister regiment and, like Greely, was wounded three times, said: "This also is the faith of the soldier, having known great things, to be content with silence." Yet, if silence is to remain Gen. Greely's fate in history, the profanation of his reputation in an official document is inexcusable. *The Armed Forces Officer* (Government Printing Office, 1950) in the chapter, "Human Nature," states:

> When the Greely Expedition was at last rescued at Cape Sabine on June 22, 1884, by the third expedition—the Revenue Cutter *Bear* and the *Thetis* under Commander Winfield S. Schley, USN—only seven men remained alive. Even in these, the spark of life was so feeble that their tent was down over them and they had resigned themselves to death . . . Until the end, discipline was kept in Greely's force. But this was not primarily due to

Lieutenant Greely, the aloof, strict disciplinarian who commanded by giving orders, instead of by trying to command the spirits and loyalties of men. That any survived was due to the personal force and example of Sgt. (later Brig. Gen.) David L. Brainard, who believed in discipline as did Greely, and supported his chief steadfastly, but also supplied the human warmth and helping hand which rallied other men, where Greely's strictures only made them want to fight back.

This account neglects to mention that Greely rose to major general and was personally responsible for Brainard's obtaining a commission. More important, the author seems to have overlooked one of the more fundamental of all Army traditions. Troops are commanded by officers who must be prepared in the extreme to order them into the jaws of death. This mandates a certain distance be maintained between the commander and his troops, lest "familiarity breed contempt." To soften this harsh reality, good commanders rely extensively on their senior noncommissioned officers—their sergeants major and first sergeants. The officer and the sergeant both strive to be leaders, but the officer should lean toward commandership, while the sergeant must often be an emissary. The best noncommissioned officers are worth their weight in gold. In the case of Sgt. Brainard, it was platinum, but this in no way detracts from the exemplary leadership demonstrated by Greely.

The account in *The Armed Forces Officer* also errs on a factual basis with respect to the condition of the survivors at the moment of their rescue. A few months after the rescue, Commander Schley wrote to Greely:

On the occasion of your rescue on the evening of June 22nd last, by the relief expedition under my command, I saw no indications of insubordination nor of division among your party. On the contrary, I was much impressed by the salutes of Brainard, Frederick and Biederbick when I approached your camp. This one slight feature bore its own testimony to the condition of your command.

Perhaps the most telling evidence of Greely's leadership and compassion centers on Sgt. Elison. Elison was the survivor who died after the rescue. Months earlier, in an heroic effort to retrieve a distant cache of food, Elison was struck with frostbite. Greely would write:

Though both hands and both feet had been lost by natural amputation, his indomitable will-power and naturally fine physique kept him alive for seven and a half months. Utterly hope-less, fed with double our ration, cared for and nursed by his starving comrades, no open word or secret insinuation ever came to me that this drain on our strength and resources was useless—this man a burden. I hardly know now whether most to admire the courage and will which kept Elison alive, or the devotion and charity of his comrades who gave so freely of their strength, food, and tender offices, knowing all the while that their sacrifices were in vain.

These sentiments are not the mark of a martinet. Moreover, Greely saw to the needs of the survivors for as long as they lived, whether this meant lecturing them like a Dutch uncle when they fell into bad habits or loaning them money without hesitation or interest, or just inquiring into their well-being.

Whether or not the account in *The Armed Forces Officer* will be rec-tified is problematic, but the Army at least owes it to the memory of Gen. Greely and his descendants, one of whom also rose to general officer rank, to set the record straight, for he was a soldier who pos-sessed a rare combination of worthy attributes with no disabling ones: outspoken when duty required it, without loss of reserve or pro-tocol; absolute integrity, without intransigence or self-righteousness; good judgment, combined with intelligence and foresight; and cour-age, both in the immediate sense of the battlefield and in the endur-ing sense of prolonged trials of strength. For the sake of his country and the Army, he made the most of every opportunity that came his way, but rarely if ever complained of adversity. When he elected to forgo tactfulness, it was because he was intolerant of injustices vis-ited upon his subordinates. He was in every sense of the word a great and good man.

PART TWO

LEADERS WITH STYLE

CHAPTER SIX

Slim

by Brenda Ralph Lewis

F ield Marshal William Viscount Slim of Yarralumla and Bish-
opston, GCB, GCMG, GCVO, GBE, DSO, MC, was the greatest
exception to the rule that in order to achieve fame, acclaim
and success a man has to be a bit of a bastard. On the contrary, Slim
was so pronouncedly the opposite that he seems almost too good to
be true.

He rose to the peak of his profession, universally liked, admired and
respected. He never failed to observe the demands of good manners,
even in the most grueling wartime situations. He was to a large extent an "establishment" figure, without ever being stuffy or pompous
about it. Even more remarkably, he inspired such affection among the
men of the 14th Army whom he led to triumph over the Japanese in
Burma in 1945, that they always spoke of fighting *with*, not *under*,
him.

When a memorial service was held at St. Paul's Cathedral in London over 30 years later in 1976, more than 2,000 of them came to honor the memory of the commander they still regarded, with enormous affection, as "Uncle Bill."

This unusual legacy of regard, unmatched by any other wartime leader, was left behind by a man whose personality was never blatant, but was rooted in the quieter virtues of integrity, humanity and reliability. Slim certainly possessed charisma, but without its usual flamboyance, and he was not a man for those who preferred their heroes to be rambunctious or nonconformist.

There was none of the dash and panache of Erwin Rommel, nor the blazing zeal of the eccentric Orde Wingate, nor the buccaneering brashness of George Patton, and certainly not the acerbity of Gen. Joseph Stilwell. Stilwell was not called "Vinegar Joe" for nothing, but he found Slim so eminently likable that for him alone among the "Limeys," he dimmed his passionate anglophobia.

What probably disarmed the prickly Stilwell was what puzzled many people about Bill Slim. He never seemed to be aware of his own stature, and progressed by outstanding ability through the halls of fame without ever quite realizing what he was doing there. Others, however, knew.

As early as 1926, when Slim was a 35-year-old captain in the Indian Army, a fellow officer referred to him, out of his hearing, as "a man who's going to be commander in chief." Slim himself would have scoffed at the very idea.

Later, in 1936, when Lord Gort, commandant of the Imperial Defence College, was recommending that Slim be made a colonel as soon as possible because he was "obviously a commander," Slim was privately starting to worry about his chances of promotion. Those worries reached such a pitch that he briefly contemplated leaving the army to seek some civilian occupation with a better future.

In the course of time, Slim rose far beyond a colonelcy, to become a knight (1944), commander in chief of Allied land forces in Southeast Asia (1945), commandant of the Imperial Defence College (1946), a field marshal (1948), chief of the Imperial General Staff (1948), governor general of Australia (1953–1960) and in his last years, until a few months before his death in 1970, governor and constable of Windsor Castle.

Throughout, he seemed to greet advancement in the same bemused mood which marked his return from a conference in Whitehall in the summer of 1945. His wife, Aileen, became worried when she saw him standing at the door of their hotel room in a silent daze, apparently dumbstruck by some piece of startling news.

"Astonishing, astonishing . . . ," Slim was muttering. "They've made me the commander in chief!"

His modesty was as genuine as it was rare among men who rise to the apex of achievement. In this, Slim remained throughout his long life the same 16-year-old who in 1908 dreamed of becoming an army officer, but realized that birth, background and social status were against him.

In those days, the higher echelons of the British Army resembled an exclusive club for the high- or nobly-born and the well-to-do. Rising from private to general had certainly been attained—by Slim's boyhood hero, "Fighting Mac" Macdonald—but it was too extraordinary to be easily repeatable.

Class-wise—and "class" was crucial then—Slim was caught between the British social strata. As the son of a small Bristol businessman, a wholesale hardware trader, he was a bit too well placed to enlist in the ranks. At the same time, his family background, undoubtedly humble, often impecunious, seemed to preclude Slim from officer status.

Regretfully, but realistically because the teetering family finances required him to find work quickly, Slim opted for a teaching job in Birmingham at 17/6d. per week (about 37 cents) and found himself face to face with some of the roughest, toughest and most deprived pupils in the entire school system.

More than one teacher, encountering such unwashed, coarse-mannered children of the slums, either recoiled in digust or turned socialist revolutionary to end their scandalous plight. Slim, who held no brief for snobbery and was never political, did neither.

He perceived the sturdy courage beneath the grime, the stoicism beneath the pinched faces of undernourishment and the quick-witted humor and loyalty beneath the misery. In later years, this teaching experience emerged as a valuable asset to Slim the military commander; he knew instinctively what motivated, what daunted and what roused the ordinary humble "other ranks" under his command.

Slim never agreed with another high-ranking British commander who once told him that it was possible to talk to officers, but not to ordinary soldiers, about the higher, more spiritual aspects of soldiering such as military traditions or duty or the secrets of morale. Nor did he believe, as some others were convinced, that such men had to be lectured by their leaders.

Slim always talked *with*, not *to*, his men. It was the secret of the undimmed loyalty and abiding regard they conceived for him. His approach was made quite clear to them before the Burma campaign in 1945 when he toured 14th Army units to sit informally on the hood of his jeep and discuss ideas about the task that lay ahead.

It was man-to-man, human-to-human talk, and Slim was as far removed as could possibly be from the great commander come down from on high to bestow his wisdom on the lowly.

Quite possibly, Slim dealt with his men in this fashion because he recalled too vividly what life was actually like at lowly levels of society. He had enough experience of it himself, quite apart from the two years he spent teaching in Birmingham. The pre-1914 business world hardly knew a lower form of life than the junior clerk, and this, for a metal tube manufacturing firm, is what Slim became in 1910.

Nevertheless, he had not entirely abandoned his soldiering ambitions. He always had a small book of military exercises and tactics about him, made favorite reading out of manuals with titles like *Field Service and Musketry Regulations* and, in 1912, joined the Officers Training Corps. He was soon promoted to lance corporal.

Slim's military life at this juncture was necessarily peripheral, consisting of evening drills, weekend and summer camps and rifle exercises practiced in the privacy of his bedroom. However, World War I, which was then brewing, gave him the chance that peacetime soldiering might never have afforded. On 22 August, 1914, 18 days after the war began, Lance Corporal William Slim was gazetted second lieutenant in the Royal Warwickshire Regiment and within a month was faced with that officer's nightmare: a mutiny.

Only 23 years old at the time, he was already an impressive figure. The embryo was already there of the burly, jut-jawed, keen-eyed "Uncle Bill" of Burma campaign days, gazing confidently and not a little stubbornly from the shadows beneath his broad-brimmed bush hat. The mutineers in question were rough, tough miners who had locked themselves in barracks over a complaint about pay.

The sergeant and sergeant major, approaching the problem as one of military discipline, failed to roust them out. Slim approached the mutineers quite differently: as men with a grievance who needed to air it. It was an unusual approach and one which, remarkably, contained no tricks. The miners let Slim inside the barracks, and they all sat down on bunks to talk it over. The upshot was that the mutineers agreed to end their strike after Slim promised to scrutinize each man's account.

This early side of command led Slim to recommend later that all officers should learn how to recognize the causes of mutiny and how to prevent them. He regarded mutiny as a human problem. His fellow officers, on the other hand, regarded as bad taste the very idea that army mutinies should be studied like tactics.

The First World War was, of course, a conflict that saw several, infinitely more serious mutinies in the armies of the combatants and in Belgium, France, Iraq, and particularly at Gallipoli, Bill Slim got plenty of experience in the holocaust horror and waste of life that produced such desperate, last-resort protests.

At Gallipoli in 1916, Slim suffered the first of several injuries in battle, and was so badly wounded in the lungs that, at one point, it seemed he would die or at least spend the rest of his life as an invalid. In fact, when Slim reached Southampton on board a hospital ship, an orderly had pinned a notice on him which read: "Dangerous. Not to be moved by train."

Nonetheless, Slim recovered and afterwards served in Mesopotamia, where he earned himself his Military Cross, even though not properly fit for active service. After the war ended, Slim joined the Indian Army as a captain in the 1/6th Gurkha Rifles. His choice was influenced by the admiration he had conceived for the Gurkhas who fought at Gallipoli. It was by no means easy, however, for an outsider like him to be accepted by such men.

The Gurkhas were military connoisseurs, fighters of compulsive valor and astounding endurance, with an instinct for military quality inborn by centuries of tradition. The currency of their regard was the ability to lead, not because the stripes or pips on a uniform said so, but because the heart beneath it was the lionheart of a leader.

While the Gurkhas were observing and assessing the stuff Slim was made of, a certain detached air prevailed in the 1/6th officers' mess. It did not last long. Not only was Slim "obviously a commander," well versed in the subtle business of maintaining discipline while retaining friendship, but there was no hint about him of the haughty "pukka sahib," a British master-type so prevalent at the time in British-ruled India.

On the contrary. Slim moved among other races as he moved among his own—as a human being in contact with other human beings. As a result, the Gurkhas quickly responded to Slim the man as well as to Slim the soldier, and accepted him in the all-embracing way acceptance means in Eastern society: as a member of their large and mutually loyal family.

It is significant that the 14th Army, from whom Slim elicited such extraordinary response, was in the main made up of Asian soldiers.

If Slim found it relatively easy to gain acceptance among a people who bestowed friendship totally but not lightly, he did not find the interwar years in India free from trial and worry. Apart from his concern that age might rob him of promotion, he was constantly bothered that lack of money made his bank statement such dismal reading. The habit of worrying about money seems to have been another facet of his modest image of himself, and was probably bred into him by his own impecunious youth and the dire poverty he had seen in Birmingham before World War I.

Even after he became an illustrious public figure, money worries still haunted him, and to such an extent that when he retired as governor general of Australia the Australian government sought to ease his mind by granting him a pension. It was an unprecedented step.

The money problem was much more pressing, though, after 1926, when Slim married and produced, in 1927 and 1930, a family of two children. His solution then was to turn writer. In the 1930s, 15 guineas (about seven dollars) a story and twice as much for an article were attractive pickings for the part-time writer and, fortunately for Slim and his bank manager, he was a successful one.

As Anthony Mills, Slim had stories and articles published regularly in British newspapers and magazines, and though by no means a master of literature, he displayed in them that knack of arousing and retaining interest, for explaining situations clearly and narrating events cogently which was later so valuable in what he called his "stump talks" with the men of the 14th Army.

World War II, in which Slim first saw service in the Sudan and Iraq, was a war in which facility with words and human communication counted for more than in any previous conflict. The need for rapport between commanders and men had been branded on the minds of men of high rank by their own experience as juniors in World War I.

Then, generals were deservedly held in contempt for remaining aloof, comfortable and safe in country houses far behind the lines while the men at the front got on with the bloody business of fighting and dying. This was why commanders in the Second War were so meticulous about visiting their own front lines, a task which Slim embraced with particular zest.

He also realized that the jungles of Burma, where he arrived in March, 1942, represented a unique battleground, requiring more than the usual care to see that the troops on the ground did not feel remote from the men at the top. He had long believed that the predominant emotion of soldiers on a battlefield was loneliness, and that emotion was greatly magnified by the eerie, claustrophobic jungle country where enemies could lurk behind every tree, every mound of undergrowth and along every overgrown path.

In the Burmese jungle, the Turkish bath of the tropics is at its sweatiest, thirstiest, most fly-infested and most enervating during April and May, and it was during those months in 1942 that the I Burma Corps, or "Burcorps," under Slim's direction, made the longest retreat in the history of the British Army. As they withdrew towards Imphal, in eastern India, the victorious Japanese were gobbling up Burma and hammering them from the air, as well as from the ground.

Obstructing the British as they went were swarms of terrified refugees. Communication and liaison consisted of wireless sets with batteries charged by bicycle wheels, or runners and messengers who might or might not get through. Psychologically, as well as physically, this protracted and harrowing disgrace to British arms might well have seen the nadir of morale and fighting spirit.

Slim instinctively understood such things, which was why he took such great pains to reach his officers and men and talk to them, in person when he could or otherwise through the makeshift wireless system.

"This is Bill speaking," was his normal introduction when wireless contact was made. The friendly, good-humored, never-dictatorial voice coming through the crackle infused so much confidence and cheer into the troops that in May, Burcorps arrived at Imphal, exhausted, decimated, but still a cohesive force with its morale and fighting spirit intact.

To a great extent, however, Slim's outward calm during the withdrawal in which the corps lost 42,000 men, half of them "missing," was something of a mask. Beneath the surface of imperturbable calm and faith, Slim was a serious-minded, sensitive and very self-critical man. Often, this inner self brought him to the point of self-torture, making him chew over thoughts of his failures in introspective despair.

Concealing it as well as he did called for mammoth efforts of self-control. In this, Slim was a typical perfectionist. To him, "the only test of generalship is success" and once the retreat from Burma was complete, he was nagged by "the contrast between my generalship and the enemy's."

"For myself," Slim concluded glumly, "I had little to be proud of . . ."

Many disagreed, for like the evacuation of the Anglo-French forces at Dunkirk in 1940, the retreat from Burma two years later was a defeat that masqueraded very well as a triumph of survival.

What was more—and Slim appeared to take insufficient account of it—it had been accomplished at a psychologically bad time. The Japanese were earning themselves a name as "invincible" in the first months of 1942 as they swept through Southeast Asia and across the Pacific in a seemingly unstoppable tide. This rampage was inevitable, in Burma as elsewhere, for British preparations for defense had been ludicrously inadequate.

Defense plans, if they could be called that, had been founded on two fallacies: the impregnability of Singapore, the fortress island which protected the Burma-Malaya peninsula, and the impenetrability of the jungles of Siam (Thialand), Malaya and Burma. No wonder that, when the Japanese, long underrated as fighters by Western military minds, scooped up the impregnable fortress and penetrated the impenetrable jungle, the myth that they were unbeatable gained so much credence.

Slim had never been one to swallow whole any myth or fact without first examining and assessing it, and he refused to swallow this one. Despite the private misery he suffered at what he saw as his own shortcomings, he emerged from the Burma retreat with a conclusion that, given the mental climate of the time, was both startling and unexpected. The retreat had shown him that the British and Indian soldier was the equal of the Japanese in jungle fighting, the very area of warfare in which the latter were presumed to be supreme.

Convincing his men of this equality comprised in fact the purpose and substance of the regular talks Slim had with them after Lord Louis Mountbatten, newly arrived in October, 1943, as supreme allied commander, Southeast Asia, personally picked him to lead the 14th Army.

As a motivating spur, Slim's exercise in public relations resembled the Fireside Chats with which President Roosevelt had cheered the Americans through the Great Depression of the 1930s. And like Roosevelt's New Deal of those years, the vitalization of the 14th Army was hinged onto a carefully formulated, overall course of action.

"War," a long standing military dictum lays down, "is movement in a resistant medium." That idea lay at the core of Slim's concept of successful jungle warfare. He envisaged few and only well-judged frontal attacks on the enemy, no attacks at all on a narrow front, outflanking maneuvers as a standard tactic, widespread use of tanks except in swampland, constant patrols to probe the jungle situation and enable columns to move rapidly and as freely as possible, stringing out the enemy to make him weaker, and the use of airlifts not only for supplies but for large bodies of men up to division size.

Implicit in all this were what Slim considered "the fundamentals of war": that soldiers must be trained before they can fight, fed before they can march and relieved before they are worn out. Above all, Slim's concept required the belief that these tactics and principles were valid and that the 14th Army could achieve success with them.

So it eventually proved, despite the disappointing results of the two trial runs in western Burma: the Arakan campaigns of 1942–43 and 1943–44. Both ended in stalemate, washed out by the May monsoons. The Japanese, quite naturally, had assumed after the headlong retreat from Burma in early 1942, that they were fighting a feeble enemy. If the Arakan campaigns did anything to reinforce that impression, however, it was soon abruptly exorcised after April, 1944, when the Japanese 15th Army invaded eastern India and invested Imphal and Kohima.

Here, the Japanese discovered that they were dealing with a confident enemy, well entrenched and lavishly armed and armored, who not only refused to be budged but thrust them back from Imphal by September, 1944, and then proceeded to chase them through the jungle-smothered hills and valleys of Burma.

To their shock and chagrin, the Japanese were taken by surprise when Slim's army crossed the mighty Chindwin, Irrawaddy and Sittang rivers, and were then thrashed to defeat in decisive battles at Mandalay and Meiktila in March, 1945, and the final showdown at Rangoon in May.

Brilliant but simple, and founded firmly on Napoleon's tenet and his own that the preeminent factor in war is morale, Slim's plan for crushing the Japanese had gone precisely as he had envisaged. He was, in fact, the only Allied general to defeat a major Japanese army and retrieve a conquered territory through ground warfare alone.

Even in Slim's own perfectionist mind, there could be no doubt this time that he had passed the only test of generalship.

CHAPTER
SEVEN

Troop Command by Intuition

by Martin Blumenson

L eadership, a military officer's most prized possession, has been
the subject of endless debate and discussion not only because
it is a vital asset but also because its exercise is extremely difficult to define. We have all seen leadership at work, but to explain
why it functions is elusive, slippery and, in the end, usually uncon-
vincing.

The normal way of attacking the issue is by studying the lives of
great leaders, then distilling from their successful activities a list of
the personal characteristics commonly displayed. Traits thus extracted through the ages are very much alike. A model leader, it turns
out, should be endowed with integrity, professional competence,
physical, mental and moral courage, the ability to communicate and

the like. These qualities, like the principles of war, are shorthand notes, reminders of what is deemed more or less universally to be useful and good.

The problem is, they miss the point. They ignore the nature of those who were led. They fail to tell us the essential thing. What made it possible for a leader to project his will? What enabled him to animate his followers to his desired goals?

To say simply that the answer lies in the personality of the leader alone or in an enigma so obscure as to defy reason is to retreat into vagueness and, furthermore, to avoid the question. What then is needed to locate the magic mainspring or whatever it is that activates the application of leadership?

The meaning resides in the behavior of any great practitioner who thoroughly knew how to produce the effects he wanted and who used his knowledge to produce the results he wished. In this regard, Gen. George S. Patton Jr. is instructive. Love him or detest him, Gen. Patton and leadership are synonymous. Few men have had his power to move people toward their objectives. How did he do it? What was his secret?

Although Gen. Patton was a unique individual and impossible to imitate, his method of leadership sprang from his profound understanding of the relationship between leaders and followers. Pursuing professional excellence with both dedication and passion, he pored over the histories of great warriors in the past and watched at close range the masters of his generation, notably Maj. Gen. Leonard Wood and particularly Gen. of the Armies John J. Pershing, and modeled himself after them. He sought to grasp what motivated troops. He collected and combed citations for valor in an attempt to discover what impelled soldiers in combat to act above and beyond the normal limits of duty. In the Army of his time and place, originally on the frontier, later in France during World War I and finally in World War II on North African, Mediterranean and European battlefields, he embodied and personified vigor, audacity and drive, and thereby demonstrated his superb leadership.

In his journals, notebooks and letters, he set down his precepts. By his performance, he revealed his actual practice. Both disclose the keys to his success.

Shortly after the Battle of the Bulge, Patton wrote, "Leadership is the thing that wins battles. I have it—but I'll be damned if I can define it. Probably it consists in knowing what you want to do and then doing it and getting mad if anyone steps in the way. Self-confidence and leadership are twin brothers."

The statement is, in part, ironic, tongue in cheek and also misleading. Although Patton's leadership was real and inspiring, almost palpable, his self-confidence was always forced, put on and less than genuine. He constantly doubted his capacities and, as a consequence, strove harder to fulfill his role. As for his disavowal of understanding the elements of leadership, he knew full well what made some men capable of leading others. Perhaps he preferred to remain silent because he thought the rules to be so simple and so perfectly evident.

Earlier, during the interwar years, Patton likened leadership to the ignition system of a gasoline engine. "The motor," he said, "is but iron sloshed with oil until fired to powerful and harmonious activity by the electric spark—the soul of the leader." The higher the grade and the larger the command, the more voltage was required "to overcome the resistance of inertia" in the unit.

If Patton seemed to fix his attention here solely on the leader, he hardly neglected the ranks. Certain wires, he said, conducted the energy of the commander, "his vitalizing power," to his men, among them the wire he labeled *habit*. He compared the habit of being commanded to repeated hypnosis or training. In other words, the imposition of a leader's will depended in large part on the readiness of soldiers who had been so molded to receive and accept it. Thus, both sides of the leader-follower equation were important.

Patton continually endeavored to strengthen his rapport with his troops. He showed himself to the soldiers as often as he could. He spoke to groups frequently. He personally taught and trained his units whenever he could. He defended his people to the rest of the world. He spent more time praising and rewarding them than he did blaming them or finding fault. He made sure that they knew what was going on. He trusted them and thus fostered their self-confidence.

Emphasizing color, tradition and esprit, he built unit cohesiveness. He insisted on cleanliness. He also demanded iron discipline. He had no hesitation to impose prompt and public punishment, which he said was "not for the benefit of the sinner but for the salvation of his comrades."

Leadership, in Patton's view, resembled a certain flow between those who lead and those who follow. The leader had to have certain skills. The followers had to be willing to listen and to act. The interaction of both parties operating on the same wavelength produced the combination termed leadership. How did Patton achieve his purposes with both himself and his men?

Some persons are natural leaders. Possessing an inborn or innate ability to lead, they have a mystical charisma, an indescribable and unexplainable personal magnetism that is compelling and defies analysis. Others become leaders by consciously cultivating and enhancing their aptitudes. They pay close attention to such matters as individual dress and bearing, voice projection and the like. Military academies, officer candidate schools and similar institutions regularly and routinely provide instruction in these appurtenances of what is called command presence.

According to Patton, a leader is created in heaven; his competence is God-given. Yet he admitted the efficacy of training to produce a "fairly good imitation."

He professed to be the former sort. He took great pride in his bloodline and cherished his martial ancestors. He had, he believed, inherited the warrior propensity as well as the ancient aristocratic privilege of leading. Exuding a gentleman's charm or a ruffian's rudeness as the occasion demanded, he commanded respect and even awe by his presence alone. He had the gift of establishing instant rapport with groups of men.

Being less than confident of his effect on others, however, and wishing to improve his image, which he thought to be defective, he worked constantly to transform himself into what he thought a leader should look like and be. He practiced in front of a mirror to put on his most ferocious face, his war mask. He used his profanity, which was never obscene, in much the same way. He wore ivory-handled pistols and a scowling visage as trademarks. He used the screaming sirens of his escort and the raucous honk of his ferryboat horn to announce is arrival.

If these were gimmicks or cheap tricks meant to impress, they were effective in stimulating the electric thrill of identity that Patton wished to inspire among his men. Others have been their own stage props—Gen. Dwight D. Eisenhower's sunny smile, Gen. Douglas MacArthur's crushed cap and corncob pipe, Gen. Matthew B. Ridgway's twin hand grenades, Gen. Omar N. Bradley's steel-rimmed spectacles, and Field Marshal Sir Bernard L. Montgomery's beret and sweater. All were personal symbols connected with their leadership.

A leader's style varies according to the nature of the person. If Patton was a patrician type, like George Washington, Robert E. Lee and MacArthur, others have represented a different tradition and appearance. Zachary Taylor, Ulysses Grant and Omar Bradley had no need for flamboyance. Their leadership was also real. All sought in their special ways to have a positive impact on their troops.

Field Marshal Erwin Rommel, one of the outstanding leaders of World War II, put it this way. "There are always moments," he wrote, "when the commander's place is not back with his staff but up with the troops. It is sheer nonsense to say that maintenance of the men's morale is the job of the battalion commander alone. The higher the rank, the greater the effect of the example. The men tend to feel no kind of contact with a commander who, they know, is sitting somewhere in headquarters. What they want is what might be termed a physical contact with him. In moments of panic, fatigue or disorganization, or when something out of the ordinary has to be demanded from them, the personal example of the commander works wonders, especially if he has had the wit to create some sort of legend around himself."

The Patton legend, its birth, growth and persistence are inherent parts of his career. From his early years, stories circulated about his prowess, daring and verve. Whether true or not, they raised him to the special dimension noted by Rommel.

Some tales arose from his tendency to test himself, to steel his nerve and to challenge his being. He always took the highest and most dangerous jumps when fox hunting. He played polo with reckless abandon, as though inviting accident. "Goddammit, Donaldson," he shouted on the field at Ft. Myer, Va., "get out of my way." In Hawaii, it was "Goddammit, Walter, you old S.O.B., I'll run you right down Front Street."

At the Military Academy, he rose unexpectedly from the pits at the rifle range and let the bullets whistle about him, because he wanted to see whether he could face fire without fear. During a class in electricity, he volunteered to let the considerable spark of an induction coil pass through his arm to be sure he could stand pain. All this hardly passed unnoticed.

Without doubt, the Patton legend received a powerful impulse at Ft. Sheridan, Ill., his first duty station. On horseback, he was drilling his men when his steed bucked and threw him. He remounted at once. The horse reared back his head, struck Patton's face and opened a gash over his eyebrow. Dazed by the blow, Patton was unaware of the cut until he saw the blood running down his sleeve. He nevertheless continued to drill the soldiers while the blood flowed. When the scheduled hour was over, he dismissed the men. He then rode to headquarters and washed his face. After teaching a class at the school for noncommissioned officers and attending a class for junior officers, he saw the doctor who closed and stitched his cut.

To the enlisted men who had witnessed the scene, his composure and continuation of duty while bleeding profusely showed courage and coolness. Here was an officer, they were sure, who would lead his men even though he was hurt. Accounts of the event were certainly embellished as they passed by word of mouth through the barracks.

Several years later on the Mexican border, Patton was riding at a trot when he fired his pistol and hit a running jackrabbit at about 15 yards. The shot was a piece of outrageous luck, but those who were with him marveled at his expertise. "My reputation as a gun man is made," he wrote to his wife.

While with Pershing in Mexico, he commanded 14 men traveling in three automobiles to purchase corn. In the course of his expedition, he and his party, as a result of his boldness and simple plan, surprised and killed three prominent *Villista* soldiers. Occurring at a time when there was a dearth of news about the Punitive Expedition, the exploit made Patton a national hero for about two weeks. His photograph and the story appeared in papers throughout the United States.

His participation in the battle of St. Mihiel and the Meuse-Argonne campaign contributed to his reputation. On foot, he directed his tankers in the heat of action and spurred them to aggressive conduct— always in the right place, his men said. At one village, he preceded his tanks across a bridge supposedly mined to prove that it was safe for them to cross—fearless, they said. At a huge trench holding up the passage of five tanks, he unstrapped picks and shovels from the sides of the vehicles while enemy bullets were striking the tank hulls and organized men to tear down the sides of the trench, thus permitting the tanks to cross and proceed. How could he have been unharmed? they asked. When he was wounded by machine-gun fire, they said it proved he was a mortal. He received the Distinguished Service Cross for his activities. His troops and the war correspondents wondered how he had miraculously survived.

The anecdotes of his later years are legion. As someone has remarked, everyone has his own Patton story. They tell of his ruthlessness in training, his single-mindedness in opening and running the Desert Training Center, his pushing with his soldiers during the Bulge to get a truck up a snow-covered and icy hill, his turning in 11 days the II Corps in Tunisia from a defeated and demoralized force into a confident and aggressive organization that won victory at El Guettar. And more.

Thus, the Patton mystique. To his men, he was an unequaled military expert, master of the technical and professional matters of warfare, spectacular yet sound in his generalship. They expected him to get them through the travail with the least amount of suffering and pain. In both world wars, they trusted him, promising to follow him to hell and back. To this day, thousands of veterans proudly say, "I rolled with Patton."

Col. George Fisher, the Third Army chemical officer, summed up the feeling of the soldiers, Fisher wrote, "Patton was a consistent winner. That was the true basis of Patton's esteem among the rank and file of Third Army. As the war progressed, he was . . . an eagerly followed commander—not because of his theatrics but simply because he had demonstrated beyond question that he knew how to lick Germans better than anybody else."

So much for the side of the equation relating to the leader as an individual. In Patton's case, he was a born leader who consciously cultivated the military virtues, developed a flair for command and had an enormous impact on his troops.

And what of the other side of the formula, that part pertaining to the soldiers, the followers?

Leadership functions best and most easily in a particular kind of social context, an environment that has been prepared to receive it and to act according to it. Sometimes called the social dynamics of command, the willingness of the group to follow determines the efficacy of the leader. The greater the cohesion of the group, the less the effort needed to lead. Ingrained discipline, military courtesy and obedience provide the setting for the application and exercise of personal leadership. The whole military structure exists to reinforce this social reality. The prerogatives of rank and the symbols of authority are integral parts of the system.

For Patton, the habit of instant, unhesitating, automatic obedience on the part of troops was the *sine qua non* of leadership. Thus he endeavored with all his might to shape his men into a unit of followers, for he wished to have an instrument perfectly tuned and available to his direction.

In his early career, as well as in his later service, Patton brought up his soldiers to be models of devotion to duty. To him, this meant fundamentally inculcating them with obedience. All his units were smart, well turned out and alert. Perhaps the clearest example is the tank brigade he commanded in France in 1918, an organization he activated, trained and led in battle.

Selected as the first officer assigned to the newly formed branch of American tanks, he vowed as he embarked on his experience, "The

73

Tank Corps will have discipline if nothing else." His Memorandum Number 1, dated 27 January, 1918, which he wrote himself, spelled out in detail what it was he wanted—"soldierly appearance and deportment." This signified, he insisted, brass and leather polished to a shine, daily shaves, short hair befitting "soldiers and not like poets," precise saluting—he prescribed meticulously how to do so—and thorough military courtesy. He warned his subordinate officers that he would hold them strictly responsible for deficiencies among their men.

The first talk he made to his assembled troops stressed discipline, which he defined not only as instant, unhesitating and automatic obedience but also as doing cheerfully what they were told to do. At various intervals, he repeated the message but always in slightly different language, stressing the importance of the habit. He fined delinquents on the spot. He tolerated no use of the word "please" when his junior officers issued verbal orders, for to him a command was not the same as a request. So well did he mold his men into the soldiers he wished to have under him that Patton's Tank Corps, as it was called, became known as the sharpest and most enthusiastic formation in the area. Patton's efforts had honed his followers to a high pitch, the better, of course, to receive his leadership.

Patton's Tank Corps displayed much more than discipline. Nicknamed the "Treat-'em-Rough Boys," the organization had spirit, motivation and proficiency. The men were well trained and confident of their ability to confront and defeat the enemy. They showed aggressiveness and drive in combat and were responsive to his command. These are all Patton trademarks.

As for the actual process of permeating his troops with his principles of execution, some mystery attaches to how he stimulated and transformed them to the extent of sharing his outlook and living and breathing by his precepts. What is remarkable is that when his wound removed him from the scene of action, his tankers continued to perform in his image. Their excellence proved the soundness and effectiveness of teaching and training. Although he was absent from the subsequent fighting, his indomitable spirit remained, imbuing his men with the will to carry on as though he were there. That is the supreme test of leadership.

Here, then, was an officer who applied his natural and cultivated attributes to gain the social context that guaranteed his success in both world wars.

CHAPTER
EIGHT

The Sergeant & The Submachine Gun

by Sgt. Maj. Lloyd Decker, USA (Ret.)

"**K**eep your mouth shut, do as you are told and do it to the best of your ability."

The words were not meant to be harsh. Oh, I experienced a brief feeling of alarm but then realized that my father had spoken without a trace of irritation. Besides, that was not his way. I was about to join the Army for the duration of World War II and had asked my father, a former Army man, how best to get along while wearing the uniform. Those words of advice were his reply.

It was good, sound advice then, and it still is. If someone asked me that question today, I would give them the same reply. But that's hindsight. I should have paid greater heed then.

A couple of weeks later, while taking infantry basic training, I was startled one day to find myself appointed an acting sergeant. That was a big surprise. I had never dreamed of such a possibility. Until then my great ambition had been to "measure up" and complete basic training with my buddies. On overcoming the feeling that someone had made an outrageous mistake and that I would be incapable of discharging my new responsibilities, I felt a faint tug of ambition, followed by a burst of pride. My ego promptly expanded several immodest sizes.

I immediately resolved to do the best job possible. And I really did buckle down—for a while. By burning midnight oil and asking questions, I learned the basic elements of required military subjects and somehow managed to pass the information along to my platoon. After a little while everything seemed to come rather easily. My knees stopped trembling and I began to believe that the business of being a noncommissioned officer was not at all difficult. Truthfully, I was simply getting too big for my britches.

Then one day I called my platoon together for a class on the Thompson .45-caliber submachine gun. I had never seen a submachine gun until the previous evening, but viewed from the lofty plateau of my newly acquired military expertise it had appeared a simple weapon. After a perfunctory examination, I had promptly returned it to the arms room. I had better things to do that evening, including a few beers with the "boys" at the PX beer garden. That proved a mistake.

The time set aside for submachine-gun instruction was almost over and I was still awkwardly trying to reassemble that obstinate weapon. There seemed to be too many parts—and thumbs. In the end I found myself inexcusably trying to bluff my way through. When I was finally reduced to perspiring perplexity, a young soldier from Montana, who had apparently run out of patience, reached over and took the submachine gun from my hands. After examining it intently for only a few seconds, he calmly proceeded to put it back together again.

Nobody made a sound or said a word, although several men exchanged looks that were as disturbing as the blunt stare of an old "top sergeant." I stood before the platoon with face and ears burning, feeling very much a fool. I would have given anything to relive the last few hours and to have done things differently.

But, in one way, the incident proved a piece of immediate good fortune: it turned out that the Montanan had spent his life with guns, loved them, and from that time forward was content to be a weapons instructor. He was a good one.

Me? I burned the midnight oil that same night and before dawn could strip down and reassemble a Thompson .45-caliber submachine gun while blindfolded. Somehow, I never got around to telling my father what a fool his son had made of himself that day, but I did thank him once again for his excellent advice.

CHAPTER
NINE

Private Minelli
Assumes Command

by Col. Daniel T. Chapman

T he "Redlegs" of the artillery are very busy in Southeast Asia
these days if we can believe such evidence as television and
newspaper pictures showing howitzers surrounded by piles
of shell cases. It's a different war than the one we fought in Korea.
Still, as in all modern wars, the artillery plays a major role. As a
veteran artilleryman once put it, "The artillery lends a note of dignity
to what otherwise might be a vulgar brawl." I am sure the artillery
is fighting a good war in Vietnam, but I am equally sure that they
sorely need Pfc. Minelli or an updated model.

Pfc. Minelli, like Prewitt in *From Here to Eternity*, was a trumpeter.
He, too, carried a trumpet mouthpiece with him to keep his "lip."
Shock-haired, dark and wiry, he was no 30-year man and he yearned

for the day when he could rejoin a jazz combo. Not that he was particularly unhappy. A product of a low-income, big-city background,
he had adjusted to life in the Army with no great difficulty. For all
his adaptability, his rise in the military was less than spectacular,
and with only six months to go he was still a private first class.

The night shift chiefs were particularly fond of Minelli in his role
as night duty clerk. His was the job of monitoring the radio and telephones for the officer of the night trick who slept in the bunker on
call during periods of inactivity. In addition to his professional competence, Minelli could turn out a fine bacon-and-egg sandwich on the
top of the diesel-oil tent stove. A nice guy, but quiet; but then, on one
cold Korean morning in 1952, he leapt suddenly from relative obscu-
rity.

All conversation stopped that day when the Old Man charged into
the bunker. He had to stoop slightly to remain in the dark, pungent,
underground room. He stood six feet, and he had longer legs than any
man I have ever seen. His informal code name among his terror-
stricken subordinates was "Skeleton Six." The bootleg message,
"Skeleton Six is on the hill," was enough to send a forward observer
into a frenzy of housecleaning and gunnery review. Right now he was
angry, and the fire support coordination crew quaked in anticipation.

"Can anyone here inform me concerning an artillery battle fought
last night?" asked the Old Man with exaggerated politeness. At this
alarming indication of how mad our leader really was the S3, who
had a nervous stomach anyway, edged through the bunker door and
disappeared. The rest of us stared open-mouthed. The Old Man was
a brigadier general of artillery, and when artillery battles were fought
he fought them or knew the reason why not.

"The division commander knew about the artillery battle," continued the general with the same sinister politeness. "He complimented
me on the conduct of this division artillery during the engagement."
He continued, "*He* knew all about it. Now why don't I? I *will* know
all about it, however, and soon. I'll be in my trailer waiting for the
after-action report."

Now, for a division artillery to fight a major artillery engagement
and leave the divarty commander and the divarty staff in ignorance
is highly unusual and extremely unconventional, as the shaken and
sweat-soaked staff well realized. The assistant S3 took off up the hill
to look up the night duty officer. The S2 grabbed for the journal and
noted with alarm that the entries took up three full pages.

When Capt. Burke, the night chief, was located he professed complete ignorance of any unusual activity. "I got the first sleep I've had
in three nights," he said. "I didn't hear a thing." The agitated captain

of the day side passed on the general's demand for quick information, demonstrating in the process a considerable flair for mimicry and dramatic interpretation. Upon hearing this, Burke, who was shaving out of a helmet liner on the tent stove, developed a fine tremor in his razor hand. "Damn it, we'd better locate Minelli, and fast," he said, staunching the flow of blood from a newly acquired cut with a wad of C ration toilet paper.

As Burke told us later, the night had been completely uneventful until midnight when Minelli performed his customary feat of skill with the bacon and eggs. Minelli's coffee was not up to his sandwiches and he customarily brewed it by dumping a couple of spoonfuls of coffee into the pot left over by the day crew, half-empty or not. Even this questionable brew couldn't keep Burke awake, exhausted as he was after three sleepless nights. He had dropped onto the duty officer's cot, handy to the radios and phones, and passed immediately into profound sleep. He lay there undisturbed until Minelli woke him at 0600 the next morning. Unusually refreshed, Burke had taken off for a shave and a change of underwear.

Minelli, of course, had stayed awake and busy. How busy, we were to find only after an intensive interrogation. It was not that Minelli was uncooperative; it was just that he was exhausted from his exertions. When the operations sergeant finally got him to sit on the edge of his cot and put his feet on the floor he launched into his story.

In order to understand the nature of Minelli's exertions one should remember that the divisions that fought in Korea were somewhat differently organized than today's. The primary combat units of an infantry division were three infantry regiments. In a relatively stable situation such as in Korea after 1951, two of these regiments were normally kept on the line with the third in reserve. The principal supporting element for the infantry was the division artillery, organized into five battalions (three "light" 105-mm. howitzer battalions, one "medium" 155-mm. howitzer battalion, and an antiaircraft automatic weapons battalion). Each howitzer battalion consisted of three batteries of six guns each. Backing up the division artillery, available on call for support of the division, were the battalions of the corps artillery. These were armed with heavier and longer-range weapons that could reach farther into the hostile area than could the weapons of the division artillery.

For about an hour after Capt. Burke had thrown himself on the cot, Minelli busied himself around the bunker, posting the maps and doing the routine paperwork required during the night shift. He worked quietly, anxious not to awaken Burke, who he knew was exhausted almost to the point of illness. At about 0100 the phone rang, and a forward observer at a company-sized outpost in front of the main line of resistance passed in some mortar shell reports. Minelli knew what to do with these; he had watched the countermortar officer on many occasions. He took them over to the countermortar plotting board and began to trace out the rays which showed the direction from which the mortar shells had come. Normally a captain performed this back plotting.

Minelli was shortly interrupted by the same observer with a new batch of reports. By now he could hear the rumble of the 105 howitzer battalion assigned to support the outpost as it began to fire at preplotted concentration points. With the second batch of shell reports, Minelli got some rays that back-plotted through previously located mortar positions. He checked by telephone with the reinforcing battalion and passed out the target locations for countermortar missions. Now, normally, the duty officer would have done this chore but Minelli knew how to do it and he knew that the captain was dead for lack of sleep.

At this point the forward observer called in to report some vehicle lights to his front and to ask for fire on their location. The direct support battalion was still fully engaged. Minelli called the third of the light battalions, passed the coordinates to the fire direction center and was gratified to hear in a few minutes that this outfit was delivering fire. Now he began to get reports of incoming artillery fire, from both the outpost and the main line of resistance positions to the rear and flanks. Minelli knew how to handle this, too; he had watched the S3 act in just such a situation in the past. He got on the phone to corps artillery, reported the hostile artillery fire, and asked for the corps artillery to begin its counterbattery fire.

It was not long until the 155-mm. rifles and the eight-inch howitzers of the corps artillery began to fire against known enemy artillery positions. The subdued thunder of artillery fire was now constant and omnidirectional. The sky was lighted by gun flashes from three quadrants. The division artillery commander and his staff slept on. Any artilleryman worth his salt can sleep through a fire mission with his cot 50 yards from the gun position, and unless he is purposely awakened will never know that the guns have fired.

If the fire fight had gone according to Hoyle, the bunker would have been filled with the staff and the activities would have been presided over by the general. The Old Man would have been adding to the excitement by passionate exhortation and imprecation addressed to the staff in general and to individuals as required.

The outpost by this time was receiving mixed artillery, mortar and small-arms fire. The infantry commander sent back word that he could hear the bugles and shouted insults which customarily preceded a Chinese ground attack. He estimated enemy strength at about two companies. The direct support battalion and the reinforcing battalion were now firing close-in protective concentrations.

The 155 howitzers of the medium battalion of the division artillery, kept advised of the situation by phone calls from Minelli, were firing at road junctions and bridges in rear of the enemy front lines. It was now about 0330. The 54 guns of the division artillery were all in action and the corps artillery with four battalions was well into its counterbattery plan. More than 3,000 artillerymen were hard at work serving the howitzers and replenishing ammunition. Minelli, in full charge, hurriedly poured himself a cup of the jet-black fluid he called coffee, sipped gingerly from the hot canteen cup and listened to the guns with satisfaction.

The outpost was now in close combat with those Chinese infantrymen who had survived the fires of the protective concentrations. A company of the regimental reserve huddled under the protection of a reverse slope and prepared to counterattack on order. Overhead, "Lightning Bug Willie," a flare-carrying C-47 of the Air Force, was sporadically illuminating the battlefield.

The concentrated supporting fires prevented the Chinese from reinforcing their infantry, and the defending doughfeet methodically and laboriously began to eliminate the comparatively few enemy who had survived the massed artillery fires. By 0415 the outpost was clear and the Chinese were withdrawing across the fire-swept slope.

As the Chinese infantry withdrew, the fire from the enemy artillery slowed and then halted and the mortar fire slackened. Minelli called the corps artillery, advised them that the hostile artillery fire had ceased, and expressed polite appreciation for the counterbattery. The corps artillery battalions dropped out of the fight one by one.

As the battered Chinese companies straggled back across the flat in front of the outpost the light battalions of the artillery stepped up their fires at concentrations along the avenues of withdrawal. As the enemy infantry reached cover along the hill line of the enemy trenches the light battalions ceased fire. By now the only artillery engaged were the 155 howitzers of the medium battalion firing to the rear of the enemy trench line at bridges and supply points. By 0515 the division front was silent and the casualties of the night were being evacuated from the outpost. Minelli completed the last entry in the journal which he kept meticulously during the night's activities. Seizing a broom, he hastily undertook one of his assigned chores, that of sweeping out the bunker. The resultant pall of Korean dust caused Burke to awaken in a fit of sneezing. The dust had accomplished what the noise had failed to do.

"Everything all right, Minelli?" he inquired between sneezes.

"Everything is fine, Captain," said Minelli. "Managed to keep busy all night," he added.

By this time the day crew had begun to straggle into the bunker and Burke went off to shave before proceeding with the day's business. A few minutes later "Skeleton Six" made his appearance.

It took the day shift chief some little time to pry the whole story out of Minelli, befuddled as he was from fatigue. When the shift chief had the whole story he took the journal in hand and in great trepidation departed for the general's trailer. The Old Man listened in stony silence to the report of the sweating major. When the story ended he drummed his fingers on the desk top and dictated two short memos. The first consisted of additional instructions to the night duty officer. The second was a directive to the adjutant ordering Minelli's promotion to corporal.

Minelli was inordinately pleased with his new stripe and his advanced rank but he was never so popular again with the officers of the division artillery. His sandwiches were still very tasty but he had now become a liability. By personal order of the Old Man the night duty officer was never allowed to let the new corporal out of his sight. As the General's memo made clear, "The officer in charge will take such steps as are necessary to prevent Private First Class (to be promoted to Corporal) Minelli from assuming command of the division and corps artillery."

Minelli was no glory-seeker. He had conducted his last artillery battle. Apparently unaware of the close surveillance exercised by the nervous staff he went about his routine duties with unabated cheerfulness. When he left Korea a couple of months later he was probably still unaware of the magnitude of his exploit as an artillerist. All unknowing, he had realized the dream of many an aspiring "cannon cracker": he had fired a division and corps artillery on his own.

CHAPTER
TEN

Mustaches

by Maj. Scott R. McMichael

During the height of the feminist movement, the male image suffered considerably. To arrest the degrading slide of the macho man into a limp-wristed wimp, some brave soul wrote the illuminating book, *Real Men Don't Eat Quiche*. The Army is now undergoing a similar identity crisis.

In the course of 1985, the "Year of Leadership," the Army's leaders were bombarded with a barrage of new ideas, concepts and, worst of all, buzzwords about leadership. As a result, a lot of fine men and women in the Army just were not sure what good leadership really is.

It is time to reset the azimuth, to put the train of leadership back on the tracks. I am talking about a return to the world of real leadership as practiced by Real Leaders.

Real Leaders have a language all their own. The Real Leader begins all of his remarks or speeches with the statement "It's a great day to be a soldier!"

Real Leaders know and use all the current buzzwords and clichés without the least bit of shame. What is more, they know which buzzwords are in and which ones are out.

OBE (overtaken by events) is now out. OE (organizational effectiveness) is also out. Real Leaders would not be caught dead asking for the OE guys to come check out their units. On the other hand, "coaching," "mentoring" and "footlocker counseling" are in.

Real Leaders do not necessarily like to talk *to* their soldiers and NCOs, but they like to talk *about* them:

"By God, sir, we've got some fine soldiers and NCOs down here in my battalion. Tough sons-of-bitches!"

"Yes, sir, got my warriors out on the range today."

Real Leaders also talk tough. They use expressions like "Go for it" and "No one ever said it would be easy, trooper."

My favorite tough talk, though, is "Make it happen." When I hear those words, a chill runs up my spine and I feel an intense desire to excel. Real Leaders talk tough even when they have no idea what they are talking about.

Real Leaders know that it is okay to make mistakes. In fact, they thrive on a mistake-rich environment.

Ask one of the officers attending the Army War College today and he will tell you, "Sure, my battalion makes a lot of mistakes every day. We were pretty screwed up, but that's okay."

One ex-brigade commander who recently addressed the precommand course at Ft. Leavenworth, Kan. (the home of Real Leadership), revealed the secret of his success. "Our motto," stated this Real Leader, "was 'total defects.' We lived it, breathed it and believed in it."

Real Leaders know that there is no such thing as a bad mistake. Some encourage their men to make mistakes because it permits them to do more coaching, mentoring and footlocker counseling.

You can always recognize a Real Leader by his personal appearance. Real Leaders do not wear mustaches, or, if they do, they shave them off before they get their Department of the Army (DA) official photographs.

Real Leaders starch their battle-dress uniforms (BDUs) and use only embroidered name tapes, insignia and badges. They always wear anodized brass on their Class A and dress uniforms.

I knew one Real Leader who had his BDU pockets taken off and reversed from one side to the other so that the accordion fold faced outside. They looked great. He also had the sleeves cut off elbow length on several of his BDU shirts so that he could get a better "roll" during the summer months. This man was idolized by everyone who knew him.

You can also spot the emerging Real Leaders in the junior officer ranks easily. They are the ones who already own mess blues and dress whites. Any officer who has a subscription to the "Cav store" (the U.S. Cavalry Store, a commercial establishment near Ft. Knox, Ky.) catalogue is probably a Real Leader.

Sometimes, the Real Leader will extend his ardor for personal appearance into the unit area. This is the officer who always has seven or eight soldiers on detail, painting rocks, trees, buildings and especially curbs. Find a unit with dirty curbs, and you can bet that the commander and first sergeant are not Real Leaders.

The epitome of the Real Leader in this regard, however, is the officer who uses a theodolite or aiming circle to line up all of his vehicles in the motor pool. Whether or not the vehicles are operational is incidental; the important thing is that they are painted and lined up properly. Real Leaders know that appearance is everything.

Real Leaders have their own style in the field, too. They use permanent call-signs like "The Dueller," "Cobra 6" or "Iceman 6."

Their jeeps have bucket seats in the front, and they take the back seat out so that an extra radio can be installed (to monitor higher-echelon communications nets). I could always recognize the Real Leaders at Grafenwoehr Training Area, West Germany, in the winter; their jeeps all had hard-top kits and a special track heater up front that always worked.

Real Leaders look good in the field. They never get cold or dirty. Underneath a Real Leader's field jacket, you will find the latest Eddie Bauer down vest. He wears his helmet chin strap down and his goggles up, with an olive-drab scarf and binoculars around his neck and a stainless steel thermos under his arm. He spitshines his .45 holster and secures it with a white lanyard. Most Real Leaders smoke cigars in the field.

The tactical operations center (TOC) of a Real Leader is a thing of beauty. It always has a duckboard floor painted in a camouflage pattern, a brand new light set and VTR (vehicle tracked recovery) headlamps mounted as spotlights.

Often, the Real Leader will have a special TOC chair, painted Branch color, with a padded seat and "CO" stenciled on the back.

Positioned in front of the situation-map, the chair is seldom used because the Real Leader is usually out visiting the TOC of a higher commander.

Real Leaders revere general officers (GOs). Being noticed by a GO is ambrosia. Being liked by a GO is comparable to dying and going to heaven. There is nothing so satisfying to a Real Leader as having a GO in his rating chain.

Thus, Real Leaders try to meet and impress as many GOs as they can. Once a GO knows him personally, a Real Leader does all he can to adopt the GO as a sponsor. Real Leaders know that you can never have too many sponsors (after all, one of those GOs may be on a selection board some day).

Real Leaders never refer to a GO by rank; they always use the GO's first name:

"Old Johnny Miller will make a great division commander."

"Men, Bill Parnell will deliver the address at our dining-in."

"Now that Jocko's got the Corps, gentlemen, expect nothing but the best."

One of the true measures of the stature of a Real Leader is the number of GOs to whom he refers by first name.

Real Leaders will be found in quantity at Headquarters, DA, in Washington, D.C., for several reasons, the most important of which is the large number of GOs to be found there. The daily contact with GOs is a source of great excitement and job satisfaction to the Real Leaders on the DA staff. The world holds few thrills which can match that of working at DA.

In addition to the joy of frequent contact with GOs, Real Leaders on the DA staff get to wear that special Pentagon badge which identifies them as the *crème de la crème*. Even better, after being assigned to the Pentagon, Real Leaders can thenceforth refer to it as "The Building," as in "When I was working in The Building, I saw the Vice at least once a week." This is a priceless claim.

DA attracts a lot of Real Leaders because it is the source of the newest acronyms and buzzwords. Long after most officers in the Army continued to think that a LID was a quantity of illegal drugs, Real Leaders at DA knew that a LID was, in reality, a light infantry division.

Similarly, the DA staff Real Leaders were deep into mentorship when the rest of the Army still thought that it was some kind of naval vessel. Being in the know before everyone else is a trait of Real Leaders.

Of course, even at DA level, the best of the Real Leaders seek out the choicest jobs where they can best serve the Army in selfless dedication. It is known, for example, that working in the Office of the Chief of Staff is restricted to certified high-quality Real Leaders (some say that a buzzword entrance exam must be passed before you are even considered for such a job).

Other top-quality Real Leaders serve as aides or executives to the "two- and three-bullet GOs in The Building." Lesser-rank Real Leaders are mere action officers.

Be on the lookout for these Real Leaders. If you are still not sure that you can spot one, look for an officer who loves formations, constantly uses a Daytimer organizer notebook and has been divorced at least twice.

If you want to succeed in today's Army, emulate these men. And remember, these Real Leaders can have a real impact on your career if you let them.

CHAPTER ELEVEN

Harry S Truman, Cannoneer

by Richard Lawrence Miller

A s Americans celebrate the centennial of Harry S Truman's birth (8 May, 1884), many will recall his decisions as commander in chief on Hiroshima, Berlin and Korea. Fewer may remember his formal military background, a calling that fascinated Truman from childhood.

As a boy, his favorite reading was a multivolume set of biographies that his mother gave him. He admired the military heroes above all, and years later he could still name the men he studied hour after hour—Alexander, Attila, Ghengis Kahn, Napoleon Bonaparte, Cincinnatus, Hannibal, Cyrus the Great, Gustavus Adolphus, George Washington, Robert E. Lee, "Stonewall" Jackson and J.E.B. Stuart.

"Of all the military heroes," Truman once said, "Hannibal and Lee were to my mind the best because, while they won every battle, they lost the war, due to crazy politicians."

Young Truman decided that great men received training in agriculture, banking and the military, and that he would follow those same paths to see where they would lead. His family apparently opposed his interest in the military, but soon after reaching the age of 21 he enlisted in a militia artillery battery newly formed in Kansas City, Mo. Truman was a bank clerk then, and the nighttime drills promoted fellowship with battery members from other downtown businesses.

Yet, in the words of a regular Army inspector, the battery aimed for "service-ability, not pastime amusement." Records of the Missouri Adjutant General show Truman's battery as outstanding, considering the limits of training time and equipment. One regular Army inspector particularly praised the battery's fastidious record keeping—Cpl. Truman was the clerk, in addition to his duties as team driver in that horse-power era.

Truman wrote of marches and summer encampments, which in retrospect he viewed as times of naive innocence. The men "learned to ride horses and caissons across potato rows the wrong way . . . acted as gunners and Numbers 1, 2 and 3 in firing the pieces."

He remembered, too, that "when you fired the old thing it rolled back 20 yards, and one of the orders in training was 'cannoneers on the wheels' to roll it back into position."

When one of the men was promoted to captain of the battery, Truman wrote, one night at camp "some of the boys to show that they still loved him took a bucket of ice water and emptied it over him in his nightgown, one of those old-fashioned long affairs that reached to his ankles. If he'd ever caught the perpetrator of that joke I am certain he'd have killed him. He never caught him."

Truman served two three-year hitches in the militia. He became uneasy about the danger of artillery accidents, but family pressure was another reason he left military service in 1911. The time and energy Harry Truman put into the peace-time militia was needed on the family farm as his father strained to meet the mortgage.

During the Mexican border action of 1916, he stayed at home, busy now with mining and oil ventures that he hoped would generate enough money to save the farm. April, 1917, was a different matter. "I was stirred in heart and soul by the war messages of Woodrow Wilson," Truman said. "I felt that I was a Galahad [going] after the Grail."

He helped organize a National Guard artillery regiment in Kansas City, and, much to his delight, the men elected him lieutenant.

This was an era of hometown companies. Some of these men had served with Truman in the militia, and a colonel over him was the former captain that Truman's old unit had once drenched with ice water.

The new National Guard artillery unit was mustered into federal service as the 129th Field Artillery Regiment and went to Ft. Sill, Okla., for training. In addition to his other duties Truman was put in charge of the regimental canteen. "I have been going like a sewing machine," he wrote home.

The canteen performed so well that top officers in the 35th Division took notice. Truman credited the canteen for his promotion to captain, but gave his sergeant, Eddie Jacobson, credit as the brains of the operation. Sgt. Jacobson, who was a Jew and a Zionist, became a close and lifelong friend. Many years later this friendship would play a crucial role in President Truman's decision to support the state of Israel.

In those days National Guard enlisted men elected their officers, and Capt. Truman labored under the stigma of "political officer" whose rank indicated nothing about military merit. He recalled that the regular Army brigade commander "took much pleasure in chewing up young officers with his false teeth and spitting them out in small bits."

Nonetheless, Truman got choice assignments. He joined the advance detail that went overseas to prepare necessary facilities for the regiment in France, became a regimental firing instructor and then battalion adjutant.

These were assignments many officers might covet, but Capt. Truman was dissatisfied. His ambition was to lead men in combat. He got his chance in July, 1918, when he was given command of Battery D.

This was a problem unit with highspirited Irishmen and several "very tough characters" imported from the Bowery of New York City to break a streetcar strike in Kansas City. The regimental commander was on the verge of dissolving Battery D and scattering the men among other units, but decided to give the young Truman a chance to turn the battery into a combat organization.

In civilian life Truman had been paymaster for hobo railroad construction gangs, had directed farmhands and mining crews, and had dealt with the street operators of the Pendergast political faction. Truman knew how to motivate men, and to the amazement of the regiment he turned Battery D into a disciplined 75-mm artillery unit.

The area of eastern France in which Truman fought had once been part of Germany. Although no guerrilla activity is recorded, the men of Truman's regiment feared they were in unfriendly territory populated by spies—an unease faintly foreshadowing conditions Americans would face years later in Vietnam.

Hiding in the day to avoid German reconnaissance airplanes, Truman's unit made forced marches night after night to reach the Argonne Forest. After firing part of the opening barrage of the Argonne campaign, Truman then "went forward for more trouble than I was ever in before." Boggy ground conditions complicated matters, as did rapidly shifting lines. The shifts were so dramatic that troop commanders occasionally misidentified the source of incoming German artillery shells and mistakenly accused Truman's regiment of firing short.

Observers in proper positions, however, confirmed that Truman and his comrades were hitting correct targets. Indeed, Truman's quick work destroyed a German battery going into position and thus probably saved many American lives. He was justly proud of his battery's ability to hit fast-changing targets, a feat hard enough on a firing range let alone under combat conditions.

The personal loyalty of Truman's cannoneers continued into civilian life. His men worked hard in the local elections that started Truman's political rise. He was loyal to them throughout the years as well, offering small loans and job assistance. After Truman died, a small file was found in his desk; it was through this means that he had kept track of his cannoneers to the very end.

After the war Truman organized a Reserve officers association in Kansas City involving men from all services. This was no mere social gathering but a professional organization keeping members in touch with military developments. Lectures were given by instructors of the Command and General Staff School located at nearby Ft. Leavenworth, Kan. The association acquired equipment sophisticated for the time, including a simulator for firing artillery problems.

Truman rose in the Reserves, eventually becoming a colonel commanding a regiment. He attended summer encampments even after becoming a U.S. senator, although he finally became inactive as his Senate responsibilities increased with the approach of World War II.

As a member of the Senate Military Affairs Committee, he surprised colleagues during a military-base inspection when he accepted a general's invitation to take over an artillery piece. Truman figured the firing data, issued the proper commands, and hit the target. His self-esteem deflated when, much to the amusement of fellow senators, someone wise in the politics of military appropriations asked whether the gun crew had received the correct settings in advance.

After Pearl Harbor, Sen. Truman vacillated about whether he could do the war effort more good as a field artillery officer or as chairman of a Senate committee improving industrial production of military goods. He decided in favor of combat and personally offered his services to Gen. George C. Marshall. Gen. Marshall turned him down, saying Truman was too old to fight a war—a statement which later drew good-natured kidding from President Truman.

Frustrated in his attempt to engage Adolf Hitler and Emperor Hirohito in combat, Sen. Truman avidly followed the adventures of friends in the European and Pacific theaters, and often expressed his desire to be in the action. Little did he or anyone else realize that political developments at home would soon give him the opportunity he sought, not as a field officer but as commander in chief.

Truman's formal military background, including both combat command and professional studies, gave him unusual confidence in the White House. His familiarity with tactics and strategy allowed him to meet on an equal basis with the Joint Chiefs. Gen. Dwight D. Eisenhower once asked if Truman fully understood the implications of a seemingly spur-of-the-moment decision, and Truman amazed the gathering with an explanation of the various strategic consequences. Gen. Eisenhower thereupon declared himself convinced.

As President, Harry Truman had no qualms about ordering atomic attacks on Japan. At first his comments about the bomb reflected his experience as a field artillery officer. Truman had used high explosives, shrapnel and poison gas in World War I. He viewed the atomic bomb as simply the latest advance in weaponry and believed effective countermeasures would soon be found for it, as had been found for all previous weapons.

Truman eventually realized, however, that nuclear weapons had drastically altered the meaning of warfare. Anticipating the possible consequences if the President's judgment were fallible on this issue, after World War II Truman never made another decision about development, deployment or use of atomic weapons until a committee of advisers concurred that he was correct.

President Truman made another famous military decision when he relieved Gen. Douglas MacArthur in the Korean War. This, too, reflected Truman's experience in World War I. As an instructor then, he had lectured, "Discipline is the instant obedience of a command— emphasis on the word 'instant.'"

While recognizing Gen. MacArthur's brilliance as a commander, Mr. Truman felt no military organization could negotiate about whether direct orders would be promptly obeyed. A World War I buddy wrote to Truman after the MacArthur incident and recalled Truman's old lectures about military discipline. In reply, Truman said that the principles he had taught in World War I had guided his decision to relieve Gen. MacArthur.

A less dramatic event, but one of far-reaching significance, was the formation of the North Atlantic Treaty Organization (NATO) under President Truman. Ten years earlier no President could have dared put the United States in formal military alliance with European nations. Truman seized the moment of postwar unity to move America into the kind of forthright involvement with Europe that he had long advocated as a senator.

NATO not only helped end the traditional isolationist foreign policy of America but helped direct the attention of the best government planners toward Europe and away from Asia—an ironic development, since in the coming years America would face its greatest military challenges in Asia, not Europe.

While trying to expedite national defense work, Sen. Harry Truman was alarmed by the lack of cooperation he found in Army and Navy operations. He spoke of examples such as Army planes being forbidden at Navy airfields—thus the Army had to construct new fields almost next door. As a senator, he created great controversy by attributing the Pearl Harbor disaster to such competition among the armed services.

He called for the unification of all armed forces under a single Defense Department, and as President he proceeded to accomplish exactly that. (Such reorganizations, however, often have less impact than proponents claim, since typically the same persons remain at the same jobs regardless of changes in paper flow. Changes in attitudes are generally more important than new flow charts.)

In retrospect, a more profound change in day-to-day military operations came from President Truman's decision to hasten racial integration in military units. From his World War I experience, he became convinced that black soldiers performed as well as whites, and World War II did nothing to alter that opinion. In the immediate postwar years and in Korea the military provided many white Americans with their first opportunity to deal with black citizens on an equal basis.

Common sense would suggest that such experiences had to affect conduct upon return to civilian life, and that through Truman the military had an unintentional and unexpected influence upon the continued progress of civil rights for all Americans.

President Truman was unsurpassed in admiration for the nation's citizen-soldiers. In awarding the Medal of Honor he once declared, "I would rather have a Medal of Honor than be President of the United States."

Although the Medal of Honor was a military award, Truman viewed it as recognition that the recipients had demonstrated the kind of selfless dedication that had always moved civilization forward. They could be depended upon, no matter what. And Truman would rather be such a man than hold a fancy title.

Such were the military background and decisions of our 33rd president. As Americans pay homage in his centennial year, they should remember not only his political achievements but the importance of his military heritage in the shaping of his life, his Presidency and the nation.

PART THREE

BY THE BOOK

CHAPTER
TWELVE

All in the Name
of Efficiency

by Lt. Gen. Edward M. Flanagan, Jr., USA (Ret.)

F rom the Army's earliest days until now, efficiency reports have
been with us in one form or another. Raters have sweated
over them; ratees, when they got a chance to see theirs, have
been glad, sad or mad; and selection board members have pored over
them by the hour or by the day, trying with honest objectivity to cull
"the best and the brightest" from the hundreds of files set before
them.

By now, probably most of us have read the first recorded efficiency
report in the files of the U.S. Army. But for those of you born after
1895, I'll repeat parts of it. It was dated 15 August, 1813, emanated
from Lower Seneca Town, and contained a list of the officers of the
"27th Regt. of Infty" and the commander's critique thereof.

The "Brig. Gen. Cmdg" kept his comments short (he even grouped a few dullards together to save verbiage) and to the point: "An ignorant, unoffending Irishman"; "All Irish, promoted from the ranks, low vulgar men, without any qualification to recommend them, more fit to carry the hod than the epaulet"; [I do take exception to those first two remarks]; "A man of whom all unite in speaking ill, a knave despised by all"; "Willing enough—has much to learn—with small capacity"; "A good officer but drinks hard and disgraces himself and the service"; "Raised from the ranks, ignorant, vulgar and incompetent"; and, finally, "An excellent officer." A promotion board would have no trouble sorting out the promotable from that list.

As one who has been a member of promotion boards at almost all levels (to include the highest—selection of officers to be promoted to permanent major general), I have read thousands of efficiency reports in all forms and all gradations. I think that I reveal no secrets of board procedures when I mention that officers or NCOs, as described by their efficiency report file, fall into three general categories: the water-walkers, the great middle mass and the also-rans.

Unfortunately, the number of water-walkers, because of inflation and the raters' honest but misguided determination to do the best by most of their officers, always exceeds the number of slots available for promotion, school selection or whatever the board is trying to decide. And the also-rans, easily distinguished from the great mass, are a very small minority. It's easy to say that only 50 percent of all officers are in the upper half in terms of quality; it's much more difficult to distinguish one half from the other.

The board's task, then, boils down to this process: read all the reports of officers (or NCOs) in the zone—including below the zone in many cases; set aside the also-rans, easily done but relatively few in number; earmark the water-walkers for intensified study; double check the great middle mass; then study, discuss, reread, reexamine the water-walkers until the select few pop to the top or jog across the Potomac one foot above the water.

Someone, who is anonymous but most probably was a red-eyed, caffeine-alert promotion board member, collected a list of gems from efficiency reports more recent, obviously, than those from Lower Seneca Town. The excerpts could have been from today's reports or World War I or on Teddy Roosevelt's Chargers. For what they are worth—and I think that they are priceless not only for their double-talk, innuendo, ineptness and inapplicability, but also for what they can teach today's raters—here are a few of the worst.

Some raters seem to have been influenced by a subordinate's alcoholic predilections:

"His drinking habits are below minimum."

"Drinks and holds it like a good recon man."

"His one fault is his overfondness for drinking beer; however, his duty never interfered in this."

"Intemperate use of alcohol has prejudiced my evaluation in Section F."

"There has been a marked improvement in this officer's use of alcoholic beverages."

Other raters have a penchant for describing an officer's interest in the opposite sex:

"Conducts himself properly in sexual relations."

"God's gift to women."

"He has allowed himself to become entangled in a web of romantic problems to an extent that they must be considered chronic rather than unusual."

"Appears to be a temporarily confirmed bachelor. While he is socially inclined and active, he is not prone to enter into entangling alliances with the female sex."

Some raters get carried away with words:

"His turpitude is a source of satisfaction."

"Handicapped by coccidioidomycosis."

"Completed battle inoculation" [Well, maybe he did].

"Like periodontis."

"Oversolicitousness for welfare of his men occasionally results in buying a 'skinny pig in a fat poke.'"

"A superior officer by any reasonable standards."

"He has failed, despite the opportunity to do so."

"Recommend promotional status to next higher grade."

"A grand chap, but he is in too deep."

Then there are those raters who seem to dwell, however vaguely, on a ratee's physical or mental characteristics:

"Has bad feet, easily frozen."

"Has black hair."

"Combs his hair to one side and appears rustic."

"A tired old man."

"A tall, beautiful blond" [sex unspecified].

"Has a prominent forehead."

"A heavy-built officer with smooth features and a conversational voice."

"Limps on one leg."

"A particularly fine appearance when astride a horse."

"Captain - - - is a lanky officer whose thin face would be dominated by a Roman nose were it not for his calm, attentive and confident eyes. They are the eyes of a man who has taken a long-range view and has prepared himself for the long pull."

"He is neat-appearing, except for his mustache."

"A tall, stocky officer."

"He is completely bald and this condition detracts from his military bearing."

"All wool and a yard wide."

Some raters describe a subordinate's religious habits:

"Seldom misses church on Sunday."

"Believes sincerely in the power of prayer and it is astonishing to note how many times his prayers are answered."

"He is a good organizer, but leans a little on the Lord to get the work done."

Some raters describe an officer's personality and traits of character in various ways—sometimes obscure, sometimes obvious:

"Tends to create the impression of unpositive personality through needless and undiscerning gentility and softspokeness."

"He is quiet and reserved in manner, but always the gentleman in mind and carriage."

"A hard-headed 'redhead' who sometimes turns purple in an argument. His country-boy-come-to-town approach, combined with an ever-present name-brand cigar and 'buck-toothed' grin, has made him a mainstay for morale within the organization."

"His leadership is outstanding, except for his lack of ability to get along with subordinates."

"A medium personality."

"A quiet, reticent, neat-appearing officer. Industrious, tenacious, diffident, careful and neat. I do not wish to have this officer as a member of my command at any time."

"He hasn't any mental traits."

"Is reluctant to have his opinion changed."

"This officer has become an expert at sitting around and doing nothing. I have to rate her low due to her failure to perform her duties satisfactorily."

"Needs careful watching since he borders on the brilliant."

"He will work 12 to 16 hours a day unless actively engaged, which is not found in but few officers."

"Of average intelligence, except for lack of judgment on one occasion in attempting to capture a rattlesnake, for which he was hospitalized."

"He consumes incredible amounts of Coca-Cola daily."

"Uses colloquialisms."

"Can express a sentence in two paragraphs anytime."

"Ardent crossword puzzle fan."

And then, finally, comes the rater who must have been drafting his efficiency reports at the end of a long, miserable day. He writes: "Some are critical of an officer who delegates authority. Others criticize the officer who does not. Seldom does a rater take into consideration the caliber of individuals to whom he would have to delegate his authority."

All of this simply proves that the lives of raters, ratees and board members are far from easy.

CHAPTER
THIRTEEN

Weapon System, S.P.Q.R.

by Richard Laurence Baron

Dtd 11 Quintilis 599

MEMORANDUM:

FROM: Decurio, 1st Maniple, 3rd Century, 2nd Cohort, 9th Legion
"Hispana"

TO: Curia of Defense, Rome

VIA: Centurion Commanding, 3rd Century Tribune Commanding, 2nd Cohort Praefectus Legio Commanding, 9th Legion
"Hispana"

REF: (a) CuDef Op. Inst. 24, Tablet 73, Para. 9
(b) Memorandum, Praefectus Provincia Gallia, dtg 03
Novembris 598
(c) MilGov Hispania Op. Inst. 23, Tablet 41, Para. 16
(d) 9th Leg. Op. Rep. 987, dtg 26 Martius 599

ENCL: (1) Stone
(2) Weapon System, Proposed, Model of
(3) Reports, Ancillary
(4) Data, Tabular

I   With permission, for background purposes, REF (d) is summarized as follows: Whilst on duty involving terrorist suppression in the area of Saguntum, in the eastern division of Hispania, 1st Maniple received an attack by approx. 200 Balearic insurgents (REF (d), Intelligence Summary). Internal Security (IS) arrangements had been set up IAW REF (c). Despite this, the attack was so swift that elements of 1st Maniple were pushed back into the camp proper.

The attack developed so quickly that no time was available to deploy standard individual or crew-served weapons. At the critical part of the engagement (REF (d), Attack on Mess Facility), Legionary 3rd Class Galba Tunctus 0377938, on duty as cook, picked up an ordinary stone (ENCL (1)–hereafter referred to as ENCL (1)), and flung it with all his might into the face of the approaching enemy. This novel idea was quickly adopted by his brave comrades (it is not for nothing that 9th Legion bears the title "Hispana"). As a result, a barrage of objects similar to ENCL (1) followed.

The rapid—and accurate—delivery of this munition-type, unfamiliar apparently to the enemy, completely disorganized the Balearics, and gave 1st Maniple the chance to go over to the offensive with standard-issue weapons. The Balearics were dispersed; the camp and surrounding area were secured; and IS arrangements reinstated (REF (d)–Body Count: 134 hostiles, 12 friendlies).

II   The use of ENCL (1) in so unconventional—and effective—a manner has led to research and development activities by elements of 1st Maniple and 3rd Century. It is believed that R&D has resulted in what may be a revolutionary new weapon system, one worthy of addition to the arsenal that is Rome.

III   First, it was discovered that while the simplest delivery system consists merely of obtaining ENCL (1), or similar, and throwing it at the target with the arm, this method obsolesces itself rather too quickly (See ENCL (3), Medical Report: "Arms, Out of Joint, Incidence of").

IV   Roman know-how, coupled with the Army's "Can Do" spirit, has led to an improved munitions system, totally consistent with the proposed munition system (Para. IX, below). After several design stages,

Harness Making Department of 2nd Century (HARMAKDEP–2) developed prototypes, as per ENCL (2). It consists basically of:

    a. Thong, leather (1)

    b. Patch, leather (1), attached to (a) above

V Several variations have of course been tried, often dependent on the type of munition used (Para. X, below). After the normal trial-and-error inherent in R&D, the current prototypes were developed, and have proved relatively satisfactory. (See ENCL (3), Medical Report: "Horses, During Training, Death of, Incidence of.")

VI Temporary nomenclature of this proposed weapon system is THRONG (an acronym for "Throwable Thong"). Designator is XM4B.

VII Use of the XM4B. A great deal of experimentation, as well as standard combat evaluation IAW REF (b), has gone into the development of the XM4B. However, it should be pointed out here that once development ceased and combat training began, there was no more difficulty in learning to utilize the XM4B effectively than there was when M43–A3 JAVELIN or 11–5–M15 SANDAL were first issued to combat troops.

Broken into operative step-functioning, the XM4B THRONG is utilized as follows:

    a. Two ends of leather thong are held in right hand, with right arm cocked upward, and thong parallel to body, perpendicular to ground.

    b. Acquire munition with left hand (Para. IX below).

    c. Using left hand, transfer munition to leather patch (Para. IVb, above) and seat firmly. Return left hand to left side of body.

    d. With required strength, begin to whirl XM4B around rapidly, keeping the plane of rotation parallel to body, perpendicular to ground. Keep head firmly cocked to the left to avoid insertion of head into weapon's rotational plane.

    e. When proper velocity is achieved, release XM4B IN THE DIRECTION OF THE ENEMY. (See ENCL (3), Medical Report: "Eyes, Being Put Out, In Training, Incidence of.")

VIII System Engineering: The Delivery Subsystem. Basically, design and bioengineering proceeds from the point at which R&D delineated the mission requirement. One advantage of this delivery subsystem: it uses off-the-shelf technology, one with which HARMAKDEP–2 is totally familiar. (See Para. IV, above; a separate report on internal development will be submitted to CuDef via Curia of Supply). Essentially, the best material for the XM4B delivery subsystem has been found to be Hide, Horse (CuSup Spec MIL–8–E401). OIC HARMAKDEP–2 has revealed that locally available Hide, Cow (CuSup/MilGov Hisp. Spec 01–MIL–75) is of poor quality, and will not meet operating specifications of the proposed weapon system. This is especially true of the tremendous torsional stress generated during the weapon's operation. Further, Hide, Cow, tends to shrink more in wet weather, a materiel dysfunction that has caused some misuse of the prototypes (see ENCL (3), Supply Memorandum: "Sandal Tie Ties, Unauthorized Replacement of").

Manufacturing is very much in line with mission requirements. OIC HARMAKDEP–2 estimates that a Supply Resource Requirement listing one (1) Hide, Horse, for every 243 XM4Bs will be quite sufficient for local manufacturing. This is certainly cost-effective, and very close to the Army's stated wish of full utilization of materiel resources. (See also CAVALRY TABLET, Vol. 8, No. 3; Virgilius Sextus Bulica: "What To Do with the Old Gray Mare," p. 31).

IX **System Engineering: Munition Availability.** Again in terms of cost-effectiveness, the munition subsystem of the XM4B could be the best deal in the entire Roman inventory. It has been discovered that munitions, similar to ENCL (1), are literally lying around waiting to be picked up. In other words, this munition-type is totally susceptible to local acquisition. (Operating elements of 1st Maniple have found that the easiest method of acquisition is to bend at the knees, keeping the back straight and face toward the enemy, and feel around on the ground for the munition.)

X **Calibration of Munitions.** Due to the wide range of locally available munitions in our various provinces (and indeed in Rome itself), some experimentation was made to determine the munition's proper size for best effectiveness and lethality. When it comes to munitions, some are too big; some are too small; and some are just right. (See ENCL (3), Medical Report: "Discs, Slipped, Incidence of"; and Intelligence Report: "Farmland Fences, Rocks in, Surprising Disappearance of.")

It has been determined that a munition calibrated IAW ENCL (1) is in fact quite excellent, and works very well over the proposed critical ranges. (See ENCL (4), Tabular Data: "XM4B Operating Ranges: Battlesight Zero, Determining of."; and ENCL (3), Supply Report: "Munitions, in High Grass and in Small Ponds, Loss of.")

NOTE: Obviously, Legionary Tunctus picked better than he knew. He has been promoted to Legionary 2nd Class and awarded a bronze stirring spoon.

XI **Evaluation.**

a. **Effectiveness of Combat-Thronging:** In actual operations against the enemy, it is evident that in the hands of highly trained operators, such as our own Legionaries, the effective capability of the XM4B in quick target contact and casualties caused is substantial. (See ENCL (3), Intelligence Report: "Casualties, Insurgent, Stone Bruises on, Incidence of.")

b. **Lethality:** On-the-spot estimation and examination of hostile casualties leads to the determination that, when the munition actually does impact against an enemy, lethality can be as high as 15%, with approximately 15% more casualties of a lesser nature being caused. In firefights against local insurgents, during which prototype XM4Bs have been deployed, as much as 5% of the total hostile body count can be attributed to the THRONG's munition-type. This may seem low. In a fight resulting in a total of four enemy casualties, perhaps a small scratch would be attributed to the lethality of the XM4B. But, multiply those casualty figures by 200%, or even 300%, and it can be seen that the **XM4B THRONG** makes quite an impact.

c. **Deployment.** In-country field testing has led to the determination that one legionary can effectively utilize up to eight (8) XM4Bs during the course of a firefight. The weapon systems can easily be carried around the neck, or looped through the corselet of the body armor.

d. **Maintainability.** Rated superb by all observers, the XM4B's ability to withstand rough handling has shown that this is a weapon system that can really take it. In addition, it is often possible to recover a portion of the expended XM4Bs after an engagement. They are readily identifiable and can easily be found in daylight, picked up, and used again. As noted in Para. IX above, the munition-type is always available.

NOTE: Unfortunate to report, but due to extensive combat testing, it is entirely possible that the enemy has recovered at least one (1), possibly two (2) XM4Bs. With so many deployed, and utilized, it is

111

hard to keep track of them. However, the resemblance of the XM4B to a sandal tie-tie is remarkable. The enemy will no doubt identify this terrifying new weapon as an innocuous piece of equipment, since Roman military technology is beyond their comprehension.

XII The XM4B THRONG has proven itself, at least initially in prototype form, to be a weapon of extremely high potential. It is a thoroughly engineered weapon system that lends itself immediately to efficient man-machine interface, high use-potential, and almost-proven lethality. Its impact on the art of war has yet to be fully recognized. In terms of system reliability, multi-functional operation, and cost-effectiveness, it is a weapon that meets the challenge of our modern army's many missions.

XIII It is hereby requested that the XM4B THRONG be considered as a closed-purchase, individual weapon system, IAW REF (a), and in line with the Roman Army's ever-expanding goal of more effective weapons for the combat soldier.

Respectfully Submitted,
AVE ATQUE VALE
/s/ Pontius Vertibris Sulla
    Decurio, 1st Maniple

CHAPTER
FOURTEEN

Breakout in Albany

by Bill Herman

T he CO thought it was a good idea, too: send our biggest tank
right into the middle of the city. An armor assault? Nope.
This was Albany, N.Y. Mopping up an urban riot, then? Nope
again. This was Army recruiting some years ago, planning to exploit
a period of direct enlistment in armor—whereas most enlistments at
the time were only for "Infantry Unassigned."

As a tanker-made information officer, I knew of a vintage M4A3E8
tank mellowing on a back lot of the nearby Watervliet Arsenal. When
my CO said the magic word, "Go!" I charged off to check out the old
crate. It needed some things like oil, lube, bath, manicure, but a few
untidy hours later it not only started, it *rolled.*

I convinced the custodians of the tank that I could, indeed, maneuver it into Albany next morning, also assuring them that I had a police road clearance. This was a slight forcing of the truth since I was

going to get the tank into town first, *then* ask for clearance in true tanker fashion.

That night I selected my crew—a local Reserve officer assigned to recruiting and distinguished in my eyes as a wine lover of unique creativity. In refurbishing his old Dutch townhouse, he placed his wine stock in a root cellar that just happened to be under his dining room fireplace. Inside the fireplace he rigged a chain hoist carrying straw baskets. Effortless turns of an ancient wheel brought up basket after basket, each nestling a cool bottle of Moselle, Tokay, Rhine and others.

When I invited him to man the turret in the morning, he stared unbelievingly at me, then rushed to the fireplace and spun the wheel furiously, snatching bottle after bottle from the baskets as they appeared from below. After several hours I convinced him that we were not going to *attack* Albany, but simply "invest" it.

In the chill, winter darkness next morning we met at the arsenal, warmed up the tank and faced our first problem: he wanted to drive. He claimed he knew some shortcuts, but he really wanted to rumble through his own neighborhood. Convinced he had made some early-morning spins on his wine hoist, I sabotaged the driver's seat so he could not get in without risking hernia. He dutifully climbed into the turret and we made our approach-march on Albany.

Needless to say, we had little trouble with the morning commute traffic; *they* had all the trouble—first, in accepting that it really was a tank rocking down the street, then to get away from it. But the police never saw us. Some torn curbs and sprung manholes later, we were safely positioned right in front of the principal department store in downtown Albany. Now to get the armor publicity campaign going.

It was mid-morning before I could get back to the tank with a sign painter (scrounged from a local movie distributorship) and found an enthusiastic crowd swarming about. They were begging to see the turret swing around, so I got in and obliged, swung it out over their heads on the sidewalk—and slashed the muzzle brake right through the department store's biggest window.

As if the resulting pandemonium were not enough, the police and store insurance adjuster demanded I leave the gun in that position—aimed menacingly at Ladies' Lingerie. The media, of course, responded energetically to the situation, but not even obliquely referred to the purpose of "The Tank in the Window" (as they called it)—the upcoming open enlistment in armor.

But, mercifully, the dust cleared—helped by the Army JAG and

IG—and the publicity campaign got under way. We had the gun tube painted and lettered ("Enlist Directly in Armor Branch") and we drew crowds but little media attention until we again suddenly had more than we wanted: one night our tank was broken into and robbed.

Supple-armed little persons unknown had reached through a periscope slot and unlocked the turret hatch. Total take: three periscopes. Result: active media interest. Reaction: we were accused of robbing our own tank for publicity, while I darkly accused the department store, which was not being hurt any by these activities.

But still no mention of "Enlist Directly in Armor."

In time, the JAG, IG—and, of course, FBI—probes were repulsed and the equipment accounted for through some fiscal logistic witchcraft. Police relations had always been chilly since we "sneaked that tank into town." But dates of the direct enlistment armor program were still not announced, and our publicity pitch was cresting ("Y'see the tank downtown?" "Yeah, I saw it—let's go to a movie").

Suddenly, I got an offer I couldn't refuse: a local entrepreneur was opening a new shopping center and wanted the tank in the act. He wanted to paint it all white (Negative!); let the kiddies ride (Oh, no!); ride the gun tube, then? (Hell, no!); let Gene Autry, who was to arrive in a chopper, step out on the tank? (We'll see). To this day I wonder why he didn't ask me to "fire a few rounds."

Well, this is where the Battle of Albany was really joined. It became the battle *with* Albany, because no sooner did the shopping center hype begin when I got a counterattack from City Hall, notifying me that the tank could not be moved—could not be moved to the shopping center because, it was pointed out, Albany streets were honeycombed with ancient Dutch sewer tunnels, now too fragile to hold an Army tank.

So everybody got in the act. The media ("snafu again"), historians ("The maps are wrong!"), antiquarians ("Army barbarians!"), engineers ("The old tunnels can hold *three* tanks!"). The op-ed and letters pages for days had a pungency of their own ("How did the tank *get* there?"; "Take it apart first"; "Leave it—plant flowers in it!").

Cooler heads attacked the problem of moving the tank without endangering the old brick tunnels, but no acceptable route could be found. The tank remained planted over the weakest part of the network and could not be moved in any direction. And the media chortled. I had myself a tank on an island in the middle of Albany!

So, again the Army's JAG, IG—and engineers—were on me and my

CO was referring to the tank as "our wart up the street." Then I got a call from a brash local contractor: "Hey—you gotta tank problem; I gotta tank problem. I gotta kid, wantsa enlist in the tanks, but first he wantsa ride in one, okay? So I got it fixed I'm gonna plank streets ahead of you over them cheap sewers so you can get to the shopping center. So you get the tank ready—and take my kid, okay?"

It was okay since it was another "00-dark" morning move and nobody knew who was in the helmet up in the turret.

And that's the way my Battle with Albany ended. But we lost the campaign: at the full swell of publicity, the plan for direct-enlistment armor was canceled. I'm not sure if the contractor's son ever enlisted. My reservist-crewman was piqued over not making the assault on the shopping center with me, but some time later wrote me, "Y'know, that turret with all those ammo racks would have made a great wine cellar."

The tank? I don't know what happened to it; I was transferred. It may still be in Albany somewhere. It may be a wine cellar. I try not to think about it anymore.

CHAPTER FIFTEEN

The Bus

by Chaplain Zane Alexander

I n the experience of humankind some things define themselves so
overtly that no adjective other than the definite article is necessary to delineate their existence. There are certain adjectives
that preceded "the bus," but if I mention them in print I will be subject to losing my ordination. No one who ever rode that particular
means of transportation would require the theologically hyphenated
adjectives to jar his memory into active duty, so I'll preserve my Presbyterian credentials and proceed with the story.

In 1967, Fifth Army headquarters was in southside Chicago. It was
a nine-story office building that guarded the misty waters of Lake
Michigan. But few people seemed to live in southside Chicago. Most
lived in Ft. Sheridan, which was adjacent to Lake Forest, a bucolic
bit of Yankee suburbia an hour's drive north—an hour's drive in "the
bus."

In Panama the buses are mobile murals. They are baptismal scenes on wheels. The colors explode in a euphony of tropic hues. "The bus" was at the opposite end of the spectrum; it was olive drab—very olive and very drab. Any hint of color would have been heretical. It rounded a corner like masculinity in motion—a down-in-the-pits, mechanical kind of maleness.

There were 52 seats on "the bus" and it's my belief that this seating capacity determined the officer strength of the headquarters. There were 52 full bird colonels (06s) assigned to Fifth Army headquarters. Seats on "the bus" were assigned by date of rank. The senior colonel had the front right seat and the junior colonel had the left rear. The pecking order was very visible.

The first bus was called the "bird cage" and behind it came the "chicken hatchery"—52 lieutenant colonels (05s), all sitting by date of rank. To violate this ordinal arrangement of seating would have been Armageddon.

At 0600 at Ft. Sheridan, senior officers look for stability in this ever-changing world. They found it in their own legally established, fully authorized, evidently earned bus seat.

You just would not have sat in one of those constitutionally or-dained seats. The chair of the papal throne was no more exclusively reserved. But I was a captain when all of this happened and I didn't know their particular law of the Medes and the Persians.

Behind the 05 bus came the majors' bus (04s). Its members were the better dressed, more aggressive, hard-charging members of that caravan. They polished their shoes daily and put on their brass with handkerchiefs—none of this was true with the first two buses. I re-member well how unpolished the 06 shoes were. But the majors had not yet made it in their chosen field of fire. They were well-dressed and on good behavior.

Logic would have dictated that I try to ride their bus, but at 0600 in the wind-chill morning of Lake Michigan, I was not very logical.

The majors' bus was followed obediently by the sergeants major bus. I have never before or since seen that many sergeants major in one place at one time—52, seated by rank and burning the air blue with the vigor of their vocabulary. I have made many mistakes in my life, but none as regretful as my failure to ride in their bus. I can only fantasize the war stories and the human interest tales that must have been told on that mobile conveyance of proud and senior soldiers.

The caboose of this troop train on rubber wheels was the enlisted bus. The senior E8 had the front right seat and the junior E2 had the left rear seat and those in between sat in their duly authorized, or-dinal positions.

There was, alas, no captains' bus. I was a captain. Someone said that I would be booed if I tried to ride the enlisted bus. That was no "officer country" and commissioned interlopers were not appreciated in this terrain of the enlisted. There were no unassigned seats on the front four buses.

I remember my quandary well as I watched those five, blunt-nose conveyances bulldog their way around a corner that first cold morning in January, 1967. They bore down on the bus stop like the Four Horsemen of the Apocalypse, except that there were five of them. The very appearance of those staggered OD boxes machine-gunning down the street could destroy one's rational processes.

There were a couple of sleepy-eyed colonels at my bus stop who were staying in VIP quarters nearby. I had been told not to invade 06 territory and my bus-stop companions confirmed the reports.

"Lord, no, don't get on that 'bird cage,'" one of them said.

"Didn't know they ever assigned captains to any Army headquarters," the other commented.

"Do you think the lieutenant colonels would mind if I rode their bus?"

"Hard to say."

"Didn't your sponsor tell you which bus to ride?" the impatient question came.

"What's a sponsor?" I wanted to know.

The rest of the conversation was erased by the roar of those five diesel engines that could rape a suburban solitude and did so with relish. My 06 sojourners climbed on the first bus and left me with my existential quandary. As I so often do, I chose the next alternative—the 05 bus.

There were a lot of wonderful people who rode "the chicken hatchery," but on that particular morning they were all in less than a cheerful mood.

"I'll be damned, a captain," was one response.

"I didn't know the Army still had them."

"They sure do, but it's obvious they don't know which bus to ride."

"Can't you junior officers do anything right?"

Some senior 05 called me over to his seat. I bent over and he whispered in my ear, "Son, you can't ride this bus."

"How about if I stand up in the back?"

"That's the worst place."

"How come?"

"Those guys don't like being assigned to that hard seat, and they don't relish anyone standing next to them and blocking their vision."

119

"What's there to see?"

"Half of Chicago get mad."

The 05 had my attention. I looked out the window at an unbeliev-able sight. Those five buses were moving through five lanes of traffic like the Tennessee single wing. They were in ordinal position—the 05 bus would never have dared to pull in front of the 06. They were stag-gered like an earthbound F-15 fighter formation and they controlled all five lanes of traffic. Early morning commuters were shaking their fists and elevating their middle fingers—all of which the bus drivers loved.

The bus drivers were a select crew of enlisted men. They were ex-empt from all special duty and work details. Their only job was to usher that caravan through big, brawling Chicago twice a day. They did. Their public relations were not the best, but their driving skills were unexcelled. None of them was the senior occupant of his bus, so from the military point of view they were not liable for the traffic violations they incurred.

Chicago police didn't exactly understand this, and the confusion was always good for the morale of the caravan. Nothing picked up spirits on the four trailing buses more than for the "bird cage" to get in some kind of trouble with the police. The whole procession would stop and the lone cop would be inundated with 250 of Fifth Army's finest.

"I always said that if I lived through 'Nam, I would never complain about anything again, but this damn bus . . . ," and there always fol-lowed a litany of the commuters' woes.

Army people are not generally required to commute to work, and much of our distress simply reflected our lack of experience with this common requirement of life in suburbia.

"Tomorrow I would suggest that you ride the majors' bus," the se-nior lieutenant colonel said. The next day I did, and I was fortunate to have a friend who was a major. He would look for some other ma-jor who was going on leave and would give me his name. I would then ask that officer if I could sit in his seat while he was gone. This arrangement worked well and provided me with a seat almost half of the time.

I learned to order my day around the bus. It left the headquarters at 1600 sharp and that elite corps of drivers was no respecter of per-sons. If you were 30 seconds late, you missed your bus. This was an emotional problem for work-addicted career officrs who had habitu-ally worked late for years and felt superior to those who did not. The bus was a great leveler. No one worked late—and it was amazing how well the headquarters ran.

I had trouble sleeping that first month at Fifth Army. It reminded me of my youth in the cotton fields of West Tennessee. When I was a boy, I would wake up at night clawing at the covers as if they were stalks of cotton. At Ft. Sheridan, I would dream that I was about to miss the bus. I would exit the bed like I had my hutch in 'Nam during a rocket attack.

"Where on earth are you going?" my wife would say incredulously.

"I'm about to miss the bus."

"At three o'clock in the morning?"

My language lost its Victorian caste. I talked soldier and crawled back to bed. After a rocket attack in 'Nam, I would try to sleep with one ear open for the next assault. At Sheridan I would try to sleep with an ear open for the bus. It was so quiet in that suburban scene that, if I were awake, I could hear them all the way across post.

After my 0300 false start, I would listen for them till five when it was time to get up. In those monastic morning hours I had time to think.

I had just changed my church membership from one denomination to another. This is no earth-shaking military matter unless you are a chaplain. Chaplains must be endorsed by the church to which they belong. If you lose your ecclesiastical endorsement, you lose your commission. The Army takes a chaplain's church relationship seriously. So does the chaplain.

The Office of the Chief of Chaplains is a busy place. They don't need chaplains changing churches to have something to do. When I walked in with my new membership, it was like getting on the lieutenant colonels' bus. The transfer of church membership doesn't happen very often and the personnel people at the chief's office had to dig out some seldom used forms and go to a lot of trouble to get everything in order. The chaplain who was in charge of my paperwork happened to be a member of the church that I was leaving.

He was exceedingly kind and gracious about the whole matter, but in a moment of frustration when he couldn't find a necessary paper, he turned to me and said, "You just wait and see where I send you."

"Look out, you're in for it now," I said to myself. But there was more mirth than mischief in the old chaplain's eye, and I didn't worry about it until I arrived at Ft. Sheridan and learned about "the bus." I'm not at all sure that he even knew about "the bus," but in my sleepless state of exhaustion the paranoid possibility crossed my mind. "This is the price," I thought, "of being a Presbyterian."

The second morning in my pilgrimage to Fifth Army, I climbed on the third bus—the majors' bus. Stepping into that mobile room of men was like entering the Nieman Marcus of military fashion. Shoes were not polished, they were spit-shined. Ribbons were not worn, they were emblazoned in Prussian splendor. My lone ARCOM was an orphan of heraldry.

All of these immaculately dressed officers were seated. I was standing. For some reason unknown to me, I cannot keep a crease in my pants. This has never bothered me except on that bus standing up across Chicago. But all matters have their consolations.

"Thank God, my socks don't show!" I said to myself. In the hectic rush to catch the bus, I considered myself fortunate if I managed to pick out dark brown or dark blue socks. It was sheer luck when I chose black ones.

"Why don't you segregate your socks by color?" a friend once wanted to know. Anyone who has lived on $300 a month knows that this kind of color management requires more than one chest of drawers. At Sheridan we considered ourselves fortunate to have a single chest.

"But it's good for your career to work at an Army headquarters," my friend changed the subject.

"It sure is," I agreed, "And someday I'm going to write a story about that bus."

"No one will believe it," he said.

I remained at Fifth Army for a year, and during that time, the headquarters was moved from Chicago to Ft. Sheridan. The office building was sold, and the bus caravan was discontinued. As the time for the last bus ride approached, I became enraptured with the historic significance of the event. I was aware that Mayor Richard Daley was unconcerned about the death of a military bus route and that most Chicago commuters would only rejoice at its demise.

I began to play with the idea of riding on the "bird cage." I would be no more illegitimate on it than on the majors' bus. I was a displaced commuter with no assigned seat anywhere. The buses pulled out of the headquarters so quickly that if I were the last one on it, they might be in heavy traffic before anyone could demand that I leave.

I toyed with the very real assumption that no captain had ever ridden on the colonel's bus. It would be like stowing away on the bridge for the Queen Mary's last voyage. I wondered what Chicago would look like from the lead bus–the 06 bus.

On the day of the last bus run, the day they closed the headquarters in Chicago, I left my desk at 1545 and took the elevator to the first-floor front door. The buses were already lined up. Those big diesel engines were running and the drivers were congregated around a tree next to the "bird cage." They looked a little down—not carrying on the way they usually did.

I was aware of their grief, but I had more important things to burn my batteries. I wondered if I could look inconspicuous enough behind the tree to wait until the last colonel got on. I decided to chance it.

It was 1557 and the buses were still not loaded. I began to sweat. Two senior 06s were talking next to the majors' bus. "Come on, get on the dumb bus!" I shouted silently.

My psychic powers must have been felt because they started moving in my direction. But just as they reached the back of the "bird cage," they stopped again. I realized that if it started rolling, they would break for the door. This would sabotage my dream. My plan would work only if I were the last one to make a mad dart for the door.

It was 1559. The driver of the "bird cage" revved his engine. This was a well-established warning. It meant that the next time he depressed the accelerator, the bus would be in motion. The two tardy colonels were well conditioned. They moved to the door and stepped inside.

My watch showed 1600. The door of the "bird cage" was still open. I saw the driver turn his head to the left and look in his rear-view mirror. Now was my chance. History held its breath. I darted for the door. It was closed as I pulled in my left leg. My heel was briefly caught, but I flexed my hamstring muscle and my heel broke free. I was in!

The bus was in motion. Three seconds later we were in traffic. The driver had been able to make his right turn onto the street without stopping. When this happened, all four of the trailing buses were so close behind that no car would challenge their exit from the Fifth Army driveway.

The colonels, however, were less reluctant to challenge me. "Holy Moses! There's a captain," rang out from the middle of the bus.

"Chaplain, what the devil are you doing on this bus?" The senior 06 wanted to know.

"Sir, this is a historic occasion and I wanted to be a part of it."

"The hell with history. Captains don't ride this bus."

The senior chaplain at the headquarters was a colonel. I could tell that he was mortified. He looked like my father had the night I dropped a plate of food at a father-son banquet.

The senior 06 had me squat down beside his seat on the front of the bus. "Alexander, I've ridden this bus for three years and no captain has dared step in it."

123

"Yes, sir, I'm aware of that."

"I want your assurance that you will never do it again."

"You have it, sir. I'll not do it again."

"Well, since you're here you might as well enjoy the view from the lead bus."

I did. Chicago had never looked more magnificent. The senior colonel pointed out some historic points that I was unaware of. I could take in a panoramic view out the front window and not see the diesel-belching back of an Army bus. And I must admit that there was a certain inner satisfaction in being up front in the lead bus. I would arrive home at least four seconds sooner than the motley herd that trailed behind us.

"But, no big deal," I told myself. "Probably won't even tell my wife. It's a new experience and I joined the Army to have experiences. Who wants to ride the same bus every day?"

Before I realized it, we were approaching the main gate of Ft. Sheridan. Just before the gate there is a wide place in the road. The driver shifted down a gear and said, "Gentlemen, this is your last view of the gate from the bus." There was a big cheer from the 52 colonels, all of whom would walk to work tomorrow.

And then it happened. No one could believe it. It was totally incredible. Never has military decorum and dignity been so blatantly abused. The 05 bus passed the 06 bus and entered the main gate first! Fifty-two angry voices were shouting as 52 clenched fists fanned the air.

"They can't do that," was a common cry.

"Who do they think they are?"

"Those bird dogs," was one of the nicer descriptive adjectives used. And no one, not a single 06, was more vehement in his protest than I was.

PART FOUR

WORLD WAR II

CHAPTER
SIXTEEN

D-Day: The Greatest
Martial Drama in History

by Hanson W. Baldwin

he time of waiting in New York and London in the spring of
1944 was time suspended. Today had little meaning; the
days crawled. One waited, plodding through the hours with
suspense, foreboding, excitement, for tomorrow.

I got to London as a supernumerary—a "scribbling fellow," as the
British called correspondents—aboard an escort carrier, one of the
Kaiser-built, merchant-hulled quickies constructed in the United
States, and sailed to England on her maiden voyage by a British crew.

The back of the German submarine campaign had been broken,
fortunately, for we sailed alone and unescorted with flight deck and
hangar deck jammed to the gunwales with inoperable aircraft being
ferried to Britain, and every empty space crammed with engines and
spare parts.

Her cabins were filled, too, with women and children. In the wisdom of their ways the British had chosen just this moment—of all moments when World War II was approaching climax—to repatriate British families who had been evacuated to America early in the war to escape the German bombing blitz.

Her crew called this initial crossing the "cargo and nursery cruise," but they enjoyed the benefits of U.S. lend-lease; the ship was completely outfitted with American gear, even with U.S. Navy blankets and bedspreads. But she also had some extra amenities in accordance with British tradition—a liberal and well-stocked wine mess in the wardroom and casks of high-proof rum ("Nelson's blood") for the traditional daily issue of a tot to each of the crew.

We steamed out of New York harbor in the dark of the night of 3 May.

I knew there was but slight chance of encountering a U-boat; we cruised singly at speeds far faster than the convoys and the U-boats had passed their savage prime. Even so, there were many uncomfortable moments (including one apparently fallacious report of a torpedo track), particularly as we moved into the shipping bottlenecks converging on the western approaches to the "tight little isle."

Perhaps because the ship was a plane ferry and was completely defenseless, or perhaps because she had a green crew on a maiden voyage, she had none of the smartness or efficiency of most of the men-of-war that flew the White Ensign. She was not, by any definition, a taut ship.

One officer, her captain, was a regular; her exec had been called from retirement; the rest of her officers, including the watchstanders, were Royal Naval Volunteer Reserves (they had wavy sleeve stripes, and were thus called the "Wavy Navy"), or Royal Naval Reserve (crossed sleeve stripes commissioned from former ratings or merchant seamen). These officers were self-characterized in the kind of wry understatement the British love as "gentlemen but not seamen, or seamen but not gentlemen."

The easy tolerance of the exec, or the presence of women and children aboard a carrier in wartime, in itself extraordinary, may have had something to do with the *laissez-faire* attitude. But the discipline was slack and my morale plummeted when I sat around the wardroom table at dinner time and watched a prospective officer of the watch—about to take the bridge in a darkened ship in a submarine zone—drink four straight whiskeys while flirting with one of the women passengers.

Ever since, I have been adamantly opposed to: (1) a wine mess aboard fighting ships, and (2) women aboard men-of-war.

128

But by guess and by God we reached England safely in early May, 1944, and I proceeded with the red tape, on the whole smartly expedited, of getting SHAEF accreditation, drawing gas mask and protective clothing, helmet and other equipment and preparing for "The Day."

John Mason Brown, who had been a New York theater critic and essayist noted for his wit (he once decribed a piece of convoluted modern sculpture as a "womb with a view"), was then a lieutenant handling public relations for Rear Adm. Alan G. Kirk, who was to command all U.S. Naval forces in the invasion of Europe. I had applied for accreditation to the U.S.S. *Augusta,* an eight-inch gunned heavy cruiser, which was Adm. Kirk's flagship and also was to be command ship for Lt. Gen. Omar N. Bradley, commander of the U.S. First Army and later of the 12th Army Group.

Checked in and resplendently attired in the correspondents' uniform (the so-called officers' pink or grayish-tan slacks and olive tunic with a "C" for "correspondent" on shoulder and brassard), I first interviewed Gen. Bradley in his London Bryanston Square headquarters and then went down to Bristol to talk to the First Army staff.

The brilliant emerald-green lawns and Gothic cloisters of Clifton College, where First Army was quartered, were quiet, incongruous background to the drab business of war.

Indeed, all of England in those fair May days—days rare for England, of sunshine and soft breezes—seemed dressed as if for festival, not for death. One entry in my notebook emphasized the gentle beauty of the stage setting for the greatest martial drama in history:

"Even the bomb-blitzed ruins seem part of ancient history. The fields are carpeted with buttercups and daisies, and yellow gorse has bloomed. England is as England was."

Back in London I wrote one or two articles and pieced together the guarded briefings I had gotten from SHAEF, from John Mason Brown and from U.S. First Army, and waited. . . .

None of us expected D-Day until the last week in May or the first in June, but all accredited correspondents had been warned to keep close to their offices or residences and not too far from a telephone. The *New York Times* office then was in the Savoy Hotel, where I had a room; the former office in Fleet St. had been bombed out.

Two memories of those days of waiting at the Savoy:

- My surrender of ration tickets for the horrible breakfasts of (a) spam, or (b) dried eggs—almost inedible—or (c) dried mushrooms on toast. There was no other choice.

129

- THE GAME. THE GAME (always in capitals) was a fad, an escape, a release then sweeping Britain, a variation of the ancient pastime of charades.

Ray Daniell was the head of the *New York Times* London bureau and a whole crew of *Times* men had been assembled to cover the invasion. We operated out of the *Times* office suite in the Savoy, where Daniell worked and lived. Sometimes we gathered there at night, hiding the increasing tension as the slow days passed by playing THE GAME.

Then, at last, I got the word: report outside the northwest entrance of the Admiralty, near the Mall, about eight the next morning, 22 May, with all equipment, ready to go.

The accredited naval correspondents—in uniform and complete with typewriters, cameras, helmets, gas masks, baggage—assembled conspicuously in the heart of London. There must have been several score correspondents: British and American and a few French, representatives of press services, individual newspapers, radio chains and stations, a few magazines and numerous photographers.

With escort and conducting and public relations officers, there were probably close to 100 people milling about in the open near the Admiralty in the midst of London's rush to work. It was a *very* conspicuous assemblage and it was meant to be.

Somehow, some of us had gotten the word. The "brass" confessed after they had herded us inside the Admiralty. This was a "dry run." We were journalistic guinea pigs, serving a three-fold purpose:

- To test the administrative machinery of assembling, transporting and escorting war correspondents assigned to the Navy.
- To provide an opportunity for the correspondents to inspect one of the crowded invasion ports.
- And most important—to try a deception ploy, a minor part of a vast cover pattern that screened D-Day, intended to fool any German spies still at large in Britain.

We played it for real. The group boarded a train bound for somewhere on the South Coast, where at every port from Dover to Land's End and around into the Bristol Channel and the Irish Sea 3,000 ships and vessels of the invasion fleet, crammed with thousands of men and the hopes of two continents, were waiting.

We were, we found, bound for the picturesque port of Fowey in Cornwall, in peacetime a fishing port and a mecca for vacationers during the August Bank Holiday, crammed now, gunwale to gunwale, with U.S. LCIs.

In Fowey we walked around the little town, inspected the congested harbor and I looked up an LCI skipper to whom I bore a message of love and a photograph from his fiancée in the states. Then, in compensation for the long and futile train trip, we were bused to Menabilly House, a *Rebecca*-like manor on the outskirts of Fowey. It was the home of Daphne du Maurier, the English novelist, master of the Gothic romantic-suspense genre, then internationally famous for her best seller, *Rebecca*.

Miss du Maurier was the wife of Lt. Gen. F.A.M. Browning, commanding British airborne troops. He was, of course, on the verge of D-Day, conspicuous by his absence. But his wife, her mother and the young Browning children took on the task of offering tea and whiskey to a clamoring crowd of correspondents.

Miss du Maurier was the epitome of graciousness and English understatement, the setting unforgettable. The Brownings lived in a half-ruined, ancient Cornish manor house and had restored to livable conditions only a part of it—as I remember, about half—before the war stopped additional restoration.

The half-ruined portion, windows blank or boarded, was very evident; the whole house was ivy-covered, the long-neglected garden here and there showed signs of cultivation and conversion from flowers to vegetables. There was a small lawn and then the tall grass, rippling in the wind off the Channel, sloped down to the high cliffs that loomed over the sea.

It was a fitting setting completely in keeping not only with Miss du Maurier's novels, but with the sense of hidden dread, prayerful hope and controlled suspense that permeated the air of England before D-Day.

The real alert, almost two weeks later, was quite different.

We gathered, inconspicuously, at various points in London in small groups, segregated, I think, by the ports in which our ships were anchored. The *Augusta* lay off Plymouth, where Sir Walter Raleigh, Sir Francis Drake and so many of the great seamen of England had left their mark on history. Again by train, we arrived in late afternoon. On 3 June, 1944, three of us boarded *Augusta*—a magazine writer and photographer, a radio correspondent (no television in those days) and I—the only reporter aboard the flagship for a daily newspaper. I had a grandstand seat for history and I hoped to make the most of it.

At 5:30 P.M., *Augusta* shifted to an anchorage in the outer harbor. Thousands waved wild goodbyes from the seawall and the Hoe, with the bomb-shattered ruins of the town behind them. As the light faded, it was, I noted in my notebook, a "sight such as I shall never forget"— the moon almost at the full; the gorse on the hills gleaming golden in the dying day and, in the skies, scores of barrage balloons tugging like silver fish at their cables. In the distance, on the headland, a light winked from a British signal station.

Immured aboard ship, along with tens of thousands of others, all was opened to us: the complete plans of the invasion, the beaches, the forces, G2's estimate of enemy strength and positions, the beach obstacles and gradients, tidal tables, ship movements, phase lines and objectives.

D-Day was to be 5 June; the Atlantic Wall was to be breached, the *Festung Europa* stormed in a single day.

Before we bunked down in uneasy sleep, Gen. Bradley himself, with Maj. Gen. Ralph Royce, deputy commander of the Ninth Air Force, and some of First Army staff briefed us in detail on the invasion plans, the hopes, the fears, the guesses.

Sunday, 4 June, with much of the invasion fleet already at sea en route to Normandy, dawned with low-hanging gray clouds, wet and foggy in Plymouth harbor. Soon after breakfast we learned the weather was down; brisk winds and high waves and low ground fog in the Channel and the Bay of the Seine would force the invasion's postponement to 6 June.

Once again the waiting, once again time suspended. Steadily, the weather worsened; by 8 P.M. it was so soupy one could barely see the Plymouth breakwater from *Augusta's* bridge.

It is like a dream now, that day at anchor off Plymouth, when it seemed the world hung in the balance. Hours drifted by studying two huge volumes of "Top Secret" invasion plans, talking to John Mason Brown, to McGeorge Bundy, then a young Army lieutenant liaison officer (later to rise to fame in the Kennedy and Johnson White House years), to Gen. Bradley and his staff, visiting the First Army command post war room, housed in a deckhouse on the main deck.

That night, shortly after dinner in the wardroom, a flash came over the radio teletype, screaming that the long-awaited invasion of France had started.

The immediate reaction in *Augusta* was shock and a sense of outraged betrayal. Before a soldier had landed in Europe, a press report had telegraphed our punch. We were certain there had been a leak; we, of the press, damned the "irresponsibility" of the press. Some of us felt that all was lost, that surely the Germans would be alerted and we would be slaughtered on the beaches.

Later, much later, we learned there had been no leak; the false report, quickly corrected, had originated, by confusion, in New York—not in Europe.

It is hard, in retrospect, to convey today the sense of consternation and awful outrage that this false news flash produced in the flagship of the U.S. invasion forces. The reaction was extreme, but it stemmed from the long, long weeks of tension and the sense of ominous dread and foreboding that underlay all our thinking. We had been thinking of the unthinkable of another war—suppose we were repulsed?

This did not seem so unlikely an outcome then as it does now with the advantage of hindsight. For months, German propaganda and Allied briefings had stressed the strength of the Atlantic Wall; the invasion plans we had just read had included in their intelligence annexes illustrations and photographs of all kind of pillboxes, fortifications, "Rommel asparagus" (heavy posts planted in open fields to prevent glider landings), mines, obstacles and devices that were intended to make the Normandy beaches impregnable to attack.

We did not know it then, but Air Chief Marshal Sir Trafford Leigh-Mallory, the air commander, had officially warned Gen. Dwight D. Eisenhower that two U.S. airborne divisions would be virtually wiped out. Somehow his pessimism, extreme and unwarranted in the light of history, had filtered out to the journalistic world. And it was buttressed by the often-grim assessments of probable casualties I had gotten from my conversations aboard ship and my London briefings and my visit to Bradley's staff in Bristol, where one senior colonel had told me "the casualties will be very heavy and there will be times when the whole thing will be wavering."

The correspondents were not alone in fearing a bloodbath; many in the military—seniors as well as juniors, very many more, indeed, than would acknowledge it today—were grim. But in England, in Washington, in New York, the sense of doom, the concept of nemesis which we pushed away from our minds again and again, emanated from the long weeks of waiting, of hopes and anticipation, postponement and fears and tension, of time in limbo.

On Monday, 5 June, *Augusta*, with hundreds of ships and craft ahead and astern of her, got under way from Plymouth Harbor, headed south into the Channel lop and then almost due east and south again towards the "Great Adventure." The sea was choppy; mists hung low over the waters as we steamed independently at about 15 knots through a swept and buoyed Channel toward the Bay of the Seine. It was an eerie passage, almost sepulchral in the light fog. Visibility was adequate but limited.

· · ·

133

On the way, the loudspeaker told us of the fall of Rome the day be-fore—brief cheers. Then, out of the mist, we passed battleship *Texas;* then *Black Prince,* and *Glasgow,* wearing the White Ensign, the Frenchmen *Georges Leygues* and *Montcalm,* a swarm of destroyers. In mid-afternoon, I was startled briefly when we test-fired our 20-mm and 40-mm antiaircraft guns.

Towards nightfall we speeded up and then sat down in the ward-room to steak, mashed potatoes, frozen green beans and creamed peas, with the usual jokes about "the last supper" and feeding the condemned men. Minute after minute, hour after hour, we passed great convoys of slow-moving landing craft, some of them making a rough crossing, all of them crammed with the youth of Britain and America.

Some men waved, or raised a hand; there was an occasional cheer or yell, but for the most part the foreknowledge of what was to come, the storming of the beaches, and the querulous pangs of seasickness, dampened overt greetings.

Few in *Augusta* slept much that night of 5–6 June; the adrenaline was flowing. It was after midnight before a smudged line, low on the horizon, revealed the coast of France. Then, as we closed, we heard the faint hum, distinct above the *Augusta's* blowers and the creaks and groans of a ship in a seaway, of aircraft engines—bombers and troop carriers bound for France.

Then, dulled by distance, the intermittent rumble of bombs and, behind the beaches, a faint pyrotechnical display: antiaircraft tracers and shell bursts speckling the clouded sky, and the great fiery glare of bomb bursts against the land.

It was about 3:35 A.M., Tuesday, 6 June, 1944, that *Augusta's* crew went to battle stations, urged to the double by the crescendo of the alarm bells. We wore steel helmets and Mae Wests, those ubiquitous lifebelts, which—when inflated—assumed the shape of the name they bore.

We climbed the ladders to a portion of a bridge, where Lt. John Mason Brown, USNR, was commencing his running broadcast of events (as he had done in the Sicilian landings) over the ship's loud-speaker system. *Augusta* was "buttoned up"; watertight doors and hatches closed; all hands at battle stations and this meant that most of the crew, except for a few topside, were locked in a steel cocoon where they could see nothing of the vast panorama in the Bay of the Seine. Brown served as their eyes.

Had we surprised the enemy?

At 3:55 A.M.—gunfire and ten chandelier flares kill the darkness on the starboard bow.

4:10 A.M.—gunfire to the port bow.

4:15 A.M.—planes overhead. German green and red ack-ack fire in the distance.

There was, as I remember, a misty overcast which veiled the scene as in a Dali painting and limited the range of vision.

Our bombers were hard at work well behind the beaches; the crump and flash and flare were constant now. Suddenly, we saw a plane was hit far to landward; it bloomed, a fiery blossom, high in the night sky, turned seaward and headed toward us. A curve of scarlet flame approached *Augusta*, veered suddenly and passed over and beyond us, banked and leveled off and crashed to seaward into the Channel.

The flame died in the waters; had the plane's crew died with it, or had they jumped? The question was posed in passing, never answered. That night, the impersonality of death was everywhere.

4:58 A.M.–another plane on fire.

5 A.M.—light in the East.

Dawn, dank and gray, came to the Bay of the Seine slowly, as *Augusta* steamed close to her gunfire support position off the beach to be forever known as "Omaha." Behind the beaches, but not on them, a barrage of bombs threw up a great curtain of flame and smoke as the Royal Air Force heavies completed their saturation bombing.

As the night died and light came to the land, the Fortresses and Liberators of the Eighth Air Force took over. And the guns spoke.

At 5:35 A.M., *Augusta's* eight-inchers roared; the concussion rocked the cruiser, smashed mirrors. Then the fleet erupted, scores of ships bombarding the land. *Augusta* steamed in to 12,000 yards offshore.

A small flight of Allied fighters passed overhead; a report reached the flagship that German E-boats had sortied from Le Havre to attack the invasion fleet; landing craft, some of them making heavy weather of it, passed us heading shoreward.

And again the waiting . . .

My D-Day notebooks tell a sparse and confused picture of those early hours; as always, the first reports of battle are slow, contradictory, ominous.

7:30 A.M.—the Rangers have taken Pointe du Hoe. *Corry*, the destroyer, is sunk off Utah beach.

8:30 A.M.—a DUKW, awash and sloshing with a 105-mm howitzer aboard, drifts slowly to seaward sinking; no men aboard.

8:40 A.M.—troops said to be moving slowly up the steep slopes of Omaha, but Bradley's worried; situation not good; most are still pinned behind the sea wall.

The ships move in close to shore to smash at point-blank range the murderous German casemates which command the draws to high ground. There's a burning LST, beached in her final berth at Omaha.

My memories of D-Day are chaotic and confused, kaleidoscopic. I remember drinking many mugs of strong coffee, rushing from my typewriter to bridge to First Army war room, talking to Col. Hall Jeschke, the senior Marine officer aboard the flagship, and—waiting. . . .

There was little hard news; what there was of it from Omaha was grim indeed. I remember, perhaps at mid-morning or later, Gen. Bradley, or one of his staff, asking me with tongue only partially in cheek:

"What do you know? We don't know anything."

The DD tanks—tanks equipped with British-designed flotation gear to enable them to swim ashore—were, we knew, in trouble. At Omaha, unprotected from the sea, the waves drowned them; only five of the 32 tanks of the first echelons hit the beach; the rest foundered, many with their crews.

Aboard *Augusta*, we saw from time to time landing craft passing us or, as our fire support missions were completed and we upped anchor and moved about the transport area, men clambering down cargo nets into the heaving boats. We saw, too, the debris of battle: craft disabled and half-afloat or abandoned or drifting, life jackets and, once or twice, a body.

I remember an LCVP, loaded to the gunwales with field artillery badly needed (as we heard later) on Omaha, foundering.

Writing furiously and waiting, I passed D-Day. It became clear as the day died that on Omaha, at least, the battle had been a close-fought thing, casualties heavy and that most of the Allied D-Day objectives were still well beyond our beachhead lines. We were ashore, but Caen, the communications center and anchor of the German line—to have been captured on D-Day—was still firmly held by the enemy.

Utah beach, where Teddy Roosevelt Jr. led the 4th Division ashore with a walking stick, was secured and casualties were light, due chiefly to the drop of our two airborne divisions in and along the base of the Cotentin Peninsula. But the various landings were still isolated and in some places we were hanging on by our toenails.

D-Day night, the night of 6–7 June, was more of the same. I remember trying to snatch a brief interlude of much-needed sleep; the adrenaline and coffee had failed. I was in a bunk for perhaps an hour when I was awakened simultaneously and abruptly by John Mason Brown's, "There's a big raid on," and the harsh, rocking bark of *Augusta's* antiaircraft guns.

A German air raid was under way—or so it was said. It was short but extensive cacophony. The gunners in the vast fleet in the Bay of the Seine were trigger-happy and from nearly every ship tracers arced against unseen targets in the night sky.

This day, 7 June, the somber reports of "pinned down," "murderous fire," "no progress," that had darkened yesterday's reports from Omaha, lightened slightly. The night before, the 16th Infantry at last took Colleville, leaving their dead behind them on the beaches and in the draws.

But Gen. Bradley, pacing nervously on *Augusta's* main deck, was somber; the wind was rising and the sea was making up. In only a few places had we reached the planned D-Day phase lines; Caen and Bayeaux were still beyond our lines; the various beachheads were not linked; supplies were backed up, ammo too short for comfort.

On 7 June, as I remember it, we of the floating press first experienced the "Nelson touch." Adm. Sir Bertram S. Ramsay, RN, was in command of all naval forces in the invasion and the British, as senior naval partners, had responsibility for all press arrangements for naval correspondents.

In Britain the role of the press, then as now, was and is entirely different from the position of the press in the United States, and English methods emphasized this. They were truly reminiscent of the days of Lord Horatio Nelson.

Steam pinnaces—tiny cockleshells of boats—were to collect news dispatches from all the ships in the invasion fleet that had correspondents embarked. One collection daily was to be made. Once the entire round of the invasion fleet had been made—from the British beaches to Utah—the pinnace was to steam back across the English Channel to Portsmouth, where the collected dispatches were to be transmitted by wire to a central censor in London, and then, variously, distributed to the London offices of the individual newspapers or press associations, or cabled to the United States.

Inevitably, the system broke down almost completely; its built-in delay factor turned into a built-in press disaster. There were not enough small boats to keep any sort of accurate collection timetable and heavy weather threw all calculations out of kilter.

Some of the tiny cockleshells, not really seaworthy enough to tackle the English Channel in its rough moods, reportedly sank or broke down en route to Portsmouth, or had to be towed to safety. Dispatches were mixed up, garbled, confused and lost; all of them were hopelessly delayed.

My grandstand seat proved to be up in the bleachers, far in left field; of the thousands of words I wrote on D-Day and the first few days thereafter only a few arrived at the *New York Times* office in New York, and most of these were so delayed they were "dated" by time of receipt.

Things settled down a little as outraged American correspondents and editors bombarded the British Admiralty with complaints, but it was not until five or six days after the fateful 6 June that dispatches started arriving at home offices from the invasion fleet with any sort of regularity. Even then, my best communication achievement while aboard *Augusta* was a two-day delay—far from good enough in those anguished days of crisis.

Not until 18 June when I returned, temporarily, to London was I able to get into the paper with negligible time lapse a situation piece headlined "Foothold in Europe Safe."

All this was in strong contrast to those press arrangements which the U.S. forces controlled. U.S. newspapers and press associations had banded together to form and support "Press Wireless," which was provided with a mobile commercial radio station ashore capable of direct communication to the United States.

Soon after, the beachhead was secured and the Army established a press camp, complete with tents, food and logistics facilities and with public affairs and escort officers and a complete censorship outfit at the scene. Dispatches soon flowed in a smooth and continuous volume direct from our beachhead to New York, with only brief delay.

This facility was not, of course, operational on D-Day, or immediately thereafter, but the Army, after some snafus, gave it high priority—news of victory was important to morale—and it opened for business very quickly, so quickly that I had a brief and heated tiff with "Rip" Struble, then a rear admiral and Adm. Kirk's chief of staff, about going ashore.

Some days after D-Day I was champing at the bit at the 19th-century British press methodology; I wanted to go ashore to see the situation for myself and to file a story, if possible, from the beach. Gen. Bradley and the First Army, who had been sending in boats to various beachheads for situation reports, were willing; Struble was not.

Struble, later in command of the U.S. landing at Wonsan in the Korean War, is a feisty man; he insisted I was accredited only as a "naval correspondent" and this meant—literally—I could not go ashore.

Struble prevailed—for a time. My most vivid memory, however, of that torn and battered coast of France shortly before I returned temporarily to England (just in time for the first of the V-1s, the buzz bombs) was of a grim stretch of Omaha beach. It was about D plus 3 or 4 and I had hooked a ride ashore with Adm. Kirk and Gen. Bradley, who was greatly concerned about the jam-up in supplies on Omaha and the delay in getting follow-up waves ashore.

The 1st and 29th Divisions had stormed the bluffs and broken the Atlantic Wall, but they were stalled in the hedgerows a mile or so inland. The beach was littered with debris and wrecked craft and equipment and everywhere, across the sands and the bluffs and the draws that led inland, were scattered thousands of Mae Wests, the discarded symbols of a hard-won landing.

A wrecked tank, singed and blackened by the fire that had devoured it, was sieved and shredded by four direct hits from 88s; even its rubber treads had melted. Damaged, disabled or foundered landing craft were half awash; foxholes speckled the beach; an unexploded bomb was marked by a red flag and the ominous German signs—*Achtung! Minen!*—warned of the buried dangers in the draws that led from beach and seawall to bluff.

The smell of the battlefield was still there—the stinking stench of oil, burnt rubber, and dead cattle and dead men.

Beneath the bluff, against the seawall of this hard-won beach, stood Gen. Bradley, Adm. Kirk and Rear Adm. "Jimmy" Hall, who was in direct command under Kirk of the Omaha naval support forces. The three were arguing explosively; faces were taut with days of tension.

I stood a few yards away; the angry voice of Gen. Bradley carried to me over the sound of the guns and the splash of surf. "God damn it! I don't care what the reasons are; I want those supplies!"

As if in silent emphasis to his words there lay, just a few yards away, almost at the feet of their commanders, in a careful line collected by a graves registration unit the bodies of about a dozen GIs, a few of the many who had died in storming Omaha. They were forever silent, but those shrouded figures with the feet sticking out beneath the ponchos spoke far more eloquently than Gen. Bradley, and they remain today, 36 years afterwards, the dominant memory of a beachhead won in blood and courage.

That—and one other image—emerges ghost-like from the cluttered memories of the storming of *Festung Europa*.

A few days later I watched a unit of the 29th Division, which had just been relieved, marching to a rest-bivouac as far from the front as one could get in that cramped and hemmed-in beachhead. These men did not look human; they moved like the living dead. They had been among the storm troops on Omaha and they had fought continuously inland through the fields and hedgerows for many days.

They walked like all battle-exhausted troops, sucked dry physically and psychologically, looking straight ahead, silent, eyes dull and staring with fatigue and horror and fear suppressed. They walked like robots; the trauma of battle had drained them. I shall never forget, nor will any other who saw them, their vacant eyes.

This, too, was the price of victory.

But it had been victory. On Monday, 12 June, one of my D-Day notebooks records: "Just saw Kirk, who is rushing off to meet Adm. King and Eisenhower. He said, 'You know I am a perfectionist; I want everything 100 percent, or at least my children say I do. But this has been an amazing success; there's no doubt about it. Power has done it. All the beachhead now, except the Cherbourg flank, is beyond the range of my guns.'"

That night at the 2000 (8 P.M.) Sitrep aboard *Augusta*, it was reported that from the initial landings to date (12 June), 97,927 troops, 12,937 vehicles and 15,582 tons of supplies had been put ashore at Omaha and 67,650 troops had been landed with 4,137 vehicles and 9,986 tons of supplies on Utah.

It was clear we were in Europe to stay.

CHAPTER
SEVENTEEN

Through the Enemy's Lines: A Platoon's Story

by Edward J. Zebrowski, M.D.

McHugh was the first one to notice the 88s. He had been standing about ten feet from the jeep, scanning the edge of the woods with his field glasses, squinting against the bright sun. When he mentioned the battery of 88s, all our men scattered, but he kept standing there describing the German soldiers busily loading the big guns.

The first shell was a direct hit on our lead jeep. The blast lifted McHugh right out of his boots like a rag doll and tore off both his legs. He was thrown 30 feet away, and he lay there in the middle of the road, crying and bleeding to death. The Germans then covered the area with a vicious concentrated machine-gun fire, and there was no way we could get to him.

Most of us followed Sgt. Sam Bailey into the thick-walled pigsty that was attached to one of the farmhouses along the road. We lay on the concrete floor on dried-up manure, listening to McHugh moaning while the shelling continued and the machine guns kept up with their high-pitched, rapid staccato bursts, sending shivers up our spines.

"This is one hell of a mess we've gotten into this time," Sgt. Bailey said.

. . .

After two months of frontline duty leading up to this incident, we men of the Intelligence and Reconnaissance Platoon of the 5th Infantry Regiment, 71st Infantry Division, thought we were ready for anything. As part of Gen. George S. Patton Jr.'s Third Army, we had been plunging through the heart of Germany in headlong pursuit of the rapidly retreating Germans. By 1 May, 1945, with a light snow falling intermittently, we seized the dam at Braunau, Austria, on the Inn River with only slight resistance. This town, Adolf Hitler's birthplace, was situated on the Austro-German border, and from the moment we took the dam, it seemed the end of the war was very near.

Over the next three days, we covered approximately 80 kilometers, driving deep into the Austrian countryside through Altheim, Ried and Pramerdorf. By 4 May, we took Lambach without firing one shot.

By then, we had already penetrated farther east than any other unit in all the Western Allied armies in the European Theater.

On Saturday, 5 May, however, with the day breaking bright and clear, we were surprised with new and unusual orders.

"Conceal your weapons," Sgt. Bailey said. "Remove the .50-caliber machine gun. This is a special mission, and we have to appear totally unarmed."

Col. Sidney C. Wooten, the commanding officer of the 5th Infantry, stood by his jeep, shading his eyes against the bright sun and impatiently tapping his riding crop against his right thigh. The holster with his .45 pistol was nowhere in sight.

His plan was to penetrate 50 kilometers into enemy territory, acting as if the war had ended. Our destination was Steyr, Austria, where we were supposed to meet the Russians at the Enns River. He was counting on the element of surprise to help us complete our mission.

Besides the colonel and Maj. Irving S. Heymont, there were two newspaper correspondents and one photographer. To add to the appearance that the war had really ended, the colonel included a captured German colonel of the 12th SS *Standarte* (regiment).

With the announcement of Hitler's death on 30 April, 1945, the German and Austrian people were in a state of mourning. Whenever we had mentioned Hitler's death the few days before this mission, the people cried openly and unashamedly. With this emotional reaction sweeping what was left of the Third Reich, Col. Wooten felt the German soldiers were ready to call it quits. Furthermore, many of the Germans felt that once the German army was subdued, Gen. Patton would incorporate it into his Third Army and then proceed into combat against the Russians.

Col. Wooten took one more precaution to ensure the success of this mission. He had ordered a motorized battalion of infantry to follow four hours behind us, with another battalion on foot.

Now, if only the Germans would cooperate, we would complete our mission without a single casualty. Unfortunately, we were not that lucky.

I shoved my M1 under the canvas on the floor of the jeep, feeling very uneasy. I saw the look of concern on the faces of the other men, and I knew they felt the same way. Morelli was in one of the jeeps ahead of me. He kept getting out of his vehicle and rearranging the rifles on the floor of his jeep. He looked back and gave me the thumbs-up sign.

Our usual patrol consisted of five jeeps and 20 men. On this day, we had a total of ten jeeps and 40 men. I patted the Luger I had concealed in a shoulder holster and felt somewhat better, even though we had been warned that if the enemy captured us with German pistols in our possession, they would probably execute us on the spot. I decided to take my chances, and I noticed the other men were checking their pistols, too.

At first, everything went along smoothly. It was a bright sunny day. The people in the villages along our route had not really experienced the savagery or brutality of the war, and they were out doing their usual Saturday chores. Steyr, however, seemed far away.

We stopped briefly in each village and spoke to the people in the little German we knew.

"Krieg kaput!" we said over and over.

"Grüss Gott," they would reply, making the sign of the cross and hurrying away with fear, astonishment and bewilderment plainly etched on their faces.

That is the way it went for the first few hours. We did not see any soldiers around, and everybody was so pleasant and polite.

Suddenly, as we swung through Wels, one of the larger towns, we found ourselves in the middle of a German military convoy, both of our columns having converged on a square in the middle of the town. There were trucks full of armed German soldiers, horse-drawn wagons and light artillery cannon, remnants of a ragged and worn-out army.

We were just as shocked as the policeman in the center of the town square, who was standing on a wooden platform directing traffic, his eyes bulging with surprise.

"Krieg kaput!" we all yelled out as we passed him.

The whistle fell out of his mouth, but his arms remained frozen in the direction of the traffic, a look of total disbelief on his face.

We continued with the convoy for about one kilometer and then turned east toward Steyr. By then, we had become bolder, almost convincing ourselves that the war, indeed, had ended.

In the next village, Kremsmünster, there were a few German soldiers on both sides of the road. Scattered among them were officers with pistols hanging from their belts. When we stopped briefly, I saw one of our men from the jeep ahead of us run up to a German officer and say, "Krieg kaput!" He then put out his hand and said, "Pistole!" The German hesitated a moment, shifting his gaze to us in the jeeps. Then he took out his pistol and handed it over.

Soon, we were all doing the same thing, and in a short time, we had more than a dozen pistols in every jeep. Most of them were Lugers and P-38s, but we also garnered some Italian Berettas, 7.65-mm Walthers, Mausers and old Hungarian semiautomatics.

Instead of a dangerous mission deep into enemy territory, this seemed to be turning into a Saturday picnic excursion into the beautiful Austrian countryside. But it did not stay that way for long. In the next village, Bad Hall, we again stopped for a short time. One of the newspaper correspondents ran up to a tall blond SS trooper and said, "Krieg kaput! Pistole!" and extended his hand to receive the gun. The SS trooper, without a moment's hesitation, pulled out his Luger, aimed point-blank at the man's chest and calmly fired three times. The man crumpled at his feet, clutching his chest, a startled look on his face. The SS trooper then deliberately and very slowly shifted his gaze to us with a look of utter contempt, returned the Luger to its holster in a sweeping motion and walked away.

"Don't move," Sgt. Bailey said in a hoarse whisper from the front seat of the jeep as we instinctively went for our rifles under the canvas. "There are too many of them."

Suddenly, from out of nowhere, the street was full of German soldiers.

We dropped off our medic to tend to the wounded man with instructions to wait for the motorized battalion behind us. He stood looking at us, a forlorn figure with the injured man lying at his feet as we left slowly and quietly to catch up to the rest of the jeeps ahead of us.

Only then did Sgt. Bailey turn around and growl, "I never saw a more stupid bunch of men in my whole life. 'Krieg kaput! Pistole!' It's lucky that we all didn't get shot in that town."

He turned away from us totally disgusted, still muttering under his breath and looking up the dust-filled road ahead of us to make sure we were not too far behind the last jeep. He knew that the Germans liked to knock off the last jeep of a patrol. Afterward, he leaned over to touch the two Lugers and one P-38 that he had stowed under the front seat. He appeared more relaxed now, but he still looked completely disgusted.

It took us six hours to reach the outskirts of Steyr. We stopped there for about 15 minutes, and some RAF (Royal Air Force) pilots came over to the jeep to greet us.

I was about to say the magic words, "Krieg kaput!" when one of them yelled out, "How is the war going, Yanks?"

They had been working in the fields as farm laborers and had been fairly well treated, subsisting on bread and soup. We gave them all our K rations since up to that time we had been living off the land, eating chicken, eggs and venison, plus all the German black bread we could find. We left them with the same instructions—to wait for the motorized battalion—and we proceeded into the center of Steyr. There were two main bridges crossing the Enns River in that area, but the Russians were nowhere in sight.

The basic mission had been completed, penetrating into enemy territory nearly 50 kilometers with only one casualty. The ruse of concealing our weapons and not engaging any of the soldiers we had met had worked without a hitch.

We remained there for about 30 minutes, then moved on north of the city. As we started up a long hill leading out of town, we saw dozens of *Hitler Jugend* of about 12 to 14 years of age in full uniform and carrying submachine guns slung from their shoulders. They all looked very determined, as if the fate of the nation rested on them alone. We did not waste any time driving past them.

We had gone only four kilometers north of Steyr, heading toward Dietachdorf on the east side of the Enns River, when a shell exploded on the cab of a German truck that had pulled up on the side of the

145

road in front of an old barn. As we passed it, we could see the driver of the truck still sitting behind the steering wheel, but his head was gone.

We drove along for another hundred yards or so and then stopped about 50 feet behind the jeep ahead. We had not yet grasped the gravity of the situation. I jumped out of our jeep and through the field glasses saw a battery of 88s in the field to my right about 500 yards away.

We later learned they were attached to the 12th *SS* Infantry Regiment along with a machine-gun company. Across the road to my left, there was a cluster of half a dozen farmhouses and barns. The lead jeep was about 200 yards ahead of us, and I could see McHugh standing there with his field glasses trained on the 88s.

Just then the first shell struck the lead jeep, wounding McHugh. This was quickly followed by another one that landed on the top of one of the houses, knocking down a portion of the roof. The area was swept by machine-gun fire, and most of us made a dash for the safety of the houses with no time to take our concealed weapons from the jeeps.

As I rushed to the pigsty, I saw Morelli jump into a trench that had been dug along the road.

Luckily, there were no pigs around. The machine guns let up periodically, and we could hear McHugh crying and moaning. Each time we started to go to his rescue, the firing began again, almost as if the Germans had anticipated our move. His crying was the most terrible sound any person could ever hear, and it was a relief to hear the machine guns drown it out.

The Germans continued to shell the farmhouses and rake the area with machine-gun fire for long periods of time, making it impossible for us to approach his position.

After an hour, his crying stopped, and we could not tell whether his crying or the devastating silence that followed was worse.

A German soldier suddenly appeared carrying a white flag with a note from his commanding officer demanding that we surrender immediately or face an unrelenting bombardment and total annihilation.

One of our officers grabbed an M1 from one of our men and shot the German in the chest. We left him lying where he fell.

After a brief hiatus, the shelling and machine-gun fire started again. The rooftops of the buildings began to crumble. After the first shell burst, Col. Wooten left for the rear to speed up the battalions following us, and he put Maj. Heymont in charge.

So there we were, huddled in the pigsty and getting edgy. Sgt. Bailey waddled over, crouching low and said:

> Zebrowski, I want you and Farkas to take up a position back down the road about a quarter of a mile in that abandoned house at that last intersection. Wait for the motorized battalion that is supposed to follow us, and let them know our position so they won't shell us.

Farkas and I crouched down and made our way back to the jeeps to retrieve our M1s. The firing became more intense, and we could hear the snapping of the bullets as they passed us and struck the ground. With good broken-field running and flopping to the ground every few yards, we reached the house amazingly unscathed in 20 minutes. Both of us had expected to be hit. Looking back, we saw that the roofs of the houses along with portions of the second floors were already demolished. The Germans, it appeared, were determined to carry out their ultimatum.

Farkas knelt down and looked out one of the windows toward the road.

"What if the Germans show up at that intersection before our own battalion?" he asked, turning around to look at me.

"Well, we'll certainly know about it before Sgt. Bailey does."

We were pinned down for about four hours before we saw advance elements of the motorized battalion drive into view, along with a bunch of Sherman tanks. We breathed much easier after that. Mortars were immediately set up, and between the tanks and mortars, it took about an hour for all firing to cease and all the Germans to walk out with their hands on their heads.

It was early evening by the time we started walking the few kilometers back to Steyr. We were happy to see each other alive, but we were sad that we had lost one of our men. We kept hearing that awful crying in the middle of the road as the shelling ripped apart the buildings we were in, while the machine guns sprayed the area. We had been only 50 feet away from McHugh, but he had died alone.

Halfway back to Steyr, we met our company clerk looking clean and fresh as a daisy. He nearly fainted when he saw me alive and well, because shortly before coming up the hill to meet our platoon, he had received a report that I had been killed by a direct hit from an 88.

After a lot of backslapping with the sheer joy of being alive, Morelli handed him one of the guns we had picked up on this mission. The company clerk, like an expert rear echelon commando, pointed the pistol at the ground, closed his eyes tightly and pulled the trigger, shooting himself in the right foot.

Three days later, on 8 May, 1945, the war was officially over. The Russians did not arrive at the Enns River until 9 May. The men of the 71st Division had traveled more than 800 miles through enemy territory in approximately two months and were officially recognized as having penetrated farther east than any other unit in all the Allied forces in Europe.

More than 107,000 enemy soldiers were captured by our division during that time, and 300 of our men were killed in battle.

Although our intelligence and reconnaissance platoon ended our last mission in Steyr, the division's cavalry reconnaissance troop had orders on 6 and 7 May to continue eastward in an attempt to meet the Russians. They were the only men of Gen. Patton's Third Army still actively engaging the enemy when the war officially ended.

The roads east of the Enns River were so jammed with German soldiers retreating from the advancing Russians that our troops were only able to reach Amstetten and Waidhofen, 38 miles from the most westward point of the Russian army.

During this time, our platoon settled down in Steyr for some well-deserved rest.

* * *

Now, almost 44 years later, when I pull out my old Luger and P-38 for occasional inspection, cleaning and reminiscing, all my old friends spring into full action, their faces bold, young, vibrant and full of anticipation, just as they were back there in 1945. The air is again charged with that same dangerous excitement that only war can create. There is Morelli smiling and flashing his thumbs-up sign. Sam Bailey is again growling and muttering under his breath. The *SS* trooper, standing fierce in the bright sunlight, is looking at us with audacious contempt after shooting the shocked newspaper correspondent in the chest. Our medic is standing beside the crumpled, dying man, lonely, worried and bewildered. Farkas is running beside me, and we are both breathing hard, racing through a storm of machine-gun fire to reach that abandoned house at the intersection north of Steyr. Our hearts are pumping wildly, for we are surprised we have survived.

The Austrian sun still seems terribly bright, forcing me to squint, and I can still taste the gritty swirling dust our jeeps kicked up from the narrow winding roads.

The tears spring too quickly to my aging eyes, however, as I see McHugh lying in the middle of the road crying and slowly bleeding to death; so I do not pull out those weapons as often anymore, and my memories lie restlessly interred.

PART FIVE

HOOVES & PAWS

CHAPTER
EIGHTEEN

O, Give a Horse a Man
He Can Ride

by Lt. Col. Robert E. Kennington, USA (Ret.)

L
ike many others of my generation, I had no idea, during my college ROTC days, that I was training for a permanent military
career. I undertook the basic two years because they were com-
pulsory, and the two advanced-course years partly because the sub-
sistence allowance of 75 cents per training day more than compen-
sated for the three-dollar cost of 13 starchy meals a week in a
boardinghouse.

Graduating from law school at Indiana University in 1937, I opted
for a year's active duty under the Thomason Act. This measure en-
acted by Congress called for training 1,000 Reserve second lieutenants with the regular Army—the objective being the commissioning
of 50 of that number in the permanent establishment's combat arms
or the Army Air Corps.

I reported for duty with the 11th U.S. Infantry at Ft. Benjamin Harrison, Ind., on 4 July and was assigned to Co. F. The initial appearance of us 11 Reserve officers in the regiment proved the accuracy of a popular saying: "Nothing looks stranger than a Reserve officer in uniform, except, perhaps, a regular officer in civvies."

Although two companies at war strength, with the band and bugle corps, were absent at expositions in Cleveland, Ohio, and Dallas, Tex., and much of the regiment was supporting a citizens' military training camp on the post, some training was in progress. I found myself performing company duty, inventorying the post exchange, taking my turn on the officer-of-the-day roster, and serving as defense counsel on a special court-martial.

Around the middle of August, I was placed on temporary duty with Co. I, which was beefed up to war strength and dispatched to Camp Perry, Ohio, for duty at the National Rifle Matches. In addition to observing the best military and civilian marksmen in competition, this duty afforded an opportunity to meet Army and Marine Corps officers from all over the country.

By the end of September, the entire regiment was reassembled at Ft. Harrison and soldiering began in earnest. To the duties already enumerated, the Reserve officers began attending formal school sessions each afternoon.

As the tempo of training increased, I began to look forward to the day when the entire regiment would take to the field for a training exercise. Shortly before the first snow, the happy day arrived. I was filled with eager anticipation as I entered the company orderly room that morning. When I reported to the company commander, he greeted me with the question, "Do you ride?"

"No, sir!"

"You'll ride today, because the battalion commander has selected you for his adjutant."

Horror of horrors! I knew that there were horses in the stables and that some people were mounted when in the field. In fact, I had intended, when time permitted, to try my hand (if that is the right word) at the art. But, to have the challenge thrust upon me so suddenly was overwhelming. Nevertheless, good soldier that I was, I staggered down the barracks' steps and headed toward battalion headquarters.

My mind was in a whirl. I had never seen a battalion adjutant and now I was one. I had never been aboard a horse and now I was a horseman. I was almost apologetic as I presented myself to the major commanding the battalion. He returned my salute with a curt, "The horses are out in back. I'll be out presently."

On the service road behind the headquarters, I found two horses held by orderlies. One, a beautiful chestnut sporting an infantry-blue bridle, was the commander's transportation. The other, a big gray, which appeared to stand as tall as the barracks' porch, wore a red bridle and was obviously borrowed from the artillery stable. He was tended by a "redleg" from the 19th Field Artillery Regiment.

I thanked my lucky star that I had attended a Reserve officers' camp the preceding year, for there I had witnessed a five-minute demonstration on mounting a horse. I didn't recall what the instructor said, only that he mounted his horse from the "near" side. So I walked to the left side of the massive steed. For want of anything better to say while I tried to figure out how to get into the saddle, I inquired if the apparition might have a name.

"Gunpowder, sir!" came the somewhat unnerving reply.

I thought, "If he lives up to his name, it's going to be curtains for this adjutant!"

I no longer recall how I did it, and I'm sure I didn't conceal the fact that I was a novice, but I found myself seated higher in the air than ever in my life, peering between two pointed ears and feeling quite exposed without a windshield before me. Realizing that I would soon need all the assistance I could get, I confessed to the orderly that this was my maiden voyage and requested that he remain at my side.

Whether he was so well-disciplined that he couldn't violate his training or whether he wanted to be where he could best see the fun, I do not know, but whenever we traveled in company thereafter he remained the prescribed distance to my rear. A help to me he wasn't.

The major appeared and led us down the concrete service road at a trot. Knowing nothing about the fundamentals of horsemanship, I was soon in desperate straits. Almost immediately, my feet became disengaged from the stirrups, and stirrups and feet were performing a wild ballet. My attempts to bring the errant items together manually only threw me off balance to the point where I was using the horse's mane for a handhold with the rein of no more help than the stirrups.

It seemed that whenever my posterior descended to the saddle it struck the pistol in its holster on my right hip or the canteen on my left, and sometimes I managed to collide with both accoutrements simultaneously. Nevertheless, I was still aboard Gunpowder as we bounced past Co. F, assembled near the post theater.

My loyal troopers, observing my exalted position and my exhibition of equestrian expertise, filled the air with catcalls and cries of "Hi, ho, Silver," "Ride 'em, cowboy," and other comments of encouragement. Appreciating their concern, I blushed exceedingly.

The next several hours passed with the regiment trudging along unpaved roads toward a distant battlefield. I was already engaged in combat with the CO and Gunpowder. The former blistered me constantly with orders to get my horse under control and the latter continued to do as he damned well pleased. Being of a reasonably religious bent, I was quite busy entreating Heaven that I might be allowed to stay aboard and thus save face and, alternately, supplicating that I might be thrown from the beast and thus end the torture.

Eventually, the major directed me to carry a verbal message of some sort to the captain of Co. G, the last company in the column. Although I longed to gallop the length of the command in dramatic fashion, I was unable to interest Gunpowder in parting from the other horses in the command group. I employed all my persuasive powers, consisting of cursing him and banging on his ribs with my unspurred heels—to no avail.

I solved the dilemma by steering the horse to the side of the road and holding him there while the other horsemen moved away and the troops marched on by. If I had a lemon to suck on, I might have resembled Stonewall Jackson reviewing his corps in years long gone, but the thought did not occur to me. All I desired was for the good men of the 11th Infantry to think I was serving a military purpose and that I had some idea of what the hell it was.

After a considerable time had elapsed, the captain of Co. G appeared, marching at the head of his organization. I delivered the message, and it was then incumbent upon me to return to my place at the side of the battalion commander. That's when the trouble really started!

By beating a tattoo on Gunpowder with my heels until my legs were sore, I succeeded in coaxing him to a position abreast of the next unit forward in the line of march, Co. H, the machine-gun company. Now, the machine-gun company was equipped with wheeled transport in the form of small, two-wheeled carts, each drawn by a mule. Each gun section, of which there were 12 in the company, I believe, had two carts, one for the weapon and one for extra ammunition in wooden boxes.

Gunpowder was overcome with a great yearning to rub shoulders with each mule we overtook. In no time, five or six carts, with mules attached, were overturned, scattering their loads in the ditch beside the road. Immediately, I was the subject of violent verbal abuse from peppery noncoms and normally passive privates alike as I wheeled the big horse about in confusion, utterly at a loss to extricate myself from this predicament and looking about for a friendly soul to rescue me.

Of course, there was no friendly soul in sight, and if one had appeared he probably would have led a lynching party. The luck of the Irish held, however, as into the shambles rode my orderly with the glad tidings that the battalion commander desired my presence forthwith. My addled brain functioned sufficiently to devise a plan to escape from the irate machine gunners.

I realized that if the orderly would take off at a gallop, my horse would follow. So I directed him to race back to the CO and report that I was on the way. The orderly, probably in fear of the cursing, screaming gunners, whirled his steed and took off in a cloud of dust. Right behind him, in a second cloud, was a great, gray horse and rider, leaving a tangled mass of mules, carts, weapons, ammo boxes and angry soldiers behind.

Never had I been propelled into the wind at such a rapid rate. My mount was completely out of control. I feared that I had been saved from one predicament, just to meet death in a more violent manner. All my earlier problems of lost stirrups, lost balance, lost reins were repeated in faster tempo.

Had artist Frederic Remington been at hand with brush and easel, he might have used me as a model for a painting of an Indian fighter, brim flattened against the crown of his campaign hat, the mighty horse's hooves throwing gravel as he fled the pursuing hostiles. But, he would not have captured the blanched cheeks and fear-filled eyes of the Reserve lieutenant aboard the loaner artillery horse that day. Such expressions of terror could never be captured on canvas.

I am unable to recall how my orderly left the scene at this point. The terror of the final episode has erased all memory of him from my mind. I recall only that I topped a rise in the road, still hurtling along at breakneck speed, and observed before me a scene which turned my bones to jelly. Squarely across the road, about 100 yards distant, the regimental commander, a tall, lean Scotsman, sat astride his mount, contentedly puffing on his pipe, oblivious to the fact that a thunderbolt was descending upon him.

I had great respect for the colonel as a man of his rank and experience. I had observed, in the regimental headquarters, how senior Army captains whom I looked upon with awe, whipped off their hats and braced themselves against the wall when he sauntered by. And, now, the Great Himself was about to be run down and killed or maimed by a go-to-hell Reserve lieutenant who could not even steer a hobbyhorse.

While offering more prayers in rapid-fire fashion, I hastily reviewed my short military career and its apparently sad end. It appeared to me that it would be regrettable to be drummed out of the service, but the years in confinement at Leavenworth promised to be worse.

But I reckoned without the skill or plain cussedness of Gunpowder. As the final great collision was about to occur—as the colonel was turning to observe his approaching doom—Gunpowder, in complete control of the situation, spun sideways and came to an abrupt halt, shoulder to shoulder with the colonel's mount. I sat wide-eyed and shaking, staring into the Old Man's face. Gentleman that he was, I do not recall being chewed out over the incident, or even being asked the purpose of my surprise visit. If asked, I certainly don't know what I answered.

When the dust settled, I walked Gunpowder (or, more properly, he walked me) over to the battalion commander nearby and, until the colonel issued his field order, I pretended that I had disappeared. When it was announced that staff officers would release their mounts to company commanders for their use in reconnoitering, I breathed a tremendous sigh of relief and lowered myself from the saddle.

I had not dared to dismount previously, even for urgent reasons, as I feared I could not get back up. The pain in my thighs and buttocks was welcomed as evidence that I was again on *terra firma*, but a rubbery sensation in my knees caused me to stroll as unobtrusively as possible to a large tree, there to brace myself until the strength returned to my legs.

The rest of the exercise and the march back to the post on foot was a welcome ordeal in spite of the agony of my sore muscles. Strange as it seems, I can't recall anyone—even my drinking buddies—taunting me about my initiation on horseback. God bless them all!

I never again rode a horse in a field exercise. In fact, I never again saw a horse ridden in a field exercise.

Sometime later, however, I became a student officer at the Infantry School. Cognizant of my shady past, and in order to properly prepare myself for combat on the scale of the Spanish-American War, I enrolled in a voluntary equitation class. After several periods of exercises in the corral, the cavalry instructor led the class out into the pine woods. There we were directed to gallop in single file around the outer perimeter of a circle of trees.

Now, all the horses were well-acquainted with each other and tended to be herd-bound, so that one had to be constantly alert against an attempt by his mount to socialize with one of its equine acquaintances. The instructor had cautioned us to "treat our horses as we would our wives and always maintain the upper hand."

Being a confirmed bachelor in those days, I accepted that silly idea as gospel. So, when my steed caught a glimpse of a particularly attractive stablemate across the circle and made a sudden move to cut through the trees, I was prepared, and pulled him back onto the trail. Feeling very pleased with myself, I was galloping along, uttering derogatory remarks in the animal's ear, when he once more attempted to break the circle. Again I whipped his head back, this time more vigorously than before.

While this sudden movement accomplished my purpose in returning the horse to the path, it did not return my upper body to its place atop Old Dobbin, so that instead of horse and rider as one, passing on the left of the next tree in the circle, only the horse was in the proper place and my face collided with the tree in a manner that was certainly not intended.

When my head cleared a short time later, I found myself sitting on the trail with the rein still in my hand and my mount staring down at me with a sardonic grin on his features. Seeing the great teeth leering at me through the haze, I momentarily imagined that I saw the ghost of my old nemesis, Gunpowder.

But, that's all in the past. Sometimes, as I ride my daughter's one-eyed gelding in California's beautiful Valley of the Moon, I meditate on the way things were and the way they now are. And, you know, allowing for a touch of arthritis and a tendency to forget whether I've taken my medication, I believe I could still perform creditably as a battalion adjutant (mounted).

CHAPTER
NINETEEN

Bearwatch

by James A. Sayler

First, it was guard duty, KP and special duties; and then it was
bearwatch. What would the Army think of next? The big
thing was to know where your fingers were. They really hurt
if you squashed them between the rocks, and it also screwed up your
timing, which was very important in a properly performed bearwatch.

Now, of course, bearwatch was nothing more than a good joke
pulled on an unlucky soldier, but the watch helped keep the others
out of trouble. For those of us who were mountaineering and survival
instructors at Ft. Richardson, Alaska, our hands were usually kept
pretty busy. Between teaching classes, handling camp logistics and,
above all, looking out for the safety of the soldiers, there was little
room in our busy schedules for soldiers needing disciplinary action.

All soldiers who were sent to Ft. Richardson were required to at-
tend either our five or ten-day course, depending on their assigned

units. The outdoor classes were taught at Eklutna Glacier, and a more rugged, intense mountain setting would be hard to find.

With few instructors and often many soldiers in camp, discipline was very important, especially at night when there were few or no classes. When a soldier needed some type of punishment, bearwatch was perfect.

Bearwatch consisted of walking the outside perimeter of camp after everyone had retired to the tents for the night. The purpose of the watch was to keep a lookout for bears.

Noise being the best method for keeping bears away, the unlucky soldier was given a softball-sized rock for each hand. Every time the soldier's left foot hit the ground, the two rocks were to come together—thus the warning for fingers. Several occasions saw the peaceful slumber produced by banging rocks shattered by the yell and curses of someone who had bashed his own fingers while on duty.

The effect of bearwatch on wrongdoers, especially with their peers looking on and making snide and humorous comments, worked wonders for controlling discipline. One example of bearwatch the first night out was usually enough to keep the other soldiers in line for the rest of the week.

Our camp had been home to the bears long before the arrival of the Army, and the bears saw no reason to leave just because a new two-legged animal was in the neighborhood. Thus, there would be the occasional four-legged visitor to camp—at what time no one could ever really say.

Usually they were daytime bears, tempted by the delicious aroma of such a large portion of military food cooking in the vicinity of the bear's home. Hypnotized by the obviously pleasant aroma of so many C-ration cans being opened at one time, the bear would come into camp only long enough to be scared away by all the noise and havoc its presence would create.

Those, of course, were daytime bears. The nighttime bears were a bit sneakier, especially with everyone asleep. Where was our bearwatch the night Blackie came around?

Remember waking in the middle of the night to the sound of the telephone? The room is dark and you are peacefully sleeping when suddenly the noise of the telephone awakens you. It usually takes a few moments to figure out what is going on and to realize what the disturbance is.

It is the same way when you awake in the middle of the night and there is a bear in your tent. It takes a few moments to get organized, but things move fast after that first second or two!

One week, three of us were living pretty well—sharing a five-man tent. Cots were against the walls of the tent leaving the central floor space for a table and a large ice chest full of good civilian food.

There were no C-rations for instructors that week. We were eating real eggs, ham and cheese sandwiches, and steaks for dinner. With all that good food someone must have gotten messy with the cleanup, for late one night Blackie came calling—or perhaps a better word would be ripping.

The canvas tent had only one door and no windows, making for a very dark interior when the lantern was not in use. Of course, no one was sleeping in front of the tent door, but Blackie did not know where the door was anyway—at least he did not use it.

The first thing I heard was people yelling, "Jim, there's a bear in the tent!" I was trying to wake up and wondering at the same time why there was a light on over my cot. The dull light of Alaska's June twilight was shining through the thin cotton liner above my cot, where Blackie's third claw had deftly created a new door through the outside canvas. Enter, Blackie.

Some people say adrenaline does wonders for the human body in a tight situation. They are right. In one fluid motion, I was out of the sleeping bag, under the previously tight tent flaps (I could not find the door either), and standing outside the tent in my long johns, only seconds ahead of the tent's newest occupant. I was the last one out of the tent. By this time most of the camp was standing around at a respectable distance wondering what was to happen next. Blackie was having a field day in the tent despite all of our verbal but hollow threats.

When it was time to leave, Blackie still could not find the real door. With his poor eyesight, he could not find the new door either. The obvious choice for Blackie was the third door which was gracefully placed somewhere between the first two. Exit, Blackie.

Of course the bear could not leave without a souvenir of its visit. Since the straps of one sergeant's backpack would not fit over the bear's massive shoulders, Blackie simply carried the pack in its mouth. Paying no attention to our continued verbal abuse, Blackie and the pack headed into the woods, not to be seen again that night.

Inside the tent, Blackie had actually been quite neat. No cots were overturned, no sleeping bags slashed. The table had been knocked over but nothing was smashed.

The food had been spilled and sampled. There was a carton of eggs with a perfect set of claw prints punched through the top, but inside not an egg was broken.

Later the next day when the pack was found, an entire loaf of white bread was missing. Blackie made only one incision the length of the plastic bag. Nothing else in the pack was touched but there were no crumbs left either. Not all bear encounters have as safe an ending, and several times a year the newspapers carry the story of a meeting that ends in injury or death. One of an estimated 30,000 bears in Alaska, Blackie was mellow; we were lucky. Since bearwatch is not always available or desirable, it is safe to assume that Blackie or friends will visit again someday. From now on, we are leaving the white bread at home.

CHAPTER TWENTY

Mascots

by Maj. Gen. A. S. Newman, USA (Ret.)

T acitus, the Roman historian, once said, "Liberties and masters
are not easily combined." The idea can be applied to an
Army-wide practice that often produces this classic conflict
of interest, which may be stated: the liberty to have pets and the
responsibilities of commanders are sometimes difficult to reconcile.
Like, for example, a happily roving dog at a guard of honor formation—especially if during ruffles and flourishes he sniffs the visiting
dignitary's legs as though they were twin fire plugs.

At my first post we had a company dog, a plebeian hound type:
back and sides black, merging into a light tan underbelly, and tan
shadings about face and ears. He didn't belong to anybody; he just
owned our company in general. But when I approached to get ac-
quainted he sidled silently away, tail drooping, and the men grinned
at my puzzled discomfiture.

It soon became clear that he avoided all officers. So I went to the man who I had quickly learned to admire, respect, trust and go to for enlightenment on things I didn't understand: our first sergeant.

"Lieutenant," he said, "it's your leggins." (At that time all officers wore either leather leggins or knee-length boots.)

When my cerebral processes still lagged he smiled and added, "Suppose the men find an old pair of leather leggins, and pass them around in off-duty hours. Then every time that little hound comes near the man wearing leggins, he gets kicked. Would that explain it?"

The first sergeant also told me about Oscar, a mascot his company had in Panama. Oscar was a very large and long snake, captured in the jungle.

Oscar spent much of his time on the dayroom pool table, lying neatly against the cushions around the edges. Apparently the green cloth-covered slate made a cool, comfortable snake mattress.

When a newcomer arrived in the company it was customary to invite him for a game of pool at which there were always kibitzers—because usually results were interesting. More than one man had taken a screen door with him on his way elsewhere after meeting Oscar face to face.

One day there was an unexpected development in the form of a husky young recruit. As he chalked his cue and approached the table, Oscar raised his head for a better look at the new arrival.

Things happened fast. The husky recruit swapped ends with the pool cue and, with a swing like Babe Ruth and an aim like Ty Cobb, scored a bull's eye on Oscar's noggin. Oscar promptly pitched a fit all over the dayroom as screen doors took another licking—this time from the kibitzers. By sundown even the tip of Oscar's tail had given up the ghost, so the company was minus a mascot but plus a recruit marked "handle with care."

Sometimes a mascot causes quakes in high places. That's what Moi did at Schofield Barracks where I was a military police lieutenant. Moi was quite a dog. He loved everybody and was known all over as "that dirty little MP dog." Apparently his ancestry was scrambled, for he resembled a bird dog in body configuration and liver and white markings, except that he traveled close to the ground on stubby legs as though there was a basset hound in his lineage.

Across the road from our quadrangle the commanding general's house fronted on the post parade. This impressive, austere soldier had no children so he and his wife set more than usual store by a highly pedigreed canine female. As you've guessed by this time, the highly pedigreed lady somehow managed to escape chaperonage at a critical time in her life—and Moi didn't miss the opportunity. Since there were several witnesses, "that dirty little MP dog" was positively identified.

There was unhappiness in the CG's house over what the resulting pups might look like, and the titillating news spread over the post. Especially when the high-level owners' unhappiness became more acute on learning kennel club rules would prevent the prospective mother from having pedigreed offspring after her morganatic liaison—for, apparently, the melody lingers on.

In war, with troops spread around the world, pets are more varied, from white parrots in New Guinea to giant lizards in Australia, and all sorts of animals. The most publicized one known to me was a small monkey named Eleanor, owned by the chief clerk in our chief of staff's office.

One morning while a brigadier general was shaving—with his removable teeth nearby—the monkey happened along and picked them up. With a muffled roar the BG gave chase and treed Eleanor, who finally flung the teeth down at him.

This not only brought a grin to weary GIs in our jungle fighting area—the combat grapevine distributed news down to the foxholes— but to uncounted thousands of Americans at home who read about it in a "human interest" dispatch from the war front.

The most memorable unit mascot in my experience was a mountain lion from the Rocky Mountains area sent to a sergeant in the 511th Airborne Infantry soon after I took command. He started out a roly-poly little fellow not much larger than a good-sized pup, but soon he was bigger than most dogs—looking even larger when approaching you in his gangly lope.

The whole regiment got a kick out of him—especially on those occasions when a stranger entered our area who didn't know we had a pet lion running lose. As regimental commander I didn't get into the act until plans were afoot to get our mountain kitty jump-qualified. But I put the kibosh on that one, having a vivid mental picture of what could happen if our lion found himself in the door of an airplane and decided he didn't want to jump—thus maybe ending up astride the pilot's neck.

Of course you could write a book about specially trained horses and mules in the Old Army. Or even about the lovable nuisance my wife and I call Kitty, who'll be in her 22nd year by the time this gets into print—every one of these years brightened for us by her presence.

Of course there are problems with pets, sometimes amplified by a few petulant people. But pets and apartment buildings don't go together. Further, some pets have inborn characteristics that get their owners into disfavor, like the penchant of dogs to bark and make devastating forays across neighbors' lawns. Or cats who catch birds when you have a bird-watcher CG—especially if he's as cantankerous as one we once had.

Perhaps the most irritating responsibility of many I endured as a lieutenant was a dog catching detail—several MPs armed with pup-tent ropes, charged with capturing any dogs running loose who might otherwise steal the spotlight at Hawaiian Division reviews. Each fido thought it was a game, gamboling just out of reach, while my red-faced and frustrated MPs, goaded by delighted comments from the crowd, kept doggedly after the loose pooches.

But it would be a sad post if any CG was so misguided as to issue a no-pets order. Further, that would be violating a basic principle of command. Proper action is to hold the owners responsible when their furry friends become an unreasonable nuisance.

It's hard to measure the place and value of pets in the Army, those privately owned as well as unit mascots. They bring a smile to the heart which, in indefinable ways, is a unifying and relaxing influence.

Perhaps it is said best in words chiseled on a small gray stone monument at Fort Benning—prominently placed for student officers over the years to see. It was erected in memory of a much-loved mutt who brightened life for Infantry School students in the 1920s. They called him Calculator, some said because he could calculate where officer classes would assemble in the field, and be there. Others said it was because, being a bit lame in one foot, he "picked up three and carried one." The inscription on his monument reads

CALCULATOR
Born ?
Died 29 Aug. 1923
He made better
dogs of us all.

PART SIX

VIETNAM

CHAPTER
TWENTY-ONE

Silent Night, Dangerous Night

by John D. Harris

The 24th of December, 1965, was a hot, humid day in Vietnam. I was a newspaper correspondent. I had been in Vietnam a few months and had been shot at by everything from Vietcong snipers to American artillery. At about 4 P.M. that day, I walked into the press tent of the 173rd Airborne Brigade, the Army paratrooper unit protecting the U.S. Air Force base at Bien Hoa, 25 miles north of Saigon.

A major sat behind a table. A few GIs, some bare chested, sat pecking at typewriters, reading newspapers and sweating in the afternoon heat—not exactly a Christmas atmosphere.

The major looked at my GI fatigues and jungle boots. I told him I wanted to talk to some of the men pulling guard duty around the base

171

perimeter for a Christmas story. The editors would go for it: our boys in Vietnam on Christmas Eve. The major nodded. He cranked up a field phone.

"Let's see what 'A' Company's got going," he said. "Hi, 'A' Company? Brigade information office here. We got a reporter who wants to talk to some of the guys on the perimeter, for Christmas and all that stuff. Can he come out now?"

A pause. The major said, "Uh-huh," then "uh-huh" again. He looked up at me. He listened for a while and nodded slowly. "Well, let me talk to him. Hang on."

The major leaned back in his chair, holding the phone. His face was blank.

"'A' Company says they don't have anyone on the perimeter today," he said. "But they have an all-night ambush patrol going out in the jungle pretty soon and they say you're welcome to join them. What shall I tell them?"

The paratroopers in the tent stopped typing and reading newspapers. The silence was heavy.

I tried to think fast—an ambush patrol . . . a killing patrol . . . a patrol looking for trouble—not like most patrols, with merely a reconnaissance function. The mission of the patrol would be to blow away enemy soldiers trying to get close to the Bien Hoa airfield.

The field had been penetrated by Vietcong sabotage squads a few months before and some F-100 fighter-bombers had been destroyed on the flight line. The U.S. command in Vietnam did not want that to happen again. F-100 operations based at Bien Hoa were crucial to American strategy in Vietnam—hence continuous patrolling around the field by the 173rd Airborne, a tough outfit that had seen continuous action since arriving in Vietnam a few months before.

But the hell with the 173rd Airborne.

An ambush patrol was not exactly what I had in mind for this Christmas Eve. My plan had been to get a story fast, telex it to the United States and then have Christmas Eve dinner with the other correspondents in Vietnam at the Caravelle Hotel roof restaurant in Saigon.

The major and the other paratroopers in the tent were still staring at me. The major gestured with the telephone, questioningly, still with that deadpan look. Okay, hotshot reporter, what are you going to do? I returned their stare. I felt my mouth go dry. I didn't have the guts to walk out of there.

"An ambush patrol?" I heard myself say. "Sure, that sounds like a great idea. Tell them okay."

Ten minutes later, a jeep pulled up outside the press tent. The GI driver took me to a row of tents on the far side of the field. He led me into the first tent in the row. Six or eight GIs looked me over.

"Here he is," my driver said, "the reporter."

A trim, deeply tanned sergeant introduced himself to me as the commander of the patrol.

"You ever spent a night in the jungle before?" he asked. His eyes bored directly into mine.

I said "no." I sat down on one of the cots. I took out my notebook: exclusive interview with S.Sgt. Charles N. Brown, 503rd Infantry, 173rd Airborne Brigade, U.S. Army, Bien Hoa, Vietnam, Christmas Eve, 1965.

Hometown? "New York." How long in the Army? "Twenty years." Seen much combat? "Seen more dead men in one day than most undertakers see in a lifetime." Ranger instructor. Parachute instructor with about 1,000 jumps. Behind-enemy-lines combat jump in Korea. Two tours in Vietnam. Decorations? "Ah, forget it." What did he think of the Vietcong? "I can handle any 12 of these bastards. It's that 13th son of a bitch who's got me worried."

End of interview.

Sgt. Brown spread a map on a cot. "This is where we're going," he said, stabbing a finger at a space designating spidery trails in the area north of the base. The 173rd was sending several patrols into the area that night, he explained. "Vietcong's in strength there," he said. "They've been pouring down these trails recently, hundreds of 'em. I lost 18 men there the other day."

I suddenly felt pretty tired. I looked around. One GI was squinting through a rifle barrel. Another was sharpening a knife. I studied them: paratroopers—tough guys—but their faces registered a certain fatalism, the look of men who have resigned themselves to death.

The soldier who had driven me in the jeep came up to me with half-a-dozen grenades cupped in his hands, as if they were hard-boiled eggs. He looked about 18 years old. "Here," he said, "you better take some of these along."

The damn things were six inches from my face. I shook my head. "No," I said, "if I take anything I'll take an M16."

The rules about arming correspondents? In Vietnam, all bets and most rules were off. Some combat outfits liked to arm correspondents so that they could pull their weight if trouble came up. I'd had weapons shoved into my hands by the Ninth Marines, the Army's 1st Cavalry Division and pilots of the 8th Bombardment Squadron (Tactical). The 173rd Airborne was no different.

"Do you have a spare M16?" I asked the kid with the grenades. He handed me one, plus a dozen clips of ammunition. Christ, I thought, how do I get out of this?

One of the men produced what was then a novelty: a Polaroid camera. He had bought it the day before in the base PX. We lined up outside the tent to have our picture taken. I was given the first copy.

I've kept it since, framed on the living room walls of the homes I have had in New York, London, Brussels, Paris, Rome and Washington, D.C. It is now in my home in Los Angeles. It shows seven paratroopers and me under a cloudy sky with some tents in the background. I have been told that most of these seven soldiers were eventually killed in Vietnam.

We went back inside the tent. After a while Sgt. Brown looked at his watch. "Saddle up," he ordered.

We were joined by some men from the next tent. We walked in single file past other tents, flaps rolled up, containing men stretched on cots, sleeping, reading, staring at us.

I found myself placed in the center of a line of 14 men. It was about 6:30 P.M. and still hotter than hell.

We walked past the dug-in military police at the camp's perimeter wire. "Hey, man," one of them said to me, "you look like a real paratrooper." I nodded. But I'm not, I told myself. I'm just a dumb son of a bitch. What am I doing here?

We continued, now with several yards distance between each man, into a wide, tree-flanked space toward a wall of thick jungle. Before the wall, a path led abruptly left for about 50 yards, then turned right into the jungle, becoming a narrow, dim trail.

We were now in the true Vietnam jungle. Giant, densely packed trees formed an interlocking canopy over our heads that blocked almost any view of the sky. The forest was enveloped in an even, sinister gloom. On either side of the trail, often wide enough to permit the passage of only one of us at a time, a tangled mass of green vegetation provided perfect cover for animal or man.

The air was still. Not a leaf moved. The humid heat was intense. I was drenched in perspiration, but that discomfort was nothing compared to the fear that tightened a vicious knot in my stomach the deeper we moved into this nightmarish world.

I've got to get out of here, I thought, I'm not going through with

174

this goddam patrol. I'll tell them I feel ill. I'll pretend to pass out. I'll fake a heart attack. Then they'll have to take me back. I'm not going to spend the night in this goddam forest.

We trudged steadily ahead.

"Listen," I whispered to my grenade-toting friend, striding before me. His grenades, instead of being cupped in his hands, dangled from his equipment. "Listen, how do we know there aren't a thousand gooks sitting a foot off this trail watching us, getting ready to zap us?"

He half turned to me. "We don't," he said without smiling. "We're the DEW line, pal, the distant early warning line. If we get zapped, that means there's enemy near the base. That puts the base on alert. That's why we're doin' this, pal."

One foot after the other. Was the trail mined? Booby trapped? Sometimes the Vietcong hid grenades at face level in the brush, controlled by trip wires. They blew heads off.

We marched for more than an hour. We reached a small clearing and another trail that crossed ours. Sgt. Brown halted the patrol. His eyes roved the fading light.

"Let's set up here," he said. "Watch the trees for snipers."

He sent two men a short distance up each of the four cross trails. I settled down, my back against a tree. I drank from my water canteen and opened a pack of C-rations. I lit a cigarette. Some of the men began to take off their packs.

A machine-gun burst stuttered, close—then another.

The men tensed, crouched over their weapons. I froze, my back riveted against the tree, the M16 suddenly in my hands. The two paratroopers who had been sent up the northern cross trail came into view. They had spotted a Vietcong scout, maybe the point man of an approaching enemy patrol. "He tried to run," one of them said. "But I got him."

Sgt. Brown nodded. He thought for a moment. He was faced with a tactical problem. He didn't look happy.

"Let's get out of here," he said. "Fast. Let's set up further back."

The other posted guards were recalled and we moved back along the trail on which we had come. Darkness was descending rapidly. The paratroopers drew bayonets and fixed them to their rifles. I moved ahead with the 14 GIs, now ghostly, nearly invisible shapes.

With the swiftness of the tropics, the darkness became total. Each man grasped the belt of the man before him. We formed a slim, human snake in the silent blackness.

We marched for about 500 yards, our eyes adjusting to the night.

175

Sgt. Brown led the patrol a few yards off the trail, to the left, through a line of trees and a thicket of bushes to a small, leaf-strewn clearing. He whispered to me that he had spotted the clearing on the way to the cross trails and had made a mental note of it in case a retreat had to be made. He peered around the clearing, into the jungle and up at the tall, surrounding trees.

"It ain't much," he said, "but it's home."

The patrol set up its ambush position for the night. Six pairs of men prone on their stomachs forming a circle, facing outward. Sgt. Brown, the other sergeant—whose name I have inexcusably forgotten—and myself squatting in the center of the circle around a radio. I looked at my watch: 8:12.

I would have been meeting my girl friend at the Caravelle Hotel bar about now.

In the darkness, the luminous hands and figures on my watch blazed like headlights. I turned the watch to the inside of my wrist. Each half hour we were scheduled to make radio contact with the Bien Hoa base. If the contact ceased, someone at the base was supposed to come looking for us. Or what was left of us.

"Charlie six to Parachute seven," Sgt. Brown muttered into the radio. *"Situation normal."*

I sipped from my canteen. The trees around us were tall, ghostly sentinels. This jungle—home of snakes, tigers, wild pigs, monkeys and birds—was also crawling with men, Americans and Vietnamese, trying to kill each other. The Vietcong, too, had its ambush patrols, each side playing a lethal game of hide-and-seek. I find you, bang, you're dead.

It was a great way to fight a war: no tanks rolling down highways, no planes, no battleships, no parades through liberated cities—just the jungle and the night.

I strain my eyes to pierce the darkness. But I can't see the surrounding GIs, just 15 feet away. I look up. Some of the leaves of the towering palms surrounding our position don't quite meet and in the gaps between them a few stars sparkle against a black sky. There's something malevolent in the way the branches part to admit a view of the sky. They seem to say, *Look at the beauty of the night, of the stars, you will never see them again. . . .*

Ten hours of darkness ahead. Seconds and minutes pass with agonizing slowness. A half hour has passed, I'm certain. I look at my watch. Ten minutes.

"Charlie six to Parachute seven. Situation normal."

I hear a sound, a rustle in the jungle. I clench my teeth.

"Ain't nothin'," the other sergeant whispers, sensing my fear. "That ain't no man. That's an animal, pig or somethin'. He movin' here an' there, this way an' that. He don't know where he's goin', just smells somethin' good to eat but can't figure out whether it's gonna eat him. So he moves, waits awhile, runs here, runs there. But a man, now you got somethin' different. You got somethin' knows what he's doin', where he's goin' an' why. He comin' to kill you, baby, an' he moves real steady, one shove at a time. He's a jungle fighter, you listen now. Easy to tell the difference."

It was a fast course in jungle warfare—learning on the job.

After a while, I hear the jungle: little snaps of twigs, rustles, the sigh of a breeze, something falling from a tree. What the hell time is it? Goddam, just 10:20. I'm bushed, but sleep is a joke. I've been scared before, but never like this. I try to measure time by the half hourly intervals between Sgt. Brown's whispered message into the radio.

I'm seated cross-legged, the M16 across my knees. I look at the thing. I make sure its safety is secured. I check the magazines at my feet.

"Charlie six to Parachute seven. Situation normal."

I hear something. The sound is faint, coming from far away.

Wait a minute. Voices singing? We look at each other. Yes, voices singing—singing, what's more, "Silent Night, Holy Night." In Vietnamese!

Must be a village with a church somewhere near . . . or maybe far. Sound carries a long way in the jungle at night. We stare at each other again. We hear bells, church bells, distant but clear. I look at my watch again.

It is midnight, Christmas Eve, 1965.

Sgt. Brown, the other sergeant and myself raise our water canteens. Merry Christmas, we whisper, Merry Christmas. "Here's to a long and happy life, pal," Sgt. Brown says.

But I have the feeling my life will be short and that it'll end unhappily—like any minute.

We'll never get out of here alive. The odds are too great. Fourteen GIs and a reporter deep inside Vietcong territory? Forget it. Merry Christmas and bye-bye. But so what? I find I'm at peace with myself and everybody else or almost everybody. It hasn't been too bad a life. There are worse things a guy can do than be a newspaperman. Right now, though, I can't think of one.

The singing and the bells cease. Silence envelops the jungle again. *"Charlie six to Parachute seven. Situation normal."*

Five, almost six, hours to go before dawn, before we can get up and begin the hike back. Maybe we'll make it yet.

I'm tired as hell, but I'm too scared to let myself drift into sleep. Yet I doze, head nodding, then jerking up in alarm. I doze again, but I'm awakened by a nearby sound. Someone is snoring. Sgt. Brown curses softly, crawls over to a pair of prostrate GIs and shoves one of them, hard.

"Shape up there, goddam it," he whispers savagely. "Shape up!"

The second hand crawls around my watch. The darkness is more impenetrable than ever.

But wait: a sound . . . then another. Something is moving . . . close—something that sounds as if a heavy weight is being dragged along the leafy jungle floor, with pauses at regular intervals.

Christ, here they come!

A GI throws out a flare grenade and a patch of jungle is brilliantly lit, as if by a powerful searchlight. We hear more rustles, confused scuffling sounds. All right, you sons of bitches, where are you? Come out and fight! Sgt. Brown is prone beside me, sighting along the barrel of his M16, finger coiled on trigger, man and weapon fused into a single, lethal machine. I find myself prone, too, gripping my M16, determined not to let down the men around me.

The flare sizzles and splutters, shedding hard, white light on tree trunks and foliage, creating ghostly shapes and dancing shadows.

Gradually, the flare subsides, then dies as if a switch has been flicked off. Once more, darkness is a shroud over our position.

Nobody moves. The silence is alive, electric.

We wait, tense to the breaking point.

But nothing happens: no charging, screaming enemy; no grenades bursting among us; no mortar shells whining in; and no streams of tracer fire.

Nothing—only the darkness and the night. I feel, rather than see, the men gradually relax. The wait resumes.

"Charlie six to Parachute seven. Situation normal."

It came slowly. There was no way to know when it began. But, as in a dream, I realized that I could now see, in grayness instead of blackness, the forms of the two GIs closest to me. The grayness increased, lightened. The trees, the foliage, the other men, the two sergeants, the radio, were now visible as dawn crept through the jungle.

It was Christmas Day.

Sgt. Brown, cradling his M16, looked up at the tree branches. "Bad time right now," he whispered. "We got to get on our feet. Anyone wants to know where we are, here's their chance. And they got a pretty good idea already, on account of that flare grenade."

A flight of birds, brilliantly plumed, came swooping and swerving low, flashing through the forest.

Now we have to get up.

The GIs rise warily, first on one knee, weapons ready, eyes scanning the jungle, the tree branches. One by one, the GIs stand up. It is a moment of mute fate. If the Vietcong are going to open up, they'll do it now. For a few seconds, nobody moves. This is it, life or death. But nothing happens.

Then there was nothing else to do but turn our backs and begin the march home.

I was placed second last in line. Every few minutes, I turned my head to see if the last man was still there, for his sake and mine. Each time I turned, he waved and I waved back. We marched in single file, a long space between each man, in case the trail had been mined during the night, in case mortar fire was directed on the trail, in case we were ambushed. . . .

With each step, my fear diminished. These guys were my friends, and I was heading home with them. This was my outfit, the 173rd Airborne Brigade. It always would be, for the rest of my life.

The sun rose, its heat filtering through the treetops, burning the night's chill from my fatigues. Tiredness vanished. I strode easily, as if I had slept ten hours.

We passed through the Bien Hoa base perimeter wire, returning the military police's Merry Christmas greetings. Yeah, Merry Christmas to you, pal.

Before leaving, I shook Sgt. Brown's hand. Take care, man. Yeah, see you around.

I thumbed a ride back to Saigon and was picked up by a jeep containing two Green Beret officers. Christmas Eve in the jungle, I grinned, gripped by the exhilaration that comes with a reprieve from death. They said nothing. They drove me to the Tu-Do, the bar-and-brothel street where United Press International had its Saigon news bureau. I sat down and wrote the story. An operator punched tape and put it on the wire.

I did not know it then, but it was snowing in New York and the wire editor did not make it to the office that day. When he came in, the day after Christmas, he saw the December 25 dateline on the story and decided it was yesterday's news. He threw it in a trash can.

• • •

Fourteen years passed.

I had left Vietnam long ago. I was based in Italy and winding up ten years as a foreign correspondent in Europe, the Middle East and Africa. After Vietnam had come more long nights. Northern Ireland, the Sinai Desert, Cyprus, Rhodesia. . . .

On Christmas Eve, 1979, the phone rang in my Rome apartment, with its view of the Spanish Steps, with its elegant, flower-decked terrace overlooking a fourteenth-century street.

The voice on the phone was terse.

"Is this the guy who spent Christmas Eve, 1965, with the 173rd Airborne Brigade?"

I was stunned. After all, 14 years!

"Well, yes, it is," I stammered. "Who's this?"

"This is Sgt. Brown!"

I froze.

"You're kidding! Where the hell are you?"

"New York. I'm out of the Army. I'm just calling to say hello. I kinda tracked you down. Any time you're in town, stop by."

My memory went back to that night, to that Christmas in the Vietnam jungle.

"I'll be there, sergeant," I said. "I'll be there."

CHAPTER
TWENTY-TWO

The Order from 'Override Eight'

by Maj. Ernest L. Webb

This is a true story and I am the major. I have written from the omniscient-narrator point of view because the incident is still an emotional thing for me and I cannot yet handle it in the first person. I feel that the related momentary lapse of sensibility on my part was my most serious mistake during two years in Vietnam.

I think the account should be told because, with only minor changes, it is the story of many men who fought in Vietnam. I also feel it needed telling because of the many detractors who currently depict the Army officer as an unfeeling, unthinking machine and egoist, concerned only with personal advancement and glory. I will not deny that there are officers who fit this description, but I object strongly to the implication that all, or even most can be so labeled.

In the main, the officers I have known are in the military be-

181

cause of a love for and a desire to serve our country. If anyone thinks that a leader can really love this country without caring for the men under his command he had best reconsider. We do not love a sterile landscape; we love the country because of the people.

The service we profess is not for the forests and the lakes; it is for the people who picnic under those trees and who fish in the lakes—and that must include all men who wear its uniform.

Unfortunately, there are many times when we fail to properly communicate this feeling and men return from the Army convinced that their leaders did not care about them. I believe that it is important for the mothers, fathers, wives and sweethearts who waited to know that the majority cared for the soldiers they led more than most could know. And we always will.—THE AUTHOR

T he new battalion commander had a reputation: mean as hell but fair and a real hard-charger. He hadn't wasted any time getting things going his way. He had talked to all the guys and told them they were good but could be a damned sight better— and he was going to give them a chance to prove it. His talk would have sounded phony from anyone else, but somehow he came across as a real guy; he was different from the field-graders the troops were used to. Maybe it was because of his boots; they looked like they had known a few rice paddies intimately and they had only enough polish on them to preserve the leather. Most of the field-graders wore highly shined boots, usually made that way by some hootch-maid. Boonie-rats didn't have hootch-maids.

During his first two days in the battalion, the major had gone to visit the companies in the field. Now, on the third day, he was en route to C Company when its commander called on the radio and reported a distant platoon in contact with a sniper. The major had his radiotelephone operator (RTO) tune the radio to the company frequency and told the chopper pilot to change course for the platoon location. As the helicopter tilted slightly for the course change and its blades groaned to keep airspeed, the major listened to the conversation on the company net.

"Tiger Three, this is Six. Anything more on the sniper?" The company commander's voice came through loud and clear.

"Six, this is Tiger Three. Negative," replied the platoon leader. "We have one KIA. No further sign of the sniper. I think I know his general area, though. Maybe we could put some artillery around the area. Over."

The major listened dumbfounded. "What the hell is going on?" he thought. "An infantry platoon of 30 healthy GIs can't find one sniper so they want to call for artillery, not really knowing where to put it. While they stand around flapping their jaws, the artillery digs holes in the rice paddies. Then he'll come back tomorrow and shoot somebody else."

"Six, this is Override Eight," the major cut in on the conversation. "Negative on the artillery. Get those GIs off their tails and find that sniper. Over."

"Wilco," came the commander's reply. "Tiger Three, this is Six. Negative artillery. Conduct search for sniper. Over."

"This is Tiger Three," came the lieutenant's voice. "Roger. I heard Override's transmission. Out."

A few minutes later the helicopter arrived over the platoon position and the major could see all its men still crouched behind the paddy dikes. It was taking the lieutenant a long time to get them moving. Time was critical, so the major violated military etiquette and bypassed the company commander, calling directly to the platoon leader.

"Tiger Three, this is Override Eight. I'm directly over your position and see no sign of your moving to get that sniper. Get moving! Over."

From the radio came a choked voice, one which did not belong to the lieutenant. Perhaps it was that of the radio operator. "But we can't leave Bobby here–alone."

Through the open door of the chopper the major could see that the men had retrieved the body of their dead comrade and had formed a perimeter around him, a number of them kneeling near the body. One soldier was holding the dead man's hand.

"Bobby," the major's voice crackled out into the still Vietnamese air, "is a goddam dead man and he's not going any place. Now get moving before that sniper has a chance to shoot someone else."

For a brief moment the platoon appeared frozen. Then they stirred, shocked into action by the major's words. But as they moved his words echoed through their minds—"Bobby is a goddam dead man!—Bobby is a goddam dead man!—Bobby is a goddam dead man!"—creating an effect not desired. The men were not aware of the major's feelings or reasons when he spoke those words; a radio transmits no feelings nor reasons, only words.

The major had momentarily forgotten that, just as he had momentarily forgotten that the life of a boonie-rat is a very limited and circumscribed sphere, and that his entire world extends no farther than the company perimeter or the night patrols. Letters from home are real, because he can hold them, but home itself is nothing more than a phantasy, a dream for which he yearns in quiet moments. His religion is also very limited but extremely personal, and his sense of religion is heightened to degrees that few men ever know. It is heightened because his God becomes manifest in those men with whom he daily shares the all-pervasive yet never-spoken understanding that death—his death—is but the flicker of a heartbeat away.

Those men are members of his squad and platoon. Each day he partakes of a holy communion with them as he breaks bread in what may well be his or their last supper. And there is no Judas at his table. Each day he walks through the garden with his God, for is not God present in every man? And in whom can this boonie-rat rest his faith and deliverance in the face of death, if not these brethren with whom he walks? And who will hold his hand when the life's blood ebbs? And who will offer the canteen with the soothing water for his parched lips when the knowledge of his own impending death brings the hot, dry breaths? And who will smooth his hair, and gently wash the mud from his face?

Unknowingly, the major had blasphemed against those boonie-rats and against their God, because a part of each of them and of their God lay wrapped in Bobby's fatigues. The platoon moved, but they hated this new major. They were convinced that he was just like the rest; he didn't understand.

The major's voice came over the radio. "Tiger Three, this is Override Eight. Give me some directions and I'll see if I can help spot him. Over."

The lieutenant contained his emotions; he wanted to tell the major to take his help and go to hell. Instead, he replied, "Roger. Approximately 400 meters to the northeast is a bamboo cluster. I think that's where the shots came from."

"OK, Three. I'll drop down and look."

The chopper dropped down to 20 or 30 feet and skimmed along the top of the bamboo while all its occupants strained to catch any signs of the sniper. The bamboo, however, paralleled a stream, and the major's hopes weakened. They all knew the sniper could have used the stream to get away without leaving any trail; they also knew that he could be buried along the stream bank. Either way it would be almost impossible to find him. The major touched the pilot's shoulder. "Set me down with the platoon. I'll call you when I'm ready."

The chopper hovered near the platoon, landed and allowed the major and his RTO to dismount, then rose to continue the search from above.

The major and the lieutenant decided that the sniper was probably gone, but they would continue to search. For another hour, the men all poked holes into the stream bank, looking for hiding places and breathing holes; they searched the bank and surrounding trails for any clues. All to no avail; the sniper had gone.

"That's the old story," thought the major. "The way it had been for a long time. Some sniper would fire one or two rounds and run like hell. Then, when he was safely away, he would watch the artillery tear up the rice paddies. It must be a great game, since no one ever shoots back at him."

The major and his RTO walked with the platoon back to Bobby's body and called for the chopper. Bobby was placed gently in the helicopter, after which the major and his RTO climbed aboard. The major nodded to the pilot and the chopper strained to rise, as the wind from the blades' wash swept over the platoon and the rice paddy they were standing in. The men turned their backs and covered their eyes to protect them from the swirling dust and tiny flying objects while the rice stalks wavered indifferently and then bent under the force of the wind. The chopper rose slightly, skimmed along for several hundred feet and then began to climb. At 2,000 feet the pilot leveled off and headed for home.

There was no conversation in the chopper, and the major listened to the whine of the engines, the *whup, whup, whup* of the blades, and the flowing, whistling sound of the wind moving past the helicopter. He noticed how the wind grabbed at the door-gunner's fatigues and whipped them into a constant rippling, like a flag flying in a brisk wind. His eyes passed to Bobby's body, lying just inside the chopper. One leg was bare to the knee, exposing the skin to the ruffling effects of the passing wind. Finally, he looked at Bobby's face, realizing that he had unconsciously avoided doing so until now.

Bobby was a good-looking kid of about 19. He had fallen in the mud when hit, the major could tell, because there was fresh mud on his fatigues. But something else troubled the major. Then, suddenly he realized: there was no mud on Bobby's face and his hair had been smoothed by some unseen hand. As he stared at the mudless face and the smoothed hair, the major's mind was engulfed by a wave of memories from when he, too, had been a boonie-rat. He found it increasingly difficult to breathe; there was a constricting pain in his chest and an uncontrollable lump rising in his throat. He tried to suppress them as he moved to sit beside Bobby on the floor of the helicopter. He smoothed the fatigues and covered the leg so that the wind could no longer tug and pull obscenely at the bare skin. Then, as he withdrew his hand, the tears could no longer be denied and they flowed down his cheek, dropping indiscriminately on both his and Bobby's fatigues. The major wiped the tears away with his hand, as his lips silently formed the inaudible words, "Oh, God! I'm sorry, Bobby."

On the ground the platoon watched the chopper grow smaller and smaller and finally disappear, carrying their friend Bobby and the major they hated because they knew he didn't understand.

CHAPTER TWENTY-THREE

Quang Tri Lady

by Michael P. Beringer

H er name was Landing Zone Sharon. Some 1st Air Cavalry Division colonel named her after his wife or girlfriend. Sharon never was reminiscent of any girl I had known.

The landing zone squatted on a chopped-off hill near Highway One, a few "clicks" south of Quang Tri City, in the Republic of Vietnam's I Corps Tactical Zone. In other words, Sharon lay about as far north as you could get in the South without risking being south in the North. She was one hot gal during both the midday sun and the midnight salvos.

Sharon looked like hobo heaven. Her perimeter sported layers of tangled barbed wire, trip-flare warning devices and booby-trapped antipersonnel mines.

Next came razor-tipped concertina wire the height of two men, plus 20-foot-tall watchtowers and ten-foot-deep combat bunkers. Positions for tanks and "dusters" (self-propelled twin 40-mm antiaircraft guns), ammunition stores and fire-fighting supplies rounded out Sharon's exterior.

Sharon's surface was dotted with a haphazard collection of jungle "hootches." These elevated plywood platforms supported two-by-four frames surrounded by sandbags halfway up, with screening above that to the rippled tin roofs. Those structures served any and every purpose we could invent.

The brick-colored landscape between the buildings contained a mixture of cases and cartons, tanks and trucks, jeeps and junk, and just about anything and everything that could be bought, borrowed, stolen or scrounged.

All the material that a twentieth-century American fighting man needed, or thought he needed, lay in a maze on the red-clay soil.

Sharon looked as though some giant had taken a big bite out of an industrialized ant hill, realized his mistake and then spat out his chewings because they tasted so bad.

Sharon tasted like a mouthful of mud. During the summer months, the slightest breeze sent fine, filtered red dust swirling into typewriters, telephones, rifles, radios and the spaces between your backmost molars.

In the fall, the rains came—and came. That summertime earth, which had served nicely as a medium-grit abrasive, now outslicked Teflon when man and machine moved across Sharon's surface.

Her red clay stuck to whatever it touched. You could scrape and scrub until your fingers ached and your mind grew numb, but boots and tires kept endlessly doubling in size and weight. The mud-cover seemed to grow faster than Vietnamese mildew.

The first odor each morning was burning diesel fuel and human waste. Sharon smelled worse than a trip through the local village on those days when *mamasans* were making *nuoc-mam*, that vile Vietnamese protein source distilled from rotting fish heads. On really heavy, humid days, the landing zone smells made it impossible to swallow anything but a malaria pill.

Sharon's perfume included the ghastly garbage dump, just beyond our wire, where peasants combed through our potable leftovers for a couple of calories.

Her scents included human remains, too: the enemy dead awaiting burial, the napalmed villagers and our own recently living soldiers in their body bags.

Sharon sounded like a rehearsal for the end of the world. The artillery batteries constantly fired harassment and interdiction rounds, combat missions and cover for air assaults. Sharon enjoyed equally the M16's bark and the AK-47's bite, as well as the 155-mm artillery outgoing and the RPG-7 rockets incoming.

There were good noises like the "thumpa, thumpa" of a Sky Crane cargo helicopter with its load of supplies and the "thwacka, thwacka" of a Cobra helicopter gunship with its load of destruction.

There were bad noises like the "pop (silence) carrump" of a mortar attack and the multisecond shriek of a 122-mm rocket racing to plant its deadly kiss on Sharon and her American lovers. Everyday sounds like tapping typewriters, squawking speakers and the KPs' punishment of pots and pans just got lost in the overall clash and clatter.

There was only one sound out of place—quiet. Sharon hated the quiet just before the first enemy sapper pierced the perimeter wire, mixing the sounds of the Fourth of July with a day at Gettysburg.

She also hated the quiet just after a chopper dropped a slingload of patrol casualties, men who that morning at breakfast had made their deep, dark death jokes. Sharon felt uneasy with quiet.

Sharon's corners and angles, never designed by natural forces, cut you physically and assaulted you emotionally. Her sights, smells, sounds, sensations and tastes reflected her bizarre moods, changing from second to second.

One minute she would carry away the drenching monsoon rains; the next, she funneled those same deluges into your sleeping bunker. One hour, she would slumber serenely in Oriental splendor; the next, she would explode into Asian agony.

One day, she would shield you from the man-searching shrapnel; the next, she would leave you naked on her smooth hillside. One week, she would reflect the sun's rays until your brain baked; the next, she would suck up solar signals until you shivered with cold.

One month, she would deposit dust into every working part of a soon-to-be-nonworking machine; the next, she would require blades of steel just to penetrate her surface.

One year, Sharon would do with you exactly as she pleased . . . because that was all she got.

CHAPTER
TWENTY-FOUR

Daryl's Last Christmas

by Maj. Mitchel L. Kotula

I was thankful the duty vehicle had a good heater as I rolled through the ghostly, now deserted streets of the 30,000-man Army training center. Had it been any period other than the Christmas holidays, I would have been a bit anxious about heading off-post to "The Corners." Notorious for drugs, brawls and the many prostitutes who worked there, it was the most depressed area of town. Only the very tough and the very poor lived there, but tonight, with most soldiers on Christmas leave, the district was quiet and nearly deserted.

It was Christmas Eve, 1972. I had returned from Vietnam less than a year before, so the pleasure of being back in the states had not yet faded. The war was never far out of sight or mind. The daily television news still carried graphic coverage of the war, as well as reports of high weekly casualties.

This night, just as I was preparing to leave for the holiday period,

191

the duty sergeant had handed me a just-received death notification requirement.

The deceased was from the small garrison town of Leesville, La., just outside the main gate of Ft. Polk. He had enlisted immediately after high school graduation and had reported for Vietnam combat duty in late October. While on patrol as an infantry private, he detonated a booby trap on 21 December and died. His death was not unusual or unique; each week many 18-year-olds died in Vietnam, some after many months in the country and others after only a few.

When a soldier dies while serving on active duty, the notification of next of kin is taken care of by the closest military headquarters. Our personnel office maintained a roster to determine who would be responsible for the notifications. With the Vietnam conflict going in full gear, there were many of these visits each week. Although it would have been correct for me to notify the personnel officer so that he could task a unit, and, in turn, that unit further task an individual to carry out this notification, I found myself telling the sergeant that I would take care of it, and I left.

The damp cold of the winter night slapped me as I stepped out of the headquarters building. It was after 1900. Notifications were required to be made immediately upon receipt, except between the hours of 2200 and 0600 the next day. If I waited, this notification would have to be made on Christmas Day, so I decided to do it myself before going home.

Following directions obtained from the few pedestrians I encountered in the area, I found myself slowly maneuvering down a rutted, unpaved dirt track of a road. I had never been here, nor had I ever before experienced a poor Southern black community.

Each house was no more than 12 feet wide with a small porch upon which there stood the metal chairs or other "sittin'" furniture common to porches throughout the South. There were no lawns or shrubs, no bicycles or toys about, just row upon row of these dark brown, tin-roofed houses, all built alike, yet each unique. Some were neatly maintained; others leaned on the verge of collapse. Most of the windows were lit up from within and the sight of Christmas trees or holiday lighting breaking through the dark monotony of this depressing community jolted me back to remembering the season and my mission.

Shutting off the sedan lights and engine, the cold reality of my situation stood sharply revealed in my mind. I, a white officer from the middle class, who had survived a combat tour as an infantry commander in Vietnam, would, on Christmas Eve, bring to a poor, black family in rural Louisiana the news that someone it loved dearly was dead. I was certain that the relatives would never forget me, the bearer of sad tidings. I sat contemplating my grim task for quite some time before I gathered my papers, triple-checked the address and approached what I hoped was the correct house.

The muffled conversation I could hear coming from within stopped abruptly when I knocked on the door. As I waited, I anticipated what the interior of the house would look like, as well as what I would say when the door was opened. My knock was answered by a middle-aged, neatly dressed black woman.

"Mrs. Williams?" I asked cautiously, secretly hoping that the Williams' had moved into another part of the country, which would spare me the burden of my mission. Her initial look reflected surprise in seeing a uniformed, white Army officer at her door on Christmas Eve, but, as her gaze shifted over my shoulder to the official sedan, panic flashed momentarily across her face. She knew.

Before I could say anything more she had my arm and, literally pulling me into the house, announced in a cheery voice, "Children, one of Daryl's Army friends has come to visit."

I was floored. My attempts to gain her attention were lost in a blur of movement stemming from the hospitality orders she directed toward the children:

"Take the captain's coat . . . here, sit down now . . . possibly the captain would like something to drink. . . ."

In spite of the flurry of activity precipitated by my unexpected arrival, I was able to take in my surroundings. The living room was not the bare, wood-floored, cheaply furnished room I had anticipated. It was clean, neat and carpeted. There were pictures on the walls, photographs and knickknacks. A scraggly pine tree on one side of the room was decorated, mostly with the kind of construction paper chains and crayoned cutouts produced by children in elementary classrooms. A string of multicolored, blinking lights, presents under the tree and pine cones stuffed with cotton to represent snow completed the holiday decor. A color photograph of a young soldier with "Old Glory" in the background sat on the television set.

As the motion in the room ceased, Mrs. Williams sat next to me on the sofa. The four children, two girls and two boys ranging in age from six to 15 years, sat in a semicircle on the floor between the sofa and the Christmas tree. All were staring with fascination at my uniform, with its decorations and shiny insignia. The children were quietly reminded by Mrs. Williams that "the captain is probably still

193

thirsty," at which the eldest daughter hurried into the kitchen. Opening a cupboard, she withdrew a pint bottle of bourbon, filled a cheese-spread-type glass to the rim and, with a quiet flourish, placed it on the low table in front of me.

Mrs. Williams, smiling in my direction, asked me for the proper pronunciation of my name, after which she announced to the children that Daryl had asked me to visit them when I returned to the United States. Her hand gently patting my knee, she asked me to "tell all of us how Daryl is doing." My questioning stare was answered with the silent communication of her eyes that pleaded, "Please bear with me."

I now realized that I had lost control of the situation. Leaning forward to take a sip of my drink, as well as to stall and reassess my predicament, I felt the unified stare of ten eyes, as well as the absolute anticipating silence of this audience, all poised and anxiously awaiting my first words.

I prefaced my remarks about Daryl by explaining that I had known him only briefly because I was leaving Vietnam as he was arriving. My description outlined how popular he was, the many friends he had, what a good soldier he was, the importance of his job and how his leaders held him in great esteem.

Mrs. Williams sat silently nodding her head, all the while maintaining a proud and knowing smile of her own while observing the smiles and flickering eye movements of her children as they eagerly absorbed my every word.

As my mind groped for further neutral praise of Daryl, Mrs. Williams seemed struck by an inspirational thought: "Since the captain has to leave this evening, why don't we open the presents that Daryl sent us?"

Daryl had apparently used the Pacific Exchange System catalogue to send presents to his family. He must have arranged for them to be sent shortly after his late-October arrival in Vietnam in order to insure that his family would receive them in time for Christmas. He could never have realized at the time how enormous this gesture of thoughtfulness would turn out to be.

Mrs. Williams continued in total command of the situation. We all held hands while she offered a prayer of thanksgiving in which blessings were sought for the country, the soldiers in Vietnam, the Army, and "the captain for taking his time to represent Daryl here at Christmas." I was asked to distribute the presents.

To the unabashed delight of the children, I numbly moved to the tree and distributed Daryl's gifts. Afterwards, we sang a Christmas hymn which I choked through rather than sang. Shortly after I said good night and wished a Merry Christmas to the children, who were now fully occupied with their presents, Mrs. Williams joined me outside on the porch.

We stood staring silently across the stark yet tranquil neighborhood, each of us deep in thoughts and feelings.

"Daryl is dead, isn't he, captain?" Her statement, more than a question, was soft and almost hopeful. It shattered the still silence of the moment, bringing us back from our thoughts as abruptly as a flash of light.

"Yes, Mrs. Williams," was all the verbiage I could muster as I handed her the message. I continued on, explaining the circumstances surrounding Daryl's death and the assistance that would be forthcoming. How easy it was to speak now that the waiting was over.

She embraced me in a mother's hug, saying into my chest, "Thank you. Thank you so very much, captain."

There was much more to say, but, instead, we briefly shared tear-streaked smiles, before I turned and walked to the sedan.

She stood on that cold, windy porch with her right hand raised in farewell, the message held gingerly in her left, as I pulled away. It had been less than an hour since I had knocked on the Williams' door, but I felt physically drained, as if I had been there far longer.

The experience remains smoldering deep within me, rekindled into bright memory each Christmas season. Since then, Christmas has taken on a meaning far beyond the exchange of gifts, as I have carried within me this touching personal experience. I find it difficult, yet deeply soul-satisfying, to reflect upon the warm gifts of strength and compassion which were shared that evening.

For as a soldier, the opportunity to serve my country is always there; but this experience granted me the additional opportunity to serve, in a very special way, a fellow countryman, as well.

PART SEVEN

THE PERSHING MYSTIQUE

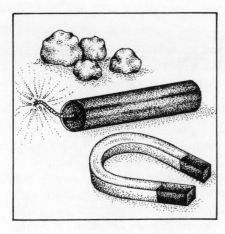

CHAPTER
TWENTY-FIVE

A Kibitzer's Guide
to Winning a War

by the Rev. Donald Smythe, S.J.

66 I am too old to fight but want to do something and thought of this plan," wrote a private citizen in Indianapolis, Ind., to Gen. John J. Pershing on 18 March, 1918, in sending in an elaborate scheme to defeat Germany. So wrote a number of others to the commander of the American Expeditionary Forces in France during World War I–all ordinary people, who had a plan, or an idea, or a new weapon, or a gadget or whatever, and sent it off to Gen. Pershing or someone else in authority. Their letters are on file at the National Archives in Washington, D.C., in a folder marked "Winning the War Suggestions." They make fascinating reading.

Most of the letters were to Gen. Pershing. "I am not making these suggestions with any reflection as to your good judgment and work," a Los Angeles citizen began, "but you know sometimes two heads are better than one." A man in Lynn Haven, Fla., prefaced his suggestion with the remark, "Reading of the many bad brakes [sic] the English, French, Russians and Italians have made in this war, we don't want you to make the same."

One suggestion was on the strategic side. Writing from Florence, Italy, a British citizen criticized "the present unintelligent deadlock-at-a-ditch method of mediocrity," and told Pershing to mobilize 12 million men (the United States mobilized four million, of whom half went overseas), and to think about attacking Germany from the Orient. "Consider whether it may not be safer to crush Prussia and blot out, or castrate, all Prussians, by *reaching Prussia overland from the East.*"

Another suggestion related more to the tactical. In the event of inevitable Allied defeat, inability to stop the German advance and the possibility of losing the English Channel ports, a New Yorker advised planting millions of tons of dynamite along a 65-mile front to a cross-country depth of two miles. He would arrange it so that an electric button pressed at Calais would detonate everything. Then he would hastily withdraw the Allied forces to a point near there, permit "the German hordes" to occupy the mined territory, and press the button.

"I would make of it such an enormous mine, such a gigantic plant, that the concussion would be felt over the entire world. I would plant so much explosive as to almost split the world in two, thereby destroying the entire German forces."

The writer admitted that this would be "an enormous undertaking and a horrible thing to contemplate," but he felt it was justified as a means to end the horrible war and that Germany deserved it as a sort of "capital punishment" for being "the great criminal" of the world. After detailing his plan to kill hundreds of thousands of human beings, he added, "I assure you I am a perfectly normal human being and one more merciful than I does not live."

A 64-year-old man wrote a letter to Gen. Pershing that was not a model of spelling and punctuation but did outline "a Yankey trick" that would make the Germans "take off their hats to you in the future." When the enemy makes a drive, "hold them back strong in the start, until you can get a force on both sides of the gap. where they will break through your line. . . . Then let the line that is holding them back. gradually give ground, not to fast in the start, but to make them think they are winning. Keep falling back slowly, till you get them where you want them in the open, then let the holding line, stand firm and go after them. Swing in the extra force on both sides of the gap in your line where they came in and *close it* regardless of cost *close it* and *hold it* then turn our Sammies [American soldiers] loos on the bunch that have come through. Close in on them from all sides, and get them dont weeken *get them.*"

A "take-no-prisoners" policy was suggested by an anonymous Californian who signed himself "A German American, over 70 and a veteran of more than one Wars, and this is why I am not 'Over There.'"

Other writers advocated retaliatory policies. One, signing himself "a crippled small French artilleryman," said that as long as the Germans shot at Paris with "Big Bertha" (a Krupp-made gun that hurled its projectile some 70 miles) Allied aviators should drop bombs on civilians in German cities. An Army captain in Pasadena advised quartering German prisoners in Allied hospitals to prevent their being bombed and doing the same on hospital ships to prevent their being torpedoed. A German "scorched earth" policy during their retreat in France and Belgium could be minimized by letting it be known that after the war German lands would be similarly devastated in reprisal, or enemy prisoners would be used without compensation to reconstruct the devastated areas. An Englishman from Southampton pointed out that the German practice of leaving behind booby traps when they retreated could be stopped by making prisoners of war touch everything first.

A number of proposals concerned offensive operations. A French *poilu* (infantryman) recommended a cloud of lime, or something similar, behind which troops might hide in making an attack. When a citizen in Uniontown, Pa., heard that Allied raiding parties had sometimes been betrayed by one of their members sneezing at an inopportune time, he informed the Secretary of War of a home remedy which "might come in handy sooner or later in No Man's land": press with the finger on the center of the upper lip just under the nose. "Thought of sending same to some publication which would give it more or less general circulation," concluded the letter, "but decided to send direct, as it is hardly the best policy immediately to acquaint the enemy with something of possible value."

One of the most more bizarre suggestions came from a doctor in Brooklyn who wrote Pershing:

"I can imagine millions of various size *stones* fired from large size guns would form a *lively stone* wall impossible for the closely formed ranks of the enemy to penetrate. . . .

If this unique way of using *stones* is feasable, then: Let *stones* be fired by the *tons.* on the heads and faces of the Huns. an answer to those savage asses. who introduced the poisonous gases. in modern warfare. to kill and scare."

The doctor added that he had already sent his suggestions to President Woodrow Wilson, Secretary of War Newton D. Baker and Secretary of the Navy Josephus Daniels, and also to General Ferdinand Foch of France, "hoping thereby to obtain attention of at least one in authority that some possible good may come from *stones*."

After quoting the Navy's reply ("Stones could be used, but with no accuracy, and guns would be ruined in a short time") the doctor rejoined:

"1st, As to accuracy: I cannot see why 100 to 1,000 stones the size of a robbins egg to a goose egg, fired at *one time* from one gun could not hit somebody or some things. 2nd, Cannot some of the old guns be used? They would ruin as well as be ruined."

Accompanying the doctor's hand-written letter was a typed sheet entitled "How to Win the War," which began with a poem:

> Shooting small *stones*, from large size guns,
> Will kill the Germans, and scatter the Huns.

Then followed a section on the history of stones, with another poem:

> Once young David slung a *stone*
> Hit the Giant on the head
> He fell dead without a groan
> All the Philistines then fled.

Next came an argument marked "T Y P I C A L": "*Goliath:* A type of the arrogant bombastic . . . Kaiser and Prussianism, dominated, and blinded by the god—Satan—of this world.

"*David:* A type of young American—and others—trusting in Jehovah, God of Heaven, and goes forth to fight in His Name."

To buttress his argument the doctor submitted several quotations from Scripture, ending with Jesus' "the *S T O N E* which the builders rejected is become the Head of the corner."

A Pittsburgh gentleman wrote Gen. Pershing that he had sent a proposal for a new weapon to the War Department which replied politely that his idea had been filed for consideration. "I am inclined to believe that it will not receive proper attention," he said, . . . and feel it my duty to bring it to your attention." His idea was a weapon constructed like a pistol, having five barrels, each slightly at an angle so that the bullets would spread. One trigger would fire all five. "It will be seen by this that if fired at a man fifty feet away, the man using the weapon would probably hit his man even though his aim were several feet from the mark, while the other bullets would stand a good chance of also finding a mark." It was the same principle as hunting rabbits with a shotgun instead of a rifle. "I devote considerable time to work on inventions," the man concluded, "and could probably work up an invention along this line, but I feel that the government has men far more competent than I. . . ."

Magnets was the key word in another proposal, this time by a French citizen. "If applied [they] would win the war in a short time and prevent conflict for a long time. It only means meeting the colossal with the colossal, by using powerful magnets to stop all projectiles (shells, bullets, bombs) and prevent them from doing harm."

Several letters advocated defensive measures. Let the enemy do the patrolling and raiding, said one, the Allies having previously prepared by placing bombs and mines just outside their barbed wire and connected with their trenches by a detonating device. "A fine wire or two placed just beyond the mines would come in contact with the crouching huns, and warn the boys in the trench, by ringing a small call bell, of their approach, and at this moment it will be possible to exterminate the attacking patrol. This may appear inhuman, but it is the proper salvation for our men."

Noting that most wounds were in the head and the upper part of the body, a Californian concluded that "the Allied forces have been fighting more with their feet than their heads," and sent this suggestion (with blueprints): a small metal dome about three feet across and extending only one foot above the ground. The soldier would dig a hole five feet straight down in which he could stand up, place the dome over his head and root it in the ground with side-projecting spikes, and fire out through portholes. A periscope in the center of the dome allowed visibility when the portholes were closed (for example, under artillery bombardment) and only a direct hit could destroy the dome. "If you will take a look at any drain under the common sidewalk, it will give you the idea of how hard it would be for men to capture a rapid fire gunner located there."

The same man who wrote about using magnets also recommended an antitank device: bombs or mines planted in the earth in front of Allied positions with only the percussion pin showing. An advancing tank would detonate the mine.

A much more complicated antitank device was a proposed system of solidly constructed dugouts or blockhouses all across the front. Between blockhouses would be a powerful bomb on a small two-wheeled caisson which could be moved back and forth by a cable connected with the blockhouses on either side. When an enemy tank approached, soldiers inside the blockhouses would pull the caisson across the tank's path and the collision would detonate the bomb.

A number of suggestions concerned water. Since nearly all heavy gases can be projected by a spray of steam or water, said a man in Oakland, Calif., why not have a small boiler on wheels that can be moved along the trenches, shooting steam or poison gas and forcing it to the ground? "Another use to which the boiler and hose would be susceptible would be to throw hot water upon an advancing enemy. While steam will not carry far, a stream of hot water will carry much farther. A number of such streams use[d] in close quarter engagements would cause much damage and confusion to the enemy."

An anonymous Frenchman suggested winning the war by flooding the Rhineland. He proposed a system of revolving paddles on a series of connecting ladders, so that when the bottom one was stuck into the Rhine River, water would be lifted to the top one and dumped into Germany.

A contractor-builder in Asheville, N.C., had the same idea, but nothing so simple. He had been studying a geological map of the Rhine Valley for six months, he said. If the American forces would drive the Germans back out of the mountains which fed the main water streams to the Rhine, engineers could build large splash dams, say 200 to 300 feet high, in the main feeders out of the mountains, "and then let them fill up in six months and then blow them up in wet weather so they will intersect at the entrance of the mouth's of the rivers all at the same time which would allow the United States Army to splash dam the Rhine River Valley and all large cities with water from seventy-five to one hundred feet deep."

Another suggestion involving water was an unsinkable boat, made by affixing steel boxes of one cubic meter to the hull at the water line; a torpedo would strike the boxes but not the hull.

From San Francisco came advice to concentrate on air power: conduct intensive, systematic and incessant bombing attacks on the enemy's communications until his armies were completely cut off from their supply bases. The writer assured Gen. Pershing that the chairman of the board of directors of one of America's largest railroad systems had informed him that such an intensive attack on communications would paralyze the transport system. "When it is realized that one bridge broken down will tie up an entire system, and also that embankments when broken down are peculiarly difficult to repair, it readily can be imagined what a stoppage of transportation would be brought about if this attack were made intensively on all communications simultaneously rather than small sectors as is done at present."

Another proposal about air power was to drop a few hundred thousand cans of gasoline on enemy trenches to force the Germans out. If an ingredient were added to the gasoline to cause "a disagreeable gas" or to "put them blind," so much the better. The gasoline would be ignited by attaching a long wick to each can and lighting it just before dropping. On hitting the ground a friction lid on the can would fly open and spread the gasoline, while the burning wick would ignite it.

A similar idea was proposed by a man in Auburn, N.Y., in an ungrammatical, bloodthirsty letter to the French ministry of war in May, 1918. "I am disgusted with the pinheads at Washington," he began. "They are alowing Millions of gallons of oil to be used here for autos for pleashure When it should be used to stop the hun. . . . I have hestated in giving this to the press for fear the Kiser Would adopt it." He advocated "oil mixed with liquid brimstone or poisonous gass of any kind," lit and dropped on cantonments munition plants and enemy attack formations. "Thousands not dozens of these shells Would Singe the wings of an intire army the more oil used the better the efert to demorlize the advancing hordes." The Allies had shown too much mercy. "The time has come when you must take off those Kid gloves and go at them. . . . I would burn them shoot them and distroy them as long as they showed any fighting spirit left I would spread burning oil . . . untill they yilded or germany Was an ash heap. . . . I Would use H—l fire and brimstone untill I Wiped them off the face of the earth if you Would rather spair the germans and slaughter our [boys] then throw this in the waste baskett or file it for future reference that is what the wise asses generaly do but if you want to whip the hun quick Singe his whings. distroy him as you Would rabid dog or he will distroy you and yours get all together and burn every thing that Will burn then blow up the rest."

As far as defense against air attacks is concerned, a doughboy in Paris thought he had the answer. Construct nets of manila rope wrapped with barbed wire, or plain wire charged with electricity, or all barbed wire, and suspend these nets in series, from balloons which would be stationed in the lane of the enemy war machines."

Psychological warfare received attention in a letter from Porter, Ind., suggesting self-destructible balloons which would float over Germany and Austria, dropping German-language newspapers printed by the Allies but bearing the heading of some German city. A time fuze on a trap door would drop the newspapers so many minutes after launch.

A variation of this plan came from a Boston lawyer: use photos. "Photograph a German prisoner just captured—thin, hungry, discouraged-looking. Photograph the same man after four weeks in a prison camp—healthy, happy, contented. Several subjects might be posed and only the best result used. Have countless copies made of the contrasting photographs with brief description on the 'before and after' order. The contrast is the whole argument. Distribute freely over German trenches. Such seed should not take long to work. Go over and reap a 'harvest' of prisoners."

Several writers devoted attention to American morale. Many American soldiers resented the nickname "Sammies" given them by some reporters; why not, then, since they were fighting for the world's liberty, "call our boys the LIBERTY boys"? Or, suggested another, why not AMSAMS (from AM SAMS), USAMS (from US AMS), or AMUSA (from AM USA)?

The most fantastic letter among the "Winning the War Suggestions" was from a Frenchman in Bagnac; he obviously had flipped. "There exists in the noble Country of France a bird which has marvelous unlimited powers," he said. "But because of the capricious eccentricities of the ignoble oppressor satellites, it remains hidden and never shows itself.

"It would have the magnetic power to stop the war. It would have the power also to spread joy throughout the world.

"More than that, it has the prodigious forces of moving mountains and the mysterious power of Satan, all existing chimeras and illicit felonies. It also has the royal authority to command the fleets of the rivers and the seas.

"At the opportune time, as a doctor it would have avoided the war fever which has resulted in such a cruel catastrophe, by combatting against the morbid microbes which have been propagated since the beginning of the war. But on the apparition of the theological doctor, those who thought themselves erudite and powerful, jealous of its supreme powers, by uniting the ignorant mundane society, proclaimed him a fool and a booby.

"Everyone wanted to know more than he did and wishing to follow their own conceived inspirations of minimum utopian imaginations, so that the fruit of their extravagant talents was to cause the onerous destruction of the peevish French people.

"And if the Czar has so passed, there are others who will pass. His destiny has been announced by the one who is called a boob. Fool and booby he is called, and the hardheaded and proud society will succumb.

"Long live the day!
"Down with the night!
"Long live love!
"Down with bats!
"Long live the day!
"Down with the night!
"Down with the bears!
"Is all I say!
"Long live America!
"Long live love!
"Down with the clique!
"And all its vultures!
— "From the perpetual global clock,
"IDEAL RUBINOFF"

Today the letters in the "Winning the War Suggestions" folder lie forgotten in the National Archives. One wonders if anything ever came of them at the time they were written or whether they were forgotten then too? Certain hairbrained suggestions like shooting stones and relying on the French booby-bird obviously deserve consignment to oblivion. Yet someone took the time to read the letters and even to translate them (as with the booby-bird); they were all given file numbers and recorded. Some, we know, were acknowledged, like the "shoot stones" letter. Gen. Tasker H. Bliss, U.S. military representative at the Supreme War Council in Versailles, forwarded to Pershing the letter about the two-wheeled boiler for squirting steam and hot water, noting on his endorsement, "Requesting such action as the case may merit."

Not all the ideas were scatterbrained. Some were considerably ahead of their time. A number of the suggestions in the letters actually were developed and used a generation later, in World War II, the Korean War and in Vietnam. They may not have appeared in exactly the same form, perhaps, but the basic idea was there back in 1918, in embryo, thought up by ordinary citizens, by patriotic people like the gentleman in Indianapolis who was "too old to fight but want to do something and thought of this plan."

If the reader will quickly review this article he will see in the list of suggestions the germ of a number of things the world later became familiar with. In the order in which they appear they are: attacking through "the soft underbelly" of the enemy, "take-no-prisoners," retaliatory bombing of civilians, slave labor, using prisoners to detect booby traps, smoke screens, rapid-fire miniguns, antimissile decoys, antipersonnel mines, antitank mines, flame throwers, antitorpedo nets, "victory through air power," strategic bombing, napalm, barrage balloons and psychological warfare.

Not all the "Winning the War Suggestions" were as useless as they seemed.

CHAPTER
TWENTY-SIX

Stature as a Weapon

by Samuel R. Davenport

O ne day in mid-October, 1942, I found myself facing General of the Armies John J. Pershing in the sitting room of his quarters in Washington's Walter Reed Army Hospital. Edward W. Barrett, director of overseas operations of the Office of War Information (OWI), had arranged our meeting.

Ed, like myself, had gone over to OWI after Gen. William J. (Wild Bill) Donovan's psychological warfare operation had been divided between OWI and the Office of Strategic Services (OSS). We were our country's dispensers of information to friend and foe alike. We sought to create doubt and fear in the minds of our Axis enemies and to keep hope alive for those in enemy-occupied areas.

Gen. Pershing seemed the one man whose words could truly make an impression on the Nazis. He and those he had led in World War I had tipped the balance in favor of victory in 1918. Totalitarians and freedom-fighters alike remembered him.

President Franklin D. Roosevelt, the Joint Chiefs of Staff and the Allied High Command conceived what we in the OWI should do, as well as when and how we should do it. These directives were passed down from OWI director Elmer Davis.

My job was to write 200-word "implementers" based on the directives. It was also my job to get the permission of internationally known Americans in our military-government-industrial complex to use implementers in their names. These short statements would be distributed as leaflets over Axis and Axis-occupied areas by the Army Air Corps and read over shortwave radio. Our intelligence sources told us that the implementers had had a strong impact on both our friends and enemies.

My mission at that time was to get Gen. Pershing's approval of the implementer I had with me, and arrange to present him with others when the occasion warranted it.

When I met Gen. Pershing that October day, he was in civilian clothes. He wasn't at all as I had pictured him: no uniform, no Sam Browne belt.

He sat stiffly erect, a sheet of paper ready on the table beside him. I read its imprint—"OWI." My dossier had been sent to the general by Ed Barrett in advance of my arrival.

The general remarked that I had been born in Nebraska, adding, "I spent happy years as a professor at Nebraska University. I see that you were also a college professor." Then, "You have worked for Gen. Donovan. He commends you. So does Gen. H. H. Arnold for what you have written about his airmen. What do you want me to do?"

I told him, and his interest in members of Congress who had served in this same capacity was sparked. It was only necessary for me to mention three. Of Karl Stefan of Nebraska, he commented, "He was the telegrapher who taught the Moros the Morse code in '05." Of Pat Kearney of New York, he said: "He was with me in France."; and of Tom Martin of Iowa, he commented, "Another professor of military strategy. I know his work on von Clausewitz."

I then handed the general the implementer I had brought with me concerning a full-force Allied landing in North Africa. He read it and reread it. "Do you know the date when this will happen?" he asked sharply.

"No," I replied, "but it will be issued when it does happen *if* you agree to it."

A moment passed, a long one for me. He had made up his mind. "I will sign it. Your pen, sir."

Arrangements were made so that when more of his implementers were needed he could be contacted through Ed Barrett. Our first meeting ended.

Gen. Pershing stood, no salute, no handshake—just an inclination of the head. I repeated that action and was dismissed. There have been a few days in my life when everything has gone right. This was one of them.

On 8 November, 1942, American and Allied forces landed on the coast of Morocco and Algeria. The Pershing statement, with those of President Roosevelt and Prime Minister Winston Churchill, was broadcast in Europe and Africa. The statements were carried behind Axis lines to the enemy and freedom-fighters alike.

OWI Director Elmer Davis called on Gen. Pershing to express the collective gratitude all of us felt for his cooperation. My presence was unnecessary. In fact, it was the middle of April, 1943, before I saw the general again. Ed Barrett had followed the procedure agreed upon immediately upon learning that Nazi Field Marshal Erwin Rommel had been either recalled by Adolf Hitler or had gone to Germany for reasons of health after the second Battle of El Alamein. His North Africa replacement was Gen. Jürgen von Arnim.

The Allies sensed a possible total victory in North Africa. Should this occur, another Pershing statement would be needed. The general's aide, however, advised Ed Barrett that the general would be unable to receive me, but in less than a week, I was asked to go once again to Walter Reed. There, the general approved and signed the North African victory statement.

On 12 May, 1943, Gen. von Arnim surrendered to the Allies, together with the 240,000 German and Italian troops under his command. Gen. Pershing's implementer shared the rejoicing of Allied leaders with President Roosevelt, Prime Minister Churchill and Gen. Charles De Gaulle. The positive effect of his contribution was especially noticeable among the French Resistance fighters.

I called again on Gen. Pershing in late May and spoke for my OWI colleagues in letting him know how much his words meant to us, to all Americans, our Allies and our friends in occupied lands. There were no other visits to the general's quarters until early 1944.

The Italian Campaign required a different psychological warfare approach. OWI was working to wean the Italian people from their Fascist leaders and to contribute to the already mounting friction between the Nazi and Fascist military. Resistance groups, especially the French *Maquis*, were restive. The Allies had supplied them with war munitions and communications, but that wasn't enough for those who risked their lives daily.

OWI had to reassure them, give them hope. Again, the Allied High

Command decided that a Pershing message was in order. The date chosen for it was the third Sunday in May, 1944, the French national day for honoring Joan of Arc.

I met with Gen. Pershing in March, 1944. Again, my mission was successful and I left with his signed statement. Two months later I was called into Ed Barrett's office. "I'm sending you up to the general this morning," he said.

I protested, "His Joan of Arc implementer isn't due for release for over a week."

Ed handed me another directive from above. I read it. "No date given," I noted.

"No date needed," he stressed. "There'll be a landing on the French coast. Americans will be a part of it. And that'll be soon."

He impressed upon me that the enemy would know that such an attack was imminent should anything connected with this directive fall into the wrong hands. I was to write the statement in Ed's office, immediately. I did so and edited it. A copy was made and the original destroyed. A meeting with the general had been arranged; I left for it directly.

When I knocked at the outer door, the general himself admitted me. That was the first break in our established pattern. He didn't explain his aide's unusual absence and I didn't mention it. I told him of the statement's security status. After reading it carefully he looked up. "Would it be possible for me to keep this overnight?" he asked.

This was the second departure from our normal procedure. "I'd have to consult Mr. Barrett on that," I replied.

He indicated the telephone and answered, "Call him."

I did and luckily Ed was in. "This isn't the way I wanted it, but do as he says," was the gist of Ed's reply. "When his aide gets through to me tomorrow, you go up after it."

I relayed Ed's message to the general and that was how I left the situation. The next morning, however, there was no word from Ed. I had a nervous lunch. When I returned to my desk I opened the letter in my "in" box. It was the general's D-Day implementer complete with his signature. It had come through the open mail. My guess was that after I had left he had approved and signed it. Without waiting for his aide, he had posted it before noon. I rushed the statement to Ed and he locked it in his safe.

I was given the second week in June off. I heard Gen. Pershing's D-Day message over domestic radio. Shortly after my return from R&R I was again at the general's quarters. I thanked him for his D-Day implementer and presented him with still another one—on the lib-

---

Pershing's D-Day Message

American troops have landed in Western Europe. The day of invasion has arrived.

As the overmastering military might of the Allies advances it will be joined by the men of the occupied countries, whose land has been overrun by the enemy but whose spirit remains unconquered.

Twenty-six years ago American soldiers, in cooperation with their Allies, were locked in mortal combat with the German enemy. Their march of victory was never halted until the enemy laid down his arms in defeat. The American soldier of 1917–1918, fighting in a war of liberation, wrote by his deeds one of the most glorious pages of military history.

Today, the sons of American soldiers of 1917–1918 are engaged in a like war of liberation. It is their task to bring freedom to peoples who have been enslaved. I have every confidence that they, together with their gallant brothers-in-arms, will win through to victory.

—JOHN J. PERSHING

---

eration of Paris. It was due to come in weeks, perhaps days. We had to have it on hand.

I watched the general sign it and delivered it to Ed. Everything had gone according to Hoyle. It was released on 25 August, 1944, upon the German surrender to French Gen. Jean Leclerc. Years later, President Dwight D. Eisenhower presented the original statement to the then President of France, Gen. De Gaulle. This was Gen. Pershing's final psychological warfare statement.

Just after New Year's Day, 1945, Ed called to say that Gen. Pershing wanted to see me. It had nothing to do with implementers—"a personal matter," he said.

Once more I sat opposite the general. "On the 26th of this month," he said, "Gen. Douglas MacArthur will be 65. We haven't always seen eye to eye. That hasn't stopped him from being a fine soldier. Will you see to it that a birthday message gets to him from me? I wish the boy health, happiness and victory."

I wrote that birthday greeting in Gen. Pershing's quarters and Gen. MacArthur received it on his birthday.

213

The Office of War Information went out of business a month and a day after V–J Day, on 15 September, 1945. Until 11 June, 1947, I was a congressional liaison officer for William Benton of the Department of State. Then, since "I couldn't lick 'em, I joined 'em," and became senior information officer for the House of Representatives.

Early in December of that year, I heard a commotion in my outer office. My name was mentioned and I investigated. A smartly uniformed Ft. Myer, Va., drill squad seemed to fill all available space.

"I'm Mr. Davenport. What can I do for you?" I asked.

"From Gen. Pershing. He wants you to have this."

A large wrapped package was given me. Before I had time to thank them, they had done an about-face and left the office.

The Pershing gift was his World War I picture—the one with the Sam Browne belt. Across that belt was his familiar signature, *John J. Pershing.*

I phoned his quarters at Walter Reed. The aide who answered was the same one who had dealt with me as an OWI writer. No, the general could not speak to me. He was confined to his bed. The aide explained that the general had asked yesterday, "What have we done for Davenport?"

This after not mentioning me for over a year. Naturally the aide's reply had been, "Nothing."

"Find him!" the general commanded. "See to it that he gets my picture!"

That had been done. I told the aide to convey my gratitude and wrote the general to that effect. He had paid what he considered his debt to me. I could never repay my debt to him.

General of the Armies John J. Pershing died on 15 July, 1948. His body lay in state in the Capitol Rotunda. I did not join the throngs who filed by his casket to pay their respects although the Capitol was just across the street from my office.

To me, the general had not died. To me, he is still very much alive.

PART EIGHT

IN OTHER TIMES

CHAPTER
TWENTY-SEVEN

Valley Forge: Where an Army Came of Age

by Col. John B. B. Trussell, Jr., USA (Ret.)

J ust two hundred years ago, during its winter encampment at Valley Forge, the American Army underwent an experience which was one of the most profound of the Revolutionary War, and perhaps one of the most significant in its history. The very name of Valley Forge has become a symbol of military endurance and dedication. It conjures up a vision of ragged, barefoot, starving Continentals, riddled with disease, shivering in a bleak expanse of gleaming snow to survive—some of them—what is popularly regarded as the severest ordeal of the war.

Without any argument, those soldiers set an inspiring example of devotion in the face of great suffering. But in terms of rags and hunger, Valley Forge differed little from any of the other winter encampments of the army under George Washington's immediate command. As for weather, the winter of 1777–1778 was probably the least severe of any which that particular force experienced. Not only was it marked by more rain than snow, but the climate of eastern Pennsylvania is hardly as rigorous as that of Boston, or the hills of northern New Jersey or the Hudson Highlands, where Gen. Washington concentrated his troops during the other winters of the war. Even the sick rate, which one month reached a peak of 36 percent, was about the same as the previous winter's, although—for reasons that will be suggested later—it never again reached such heights.

Yet Valley Forge fully deserves its special status: not because the ordeal there was exceptionally great compared to the other winter encampments, but because Valley Forge saw come into actual being an American Army that was for the first time worthy of the name.

For nine days, the troops had camped at Gulph Mills, on the south bank of the Schuylkill about 12 miles above Philadelphia, while various locations for a campsite for the winter were considered. The choice fell on Valley Forge, six miles farther upriver, for a combination of valid reasons. It offered good defensive terrain: the western boundary of the encampment was a high ridge running north and south, with a creek to the west and high ground beyond. The creek ran through a gorge and the ground running from the lower ridge was rolling farmland.

The camp was close enough to British-occupied Philadelphia to discourage the enemy from ranging far from his base, but it was far enough away to be secure against surprise. And it lay in a rich farming area which should provide a source of provisions.

The day fixed for the move was 19 December, 1776. Much of that morning was taken up by loading wagons with the sick and starting them toward hospitals further in the interior. The rest of the troops, totaling somewhere between 11,000 and 18,000, began to move out at 10 o'clock. Although there was a fine, needle-like snow with wind behind it and the ruts of the road were frozen, at least 2,000 of the men without shoes, and all of them miserably hungry, they hit a good, steady pace. But, with the troops knowing no formation but Indian file, the column stretched out so far that its head reached the new campsite before the tail left Gulph Mills, and dusk was falling (it would have been about 4 P.M. or a little after) when the final elements closed on their destination.

Each brigade had been assigned a defensive sector, but no guides had been provided to direct the units to their respective areas. There were no rations to issue, and no one even knew where to get water.

218

The tents that had been brought along offered little protection against the cold, so many of the men sat up all night, huddling together around their fires.

While these troops were veterans of several months of campaigning, marked by a good deal of hard marching and (at Brandywine and Germantown) two major engagements, they were for all practical purposes untrained. Most of them had less than eight months' service. The fact was that over half of the members of the original 12-month regiments, whose tours had ended the previous January, had not reenlisted in the new three-year regiments formed to replace the short-term units.

Manned chiefly by new recruits, the new regiments had reached the field only in the spring, and the operations of the summer and fall had left no time for training. Even more serious than the ignorance of tactics and field-craft was the absence, on the part of officers and NCOs as well as privates, of a disciplined attitude: there was nothing that could be called a reliably functioning chain of command, little acceptance of the requirement for subordination to authority, and no sense of personal responsibility toward the organization as a whole.

Organizationally, too, the force was a hodge-podge. There was no single organizational structure for a regiment, even in theory. And whatever its particular theoretical makeup, no regiment came even close to its prescribed manning level. Even in *assigned* strength (not to mention the lesser totals actually present for duty), regiments varied from as few as 86 officers and men to as many as 600.

The basic infantry weapon was the musket, accurate for little more than 50 yards and requiring some 19 motions for reloading. The only way to obtain effective firepower was through volleys by similar weapons (to minimize dispersion), discharged on command; but within any company could be found muskets, rifles, carbines and fowling pieces, most of them poorly cared for. The limited-range capability and the long reloading time put a premium on the bayonet for close work when contact was actually made, yet only about half of the men had bayonets, and few knew how to use them. Indian file was a poor way to move large bodies of men, and it was almost hopeless on the battlefield: a file of troops could be faced to the right or left to bring fire to either flank, but not to the front or rear, and confusion approximating chaos was almost inevitable when commanders tried to maneuver bodies of troops rapidly in action.

Given the situation, it is obvious why Gen. Washington was eager to use the winter, which could be expected to be quiescent operationally, to carry out sweeping reorganization and training programs. But the army's first priority was to survive, which posed immediate requirements for food and shelter. In both respects, the situation was so desperate that Gen. Washington told Congress that "unless some great and capital change takes place ... this Army must inevitably ... starve, dissolve or disperse."

With regard to food, the commissary's entire reserve consisted of 25 barrels of flour—no meat, no vegetables and almost no rum. Permanent forage details were promptly fanned out into the countryside for a radius of some 15 miles to find what provisions they could and forward them into camp. If nothing else, the men on these details could live off the country, thereby reducing the number to be fed at Valley Forge. For the same reason, most of the cavalry was relocated, moving to Trenton.

The local farmers were friendly and except for horses, which they hid, assisted the details with their official requisitions where and when they could. Gen. Washington had issued strict orders against looting and even placed a guard around the encampment to prevent the men from roaming at will; this inhibited but could not completely prohibit looting as supplies became scarcer.

Within a matter of days, some supplies began trickling in, but it would be March before the specter of imminent starvation would disappear. The problem was not a shortage of food in the area but the stupendous difficulties of transporting it. The civilian wagoners, upon whom the army had to rely, were reluctant to risk their wagons on the abominable roads; they demanded substantially more money than Congress was willing to pay; and those who did accept contracts were slowed by frequent breakdowns. Somehow, although there were times when men had to go for well over a week with nothing to eat but "firecake" (a concoction of flour and water baked on a griddle), the army survived.

The men did what they could for themselves. Although they never brought themselves to eat their horses, they denuded the area of squirrels, rabbits and other small game. Gen. Washington arranged for a farmers' market, operating six days a week, where men with money or trade goods could buy or barter for provisions. To encourage local farmers to sell to the Americans rather than to the British, who paid in gold instead of inflated Continental paper, civilians caught trading with the enemy were tried by military courts authorized by Congress. Some were flogged, some were imprisoned, and some were fined.

As for shelter, Gen. Washington ordered that each twelve-man squad was to build a log hut, the huts to be neatly aligned in company streets, with the housing area of each brigade to be immediately behind its assigned sector. The orders were explicit, prescribing that the huts would be 14 feet wide, 16 feet long, and 6½ feet high, with a door in the front and a fireplace in the rear.

The troops set to work to build their shelters as rapidly as the limited tools permitted, denuding the wooded hillsides in the process. In no respect, however, is the nonconformist individualism of the men at that stage more conspicuous than in the huts they actually erected. Archaeological excavations have found that there was little alignment and practically no uniformity. Almost no hut was as large as Gen. Washington had specified, and one has been found that was only eight by ten feet. Many were essentially roofed dugouts; their lowered profiles reduced the area exposed to the wind, but only at the price of damp, chill interiors. Some had the fireplaces on one side or in a corner. Doors were placed in whichever wall suited the builders' fancy.

Considering the difficulties, the shelters rose rapidly. By 29 December some 900 were under construction, but it was 8 February before Gen. Washington could report that "most of the men are now in tolerably good Hutts."

Gen. Washington established his own headquarters in a farmhouse belonging to one of the Potts family, Quakers who were yet friendly to the Revolutionary cause.

Clothing shortages were another major problem. In January, almost 4,000 of the privates and corporals—about 23 percent—were so nearly naked that they had to be classed as unfit for duty. Gen. Washington appealed to the states for clothes, and set up a system for obtaining shoes by bartering rawhide from the cattle slaughtered for food. But one pair of shoes cost 30 pounds of rawhide; with over 2,000 men barefoot, improvement was necessarily slow.

Indeed, through February all that could be done was to try to keep alive, and for many the struggle was too great. Malnutrition and exposure took a considerable toll. Filth compounded the problem. To some extent this was unavoidable, because no one had anything to wear while dirty clothing was being washed, and the cold was too great for men to give up even the limited comfort provided by their rags. Another major factor, though, was the lack of discipline: despite orders to keep their quarters clean, men threw the inedible parts of their rations into the corners of their huts; directives for each brigade Officer of the Day to inspect the huts in his area for cleanliness twice daily were largely ignored; and Washington's running battle to compel the men to use the latrines he had ordered dug ended in a clear defeat.

Consequently, in addition to respiratory ailments the troops fell victim to scabies, dysentery, typhoid and typhus. Lack of medicines and the primitive state of medical knowledge made the situation worse, with the result that before the encampment ended an estimated 3,000 men had died of disease.

March, however, saw the beginning of major improvements. There was a snowfall as late as 10 March, but in general the weather was moderating. Supplies of food and clothing increased. Most important of all, however, was the arrival of a Prussian volunteer called Friedrich von Steuben, represented (falsely) and accepted as a baron and a former lieutenant general in the army of Frederick the Great. Whatever he was *not*, he was a superb drillmaster; he understood soldier psychology and he had a pragmatic and adaptable mind. It was a combination which would prove invaluable.

It would be wrong to believe that Gen. von Steuben was solely responsible for the virtual transfiguration which followed. He did work out the details, and he saw that they were carried out. A good deal of the groundwork, however, had already been laid. Weeks before, Gen. Washington had proposed a standardized structure for his regiments. Because it would require extensive consolidation of existing, understrength regiments—which meant that numbers of officers from second lieutenants to colonels would be "riffed" (the term used then was "deranged")—he was running into congressional opposition, although his struggle would eventually be successful.

He had taken extensive steps to procure additional small arms and repair the large number of defective ones on hand. Directives to initiate individual training had long been issued, although they had not been carried out. Part of the problem had been the soldiers' preoccupation with survival. Another factor had been a high-level clash of personalities which had a direct effect on what could be done.

For the record, in Maj. Gen. Thomas Conway the army already had a director of training, or in the term of that day, inspector general. Irish-born, Gen. Conway had 28 years' service in the French Army, in which he had risen to colonel, before coming to join the American struggle. He was a competent officer, but he was arrogant and super-cilious. He had been known to approach American brigadiers and ask disdainfully, "Did Congress *see* you before they commissioned you?"

Not surprisingly, the American officers were so antagonized that Gen. Conway's suggestions for reform, many of them sound, had been rejected arbitrarily. Disgusted, he left Valley Forge only days after arriving and went to Congress, at York, Pa., where he became the prime mover in an unsuccessful scheme to obtain Horatio Gates's ap-pointment as commander in chief in place of Washington.

Since Gen. Conway was still nominally the inspector general, Gen. von Steuben could be given only acting status, but he undertook his duties with Prussian thoroughness. After analyzing what he saw as the requirements, he drafted a comprehensive program, which Gen. Washington approved. He then began writing a basic manual, com-bining the features of drill regulations, School of the Soldier, and of-ficer's guide. He spoke no English, so he wrote in French, which his aide translated. Gen. von Steuben would write a section of the man-ual at night, spend the next day teaching it, then that evening write the section for the next day's training. For a model and demonstra-tion unit he used Gen. Washington's Life Guard, a sort of honor com-pany, and he arranged for each brigade to designate an officer for him to train to serve in turn as a brigade instructor.

The key to Gen. von Steuben's drill was simplicity. He devised a manual of arms of only ten motions and reduced the number of mo-tions to reload by four. He adopted a standard pace of 24 inches and a cadence of 75 steps per minute—previously, although the troops had learned to keep step, pace and cadence had varied almost from regiment to regiment. He introduced platoon columns and drilled the men in wheeling into line to right or left and in moving quickly from column into line to front or rear. He reallocated weapons to make each company as uniformly armed as possible. And he included bay-onet training in every day's instruction.

In doing all this, he instructed the men personally, taking a musket into his own hands to demonstrate what he wanted. The American officers, oriented in the British tradition, were scandalized. Their concept of their responsibilities was limited to leading the troops in battle. Not only training, they believed, but such matters as troop welfare, living conditions and health were properly the exclusive functions of the sergeants. Both by his example and by the instruc-tions in his manual, Gen. von Steuben corrected this misconception, placing responsibility for the men's well-being prominently at the be-

Von Steuben, the Drillmaster

The figure accepted by the Continental Army as Baron Friedrich von Steuben, Knight of the Order of Fidelity of Baden, former lieutenant general in the army of Frederick the Great, was largely an invention of Benjamin Franklin, who had cleverly blended fact and fiction in a cover story designed to impress his fellow countrymen.

Son of a Prussian engineer officer, Steuben was born in 1730. Although his mother and grandmother were from aristocratic but impecunious families, his grandfather, a minister in the German Reformed Church, was the son of a tenant farmer named not Steuben but Steube. It was Friedrich's grandfather who, trading on his wife's connections, spuriously added the particle *von* to his name. Later Friedrich's father changed *his* name to Steuben, preempting the name of a noble Prussian family which actually had died out a century earlier.

Fredrich entered the army in 1746 and served through the Seven Years War, first in the infantry and then as a deputy quartermaster on the general staff (in German terminology, the quartermaster was a combination G2/G3, not a supply officer.) Wounded three times and captured once, he won marked distinction and at the end of the war, as a captain, was appointed junior aide-de-camp to the king.

Within a year, however, he had quarreled with one of Frederick the Great's favorite senior aides, and the postwar demobilization was used as an excuse to terminate his commission.

For the next 12 years Steuben was chamberlain at the court of Hohenzollern-Hechingen, a minor German principality. During that period, the neighboring principality of Baden awarded him a knighthood and the Prince of Hohenzollern-Hechingen granted him the title (but no estates) of baron. By early 1777, however, bankruptcy compelled the prince to close his court, leaving his chamberlain unemployed. Steuben then tried successively (but unsuccessfully) to obtain a commission in the French, Austrian and Spanish armies and a post at the court of Baden. Finally, hearing that the American commissioners in Paris were looking for experienced officers, he applied to them.

Frederick the Great's army had the reputation of being the world's finest military machine. Steuben's exceptional record in that army in both line and staff gave him impeccable credentials; but an ex-captain, Benjamin Franklin suspected, would command little attention from American generals.

Hence the cover story, which Franklin and his fellow commissioner Silas Deane propagated in letters to Congress and to Gen. Washington.

Evidently Franklin also briefed Steuben on the American Army's resentment of the appointments to high ranks that a dazzled Congress had already granted to many European applicants. Consequently, when Steuben reached York, Pa., he told Congress that he asked only for expenses; he wanted merely to serve as a volunteer, and when Congress and the army had seen his work they could grant him such rank and pay as they thought just.

In the event, the worth of his services was quickly recognized. Thomas Conway resigned on 28 April, 1778, and Steuben was appointed major general and inspector general to fill the vacancy. In that capacity and as a division commander, he served through the rest of the war. After peace came, he divided his time between New York City and an estate the New York authorities had granted him north of Utica, where he died late in 1794.

ginning of the duties he listed in his manual for each grade from corporal to colonel.

Trying to train such clumsy individualists had its frustrations. Reportedly, the first English words Gen. von Steuben learned were "God damn." Occasionally, in exasperation at the inadequacies of his vocabulary, he would turn to Capt. Benjamin Walker, his French-speaking American aide, and implore, "Curse dem for me, Valker, I giff up!" Soldier-like, some of the men groused at the increased demands upon them.

"I was kept constantly, when off other duty, engaged in learning the Baron de Steuben's new Prussian exercise," a Connecticut private wrote; "It was a continual drill." But no one resented Steuben's profane explosions. On the contrary, his broken English and noisy bluster tickled the men and made him popular as a "character" as well as respected for the manifest progress he was bringing.

And it was not merely in drill and the tactical potential it reflected that progress showed. The troops took new pride in themselves. Police of the camp improved. A genuine chain of command, with intermediate officers not only relaying orders but following up on their execution, came into being. Personal hygiene was vastly improved, with the troops being marched to the river for weekly baths—but with strict orders that no man would be allowed to remain in the water for more than ten minutes "lest it be injurious to his health." The sick rate, although still high, dropped to the lowest level in months.

There were significant improvements in the general situation. Early in May came word that France had recognized and formally allied itself with the United States. Recruits brought manning levels higher. On 27 May Congress approved a standard regimental organization. And just a week before, an event had occurred in which the troops demonstrated to themselves just how far they had come.

Rumors had reached Gen. Washington that the British were about to evacuate Philadelphia. To learn if the reports had any foundation, he sent the Marquis de Lafayette with 2,000 men on a reconnaisance in force across the Schuylkill and downstream to Barren Hill, near the British outpost line. As it happened, the rumors were premature; the British learned that the Americans were at Barren Hill, and a strong British force under Sir William Howe himself set out to cut them off.

The British movement was undetected until the last minute (the local militia detailed to patrol the approaches had gone home), but there was no panic in the American camp. Being heavily outnumbered, Gen. Lafayette was compelled to order a withdrawal, but the movement was carried out calmly and in good order. The rear guard held off the closely pursuing enemy until the main body of the Americans forded the river and deployed. Watching the professional manner in which these maneuvers were carried out, Gen. Howe abandoned the operation and returned to Philadelphia empty-handed.

Four weeks later, on 18 June, the British did evacuate Philadelphia, starting across New Jersey toward Sandy Hook, where they would move on to New York by ship. That same afternoon, one American division started in pursuit. The next morning, six months to the day after the troops had marched through the driving snow into their winter camp, the rest of the army left Valley Forge.

Nine days afterward, the leading American elements caught up with the British near Monmouth Courthouse, bringing on the largest pitched battle of the Revolution. Before poor generalship by Charles Lee brought the action to an inconclusive halt, the American troops' newly acquired discipline and tactical skill had been on the verge of winning a definite victory.

It was not until the Yorktown campaign more than three years later that the units immediately under Gen. Washington were again tested in large-scale combat. Consequently, there is no dramatically convincing evidence that it was Valley Forge that brought the transformation of an agglomeration of raw, untrained men into a responsive, proficient army. But in subtler, less spectacular forms, the evidence clearly exists.

It can be found in such brilliantly conducted, if limited, engagements as Stony Point and in the daring and highly professional execution of Gen. John Sullivan's massive expedition deep into the Iroquois country of upstate New York. It can be found, too, in such indices as the sharp drop in winter sick rates, which never again approximated the levels which, until Valley Forge ended the pattern, had invariably imposed an appalling toll in death and disability. Most fundamentally, it can be found in the fact that, despite persisting adversity and discouragements and tactical defeats, the army had learned lessons that held it together and made it a cohesive, viable and dangerous military force.

It was the experience of Valley Forge that made the difference. George Washington would never again have to repeat his gloomy warning of December, 1777, that the army's very survival was in jeopardy. And so long as that army remained intact, strong in discipline and proficiency, there was no possibility that the cause of national independence to which it was dedicated could be suppressed.

CHAPTER
TWENTY-EIGHT

Cortes in the Valley
of Anáhuac

by Richard T. Bevevino

T he conquest of Aztecs of Mexico by a relatively small contingent of Spaniards ranks as one of the greatest and most daring military exploits in history. This feat is spectacular because the Spaniards were overwhelmingly outnumbered by opposing
forces, they were fighting on foreign soil and they confronted a society that was highly militaristic.

In 1519, the Valley of Anáhuac contained one of the densest populations in the world. It is estimated that the population for all of Mexico was 30 million people, with Central Mexico having approximately
20 million. The valley alone contained several million inhabitants.
Tenochtitlán (now Mexico City), the powerful Aztec city-state which
ruled the valley, housed a population of between 200,000 and 300,000.

In addition to Tenochtitlán, there were several other Indian towns in the valley with considerable populations: Texcoco, Tlacopan, Xochimilco, Culhuacan, Azcapotzalco, Ixtapalapa, Coyoacan and Tepeyacac. Into this mass of humanity would arrive, initially, some 500 Spaniards. Not only would the Europeans be drastically outnumbered, but they would be hundreds of miles from their base of operations in Cuba.

From the Gulf Coast to Tenochtitlán, the conquistadores would have to penetrate 400 miles into the interior. This arduous journey would require the Spaniards to travel through some of the harshest terrain in Mexico; from the hot lowlands of the Gulf Coast through the Sierra Madre Oriental, crossing elevations in excess of 10,000 feet.

They would oppose an indigenous culture which was acclimated to war; one that had tens of thousands of warriors at its disposal. How, then, were these men able to overcome seemingly impossible odds and achieve victory over an adversary at the zenith of its power? In order to fully comprehend the magnitude of this military accomplishment, the following must be analyzed: military strategy, armaments, religion, communications and intelligence, legends, allies, command leadership and disease.

When Hernando Cortes and his troops disembarked on the Gulf Coast in 1519, the Aztecs were the main force in the Valley of Anáhuac. Aztec power and dominance emanated from their magnificent capital of Tenochtitlán, located at that time on an island in Lake Texcoco. (Modern Mexico City—population, 16 million—is on the site of Tenochtitlán.)

According to the Spanish, the Aztec Empire's capital was impressive. Bernal Diaz de Castillo, a soldier with Cortes who later wrote of the conquest, stated:

> Some of our soldiers asked whether what we saw were not a dream. I do not know how to describe it all, for we were looking at what had never been heard of or seen before, nor even dreamed about.

From Tenochtitlán, Aztec hegemony spread its tentacles throughout the valley, reaching the Gulf and Pacific coasts. Aztec military prowess was such that supposedly about 350 Indian towns were subjected to tribute demands from their masters in the valley. The tribute system was the principal method employed by the dominant city-states of Mexico of acquiring merchandise for their people.

In order to acquire merchandise from other Indian towns, force had

230

to be imposed. Failure to comply with stipulated demands elicited severe reprisals from Aztec forces. Tribute became essential for the Aztec state. Without it, the state would have ceased to exist.

The environs of Tenochtitlán were becoming deforested and game was becoming scarce. Consequently, Indian towns had to be subjugated and forced to render payment. Tribute of all types (slaves, sacrificial victims, food, clothing, firewood, animals, precious gems, feathers and armaments) flowed into the Aztec capital to satisfy the growing needs of a powerful and burgeoning metropolis. However, many subjugated towns despised Aztec oppression and their burdensome tribute demands.

Aztec religion also reinforced the constant need for the tribute system. Human sacrifice had been practiced by the Aztecs since their arrival in the valley. Because their religion was predicated on sacrifice to appease the gods, victims had to be found continually. The Aztecs attributed their growth and success to their deities, and, as a natural conclusion to this logic, the gods had to be rewarded constantly with blood sacrifices.

As time elapsed, more sacrifices were needed to placate the capricious gods. If the gods were not satisfied, the cosmic forces of destruction would terminate the world; the sun might not rise, the rain might not come and the wind might not blow. After the Great Temple of Tenochtitlán (discovered in 1978 in Mexico City) was completed in the late fifteenth century, 20,000 to 40,000 people were sacrificed at the consecration ceremonies, which lasted four days and nights. The victims were prisoners taken in combat and those who were part of the tribute owed to Tenochtitlán.

An example of Aztec dependence on their gods is the "Wars of Flowers." When harsh winters and severe summer droughts descended on the valley in the mid-fifteenth century, the Aztecs beseeched their priests for an explanation as to the cause of wide-spread starvation. The priests' interpretation was that the Aztecs were made hungry because the gods were also hungry. Therefore, difficult times were perpetrated by angry and starving gods. If the gods were properly nourished with increased human sacrifices, however, they would become benevolent once again.

So the Aztecs and their allies sent a message to three other city-states that were also experiencing the same hardships. They were to start a war for the expressed purpose of capturing prisoners to be sacrificed on the altar. When a sufficient number of prisoners had been captured by both sides, the opposing commanders would call a halt to the hostilities. To die in battle or on the altar stone was known as the "flowery death"; hence, these battles came to be known as the "Wars of Flowers."

Incredibly, after thousands were sacrificed, the difficult times ended. The Aztec assumption, naturally, was that the gods had been gratified with the additional sacrifices. As a consequence, the number of sacrifices increased alarmingly from then on. The Aztecs wanted to make certain that difficult times never occurred again.

Thus, a paradox arose: peace became a dangerous state of affairs. War had to be maintained so that victims could be provided to the gods. Not to placate the gods would surely bring ruin. Since people would not come willingly to the sacrificial altar, force had to be imposed. Motivated by sacrificial appeasement, the Aztec state had to be militaristic.

Along with this militarism went cannibalism. When the "Wars of Flowers" ended and the prisoners were sacrificed, various parts of the bodies were cut up and distributed to a starving populace.

The Spaniards, who were shocked and frightened, witnessed the bodies being carved and prepared for consumption.

The military spirit was imbued in the Aztec male from an early age. Upon the birth of a male child, the umbilical cord was wrapped around a miniaturized wooden battle shield and given to a warrior who then buried the contents in the nearest battlefield.

The majority of male children attended school where military precepts and the use of weapons were taught.

Basic weapons used by the warriors were the bow and arrow, sling, spear, lance, club and the "hunting wood." A short spear was launched by means of a spear thrower, a piece of wood with a grooved middle section and a peg at the end to hold the spear. The spear thrower was then attached to a warrior's arm. Thus, the spear was only long enough to fit inside the grooved section. Once the spear was launched, another was placed in the spear thrower. The Aztecs were adept and accurate with these projectiles.

The hunting wood, employed for hand-to-hand combat, was a club of the hardest wood with the shaft or handle shaved to fit the individual warrior's grip. What made this weapon so lethal were imbedded flakes of volcanic glass. A blow from the hunting wood proved effective in disabling an opponent.

Aztec military strategy was somewhat simplistic in that it relied, for the most part, on an all-out frontal assault when attacking enemy forces. These human-wave assaults usually sufficed because Aztec warriors were excellent fighters. They overwhelmed their opponents simply by sheer weight of numbers.

232

Before launching a frontal assault, the warriors worked themselves into a frenzy by screaming, blowing conch shells, beating drums, performing frightful dances and making threatening gestures. Often, the enemy would be so terrified before the battle started that, psychologically, victory belonged to the Aztecs. On signal, the warriors moved forward, arrayed in their suits of cotton "armor." As they approached their adversaries, the lance, the club and the hunting wood were brought into play.

One aspect of the Aztec military philosophy that proved disastrous with the Spaniards was an emphasis on capturing an enemy rather than killing him. The captured warrior could then be transported back to Tenochtitlán for sacrifice.

In fact, advancement in military rank depended on the acquisition of captives. Once a warrior captured four prisoners and displayed courage in doing so, he could be invited to join one or two elite warrior groups: the eagle or jaguar knights. All high military officers were selected from one of these two groups.

The Spaniards would become frightfully aware of the Indians' desire to capture them alive for subsequent sacrifice and would fight with herculean efforts so as not to be taken alive. Bernal Diaz later commented that "it was dread that one day or another they would do the same to me. Afterward, I used to feel terrified before going into battle."

Into this environment arrived the Spanish conquistadores in search of fame, fortune and, in due time, slave labor. Unburdened of the Moorish threat and fearful of Portuguese trade ambitions, King Ferdinand II of Aragon and Queen Isabella I cosponsored the voyages of Christopher Columbus.

Because the voyages of Columbus were predicated on discovering a shorter route to the Orient for the purposes of trade, the islands in the Caribbean proved disappointing. There was little gold and silver to be found, but the Spanish did employ the island inhabitants as slave labor. They would become fervent in their desire to convert the natives to Christianity. Proselytism would go hand-in-hand with their quest for gold and silver.

After colonizing Hispaniola and Cuba, the Spaniards looked beyond the islands for precious metals and other trade items. Consequently, explorers were dispatched westward in the hope of locating lands that would prove worthwhile financially. These probes resulted in the discovery of Mexico's Yucatán Peninsula.

The explorers returned with reports that the natives on the coast were more highly civilized than those encountered on the Caribbean islands. Intrigued by the possibilities of finding gold and of convert-

233

ing the natives to the Catholic faith, the governor of Cuba, Diego Velazquez, designated Cortes to lead an expedition to the newly discovered lands.

Diego Velazquez, for political or personal reasons, later attempted to rescind his appointment of Cortes as leader of the expedition. There is some question as to when the order relieving Cortes of his command was issued—before his departure from Cuba or after he had landed in Mexico.

However, Cortes's hasty embarkation from Cuba would suggest that he, at least, was informed of the governor's change of mind. Cortes was not about to relinquish command. So, in February of 1519, Cortes and his men sailed for the Yucatán. His forces consisted of approximately 550 men, 16 horses, 32 crossbows, 13 harquebuses, ten brass cannon and four falconets.

Disembarking on the island of Cozumel near the northeastern tip of the peninsula, Cortes learned from the natives that two Castilians had been living with the Mayans. Cortes sent natives in search of his two countrymen. One, Jeronimo de Aguilar, was found and joined the Spanish. The other, Gonzalo Guerrero, refused to leave his Mayan wife and family.

Jeronimo de Aguilar recounted his adventure for Cortes. He was on a ship destined for Panama, but a violent storm at sea ran the ship aground. All the other Spaniards aboard had been killed by the natives. Since that time, 1511, he had been living with the Mayans. Hence, he was fluent in the Mayan language and familiar with native customs. He was indispensable as an interpreter from the start of the conquest. Cortes had the means then with which to communicate with the coastal Indians.

Proceeding westward, the Spaniards weighed anchor near the Indian state of Tabasco. Here the Europeans had their first military engagement with Mexican natives. An indigenous force estimated at 20,000 attacked the Spaniards. Strategically deploying his men with a frontal assault and a flanking move, Cortes managed to route the hostiles. European weaponry played an important role in discouraging the natives.

The horses, previously unknown to the natives, proved to have a devastating psychological effect. The Indians, at first, believed that the rider and horse were one terrible creature. Spanish armor prevented native weapons from inflicting disabling blows on the conquistadores while the European sword rendered blows that incapacitated many of the enemy. The cannon and harquebuses belched flame and thunder with lethal results, and the primitives were awe-struck by the white man's power.

Although Cortes's men were greatly outnumbered, native armaments paled against steel and firepower. European weapons, here witnessed for the first time in the Americas, proved decisive in subsequent encounters. They had such a demoralizing impact on the natives that the Indians assumed the Europeans were invincible. The Spaniards, numerically at a disadvantage, had one obvious advantage: superior technology in weaponry.

Stunned and terrified by the ferocity of the strangers and their arms, the natives of Tabasco pleaded for peace. As a gesture of friendship, the Indians presented the Spaniards with gifts, among which were 20 Indian women, one of whom, Malinche, was destined to play a pivotal role in the conquest. Malinche, renamed Dona Marina by the Spaniards, was an Aztec who had been sold into slavery to the Mayans. Thus, she was conversant in the Mayan tongue and, more important, in *nahuatl*, the Aztec language. She was the component that completed the communication cycle.

Initially, communications with the Aztecs were established in an awkward manner: Cortes spoke in Spanish to Jeronimo de Aguilar; he translated the Spanish to Mayan for Malinche; Malinche translated the Mayan to *nahuatl* for the Aztecs. When the Aztecs wanted to speak to Cortes, the translation process was reversed. Later, Malinche acquired sufficient fluency in Spanish.

Malinche's importance cannot be emphasized enough. Not only did she accurately translate Cortes's remarks, but she did so in a tone and with a forthrightness that left no doubt in the listener as to Cortes's intentions. Her acquaintance with Aztec customs and culture provided Cortes with invaluable insight, an intelligence advantage that the Aztecs did not possess with regard to the Spaniards.

Bernal Diaz, in his memoirs, wrote that without Malinche, the conquest would not have been possible. However, because of her aid to the Spanish, she is treated as a traitor in Mexican history. Fortunately for the Spaniards, she sided with them. Before Cortes embarked on his great adventure into the interior of Mexico, he had the distinct advantages of superior weaponry and communications and intelligence.

Another factor that aided Cortes was the belief of the coastal Indians, especially the Aztec emperor Montezuma, that Cortes was Quetzalcoatl—the long-awaited god who had once vowed to return. According to native legend, Quetzalcoatl (Feathered Serpent) had reigned near Tula hundreds of years earlier. Forced to leave because of some indiscretion he had committed, Quetzalcoatl departed for the Gulf Coast and embarked on a magic raft promising to return in a One Reed year.

Aztec civilization functioned in 52-year cycles, at the conclusion of which there was widespread fear that the world would end. To forestall the destruction of the world, religious festivities were to be held at the end of each cycle. Within this 52-year cycle were Reed years. A One Reed year occurred every 52 years. One Reed years occured in 1363, 1415 and 1467; Quetzalcoatl had not returned, however. The next One Reed year was 1519.

Legend was also specific concerning the appearance of Quetzalcoatl: he was a white man with a beard. This legend was so entrenched in Aztec culture that Montezuma dreaded the approach of a One Reed year because, if Quetzalcoatl did return, Montezuma's reign would end.

Messengers from the coast eventually arrived in Tenochtitlán to present Montezuma with a message. This "picture writing" depicted the moving white pyramids (ships) that housed fierce beings. After seeing the writing and listening to the accounts of his messengers, Montezuma became hysterical.

If the fierce beings on the coast were indeed Quetzalcoatl and his followers, how could Montezuma dare attack a god? He vacillated. A One Reed year and the landing of the Spaniards in 1519 favored Cortes. It was sheer coincidence, but one that prevented Montezuma from taking action immediately against the Spaniards.

As the conquest unfolded, command leadership became crucial. In retrospect, Cortes demonstrated decisiveness where Montezuma remained indecisive. Cortes was bold to the point of recklessness, resolute, courageous, astute and discerning, capable of accurately assessing a situation and able to exploit every advantage.

For example, while at Cempoala, an Indian town not far from the coast, he learned of the dissatisfaction of tribute-paying tribes. They chafed at providing material and people as tributes to the Aztec state. Nonetheless, the Aztec armies were so powerful that the subjugated did not have the means with which to throw off the yoke of their oppressors.

Recognizing the apparent dissension among the indigenous inhabitants toward the Aztecs, Cortes ascertained correctly that the diverse native groups did not form a cohesive unit. He could exploit this lack of solidarity to his advantage. The disenchanted Indians could be used as allies, thereby augmenting his own forces.

Furthermore, while at Cempoala, he was informed of an Indian nation in the interior, Tlaxcala, that had continually defied Aztec forces. Cortes once again interpreted this information as signaling a propitious opportunity to increase his army. If, as the coastal Indians suggested, the Tlaxcalans and the Aztecs were foes, why not employ the Tlaxcalans as allies?

Cortes's compatriots did not share his enthusiasm. They were in unfamiliar terrain, were outnumbered and knew that larger Indian forces resided in the interior. Many of his men balked at continuing. They preferred to return to the islands for reinforcements because there were too many Indians for their small force to fight. Some protested that Cortes was exceeding his orders. They were not charged with exploring the interior. Others feared that by marching inland, their position would be untenable; that they would be cut off from the coast and surrounded by hostile forces.

Cortes was determined not to return to the islands when wealth and fame seemed so close at hand. In one bold stroke, he suppressed the mutinous undercurrent. He ordered Spaniards loyal to his cause to strip and scuttle the fleet. They could remain at the coast or proceed inland to wealth, fame and glory. Using his powers of persuasion, coupled with Montezuma's inadvertent aid, Cortes convinced his men to accept his course of action.

Montezuma's inadvertent aid to Cortes came in the form of gifts delivered to the Spanish. Detailed accounts of the progress of the strangers had been reported to Montezuma. Fearful that the Spanish would venture into his domain and aware that they coveted the yellow metal, he sought a means of diverting their attention away from Tenochtitlán. Presenting the conquistadores with gifts of the metal they desired would perhaps sate their appetites.

Aztec messengers, dispatched by Montezuma and bearing valuable articles, presented the items to the Spaniards at an opportune moment for Cortes. The gifts of gold and silver bolstered Cortes's reasons for continuing the journey to Tenochtitlán. The Spanish naturally concluded that the Aztecs possessed even more wealth.

In August, 1519, after establishing a base of operations on the coast (Villa Rica de la Vera Cruz) garrisoned by 150 Spaniards, Cortes departed for Tlaxcala. His forces consisted of some 400 Spaniards and 1,000 Totonacs from Cempoala, who were employed as porters. After traversing the difficult, mountainous area of the Sierra Madre Oriental, Cortes approached the kingdom of Tlaxcala.

Messengers were sent ahead to inform the Tlaxcalans of Cortes's peaceful intentions. Cortes wanted, if at all possible, to avoid hostilities. He could ill afford to lose men or horses. Diplomacy, he assumed, would be the tactic to win over the Indians.

The Tlaxcalans, however, were not receptive to peaceful overtures. Fearful that the new arrivals were friends of the Aztecs, the Tlaxcalans prepared to attack. With no alternative, Cortes engaged a Tlaxcalan army of between 30,000 and 50,000.

Luck, perseverance and military skill enabled Cortes and his remarkable soldiers to extricate themselves from a potentially disastrous predicament. Although the Tlaxcalans mounted an offensive with thousands of warriors, their leadership was divided as to the proper course of action to take against the Spaniards.

Some believed the Europeans were gods. As a result, the force did not present a solid, unified front. In addition, they employed the Indian tactic of charging en masse. The frontal onslaught allowed the Spaniards' cannon to mow down large numbers of Indians.

Spanish weapons, novelties to the Tlaxcalans, were again a decisive factor. Not only were they superior, but the Spaniards were extremely proficient in their use. Although Cortes and his men were suffering from the attacks, he believed in taking the offensive, even against so numerous a foe. Referring to the battle at Tlaxcala, Bernal Diaz wrote:

> One morning when we awoke and saw how many of us were wounded, some even with two or three wounds, how weary we were, how many sick and in rags, and how already 45 had died in battle or from disease or chills, and how the captain himself was suffering from fever, we began to wonder what it was all leading to.

Cortes pressed onward until the Tlaxcalans, like the natives of Tabasco, petitioned for peace. Cortes, through determination, confidence and aggressiveness, had converted a belligerent adversary into a dependable ally. His command leadership, with the bravery and resourcefulness of his compatriots, allowed the conquistadores to attain victory when defeat and annihilation appeared imminent.

Montezuma, conversely, exhibited behvaior that was ultimately detrimental to the Aztec state. Indecisiveness, fear and resignation characterized his actions. Not desiring the presence of strangers, who were perhaps gods, Montezuma again sent emissaries with gifts for the Spaniards.

The Aztec messengers were to inform Cortes that the trip to Tenochtitlán was long and arduous, and that such a trek should not be undertaken. Montezuma's action was one of appeasement. He hoped to placate the European lust for gold. When Cortes informed the Aztec messengers that he was definitely going to Tenochtitlán, Montezuma panicked on hearing the news.

Montezuma, like Malinche, is not held in high esteem by Mexicans. He is criticized for permitting the Spaniards to enter Tenochtitlán and for not immediately implementing military action against the invaders.

In early November of 1519, the Spaniards, accompanied by 5,000 to 6,000 Tlaxcalan allies, entered Tenochtitlán. Cortes finally came face-to-face with Montezuma. The Aztec leader's attitude was one of resignation. In his welcoming speech to Cortes, Montezuma, in essence, abdicated his authority. Speaking to Cortes through Malinche, Montezuma explained how their coming had been foretold. He was still uncertain as to who the new arrivals were.

Another example of Cortes's ability to assess a situation and to implement drastic action to rectify a potential problem occurred shortly after the Spaniard's arrival in the capital. While approaching the city on one of the causeways (three causeways connected Tenochtitlán to the mainland), he realized the precariousness of his military position.

If the causeways were disassembled while the Spaniards were inside the city, it would be difficult for them to escape. Compounding the problem was the fact that the Aztecs controlled the lake, as evidenced by their many ships. The conquistadores had placed themselves in a militarily inferior posture. If hostilities broke out, Cortes and his men would be trapped inside the city.

In order to neutralize this disadvantage, Cortes urged Montezuma to remain with the Spanish in their quarters. Montezuma, after feeble protestations, submitted. The Revered Speaker of the Aztec nation became, in effect, a prisoner in his own city. Cortes's actions substantiate, again, his decisiveness and determination; Montezuma's displayed resignation and submission.

In the spring of 1520, while in Tenochtitlán with Montezuma under Spanish guard, Cortes was notified that a Spanish force of some 1,000 men had landed on the coast. This force had been sent by the governor of Cuba, Diego Velazquez, with explicit orders to bring Cortes back to the island. Cortes's determination again manifested itself. He would not relinquish command after having endured so many hardships and having discovered Aztec riches.

By sending a conciliatory message and gold and silver to Panfilo Narvaez, leader of the force ordered to arrest him, Cortes attempted to persuade his countrymen to join him.

Leaving a small detachment of Spaniards in Tenochtitlán under the command of Pedro de Alvarado, Cortes set off for the coast. There he confronted his Spanish adversaries and, after some heated discussion, swayed them to his cause. Spanish forces tripled with the addition of Panfilo Narvaez's soldiers.

The Spaniards who stayed in Tenochtitlán soon came under siege. After learning of events inside the capital, Cortes rushed back.

He confronted Montezuma and ordered him to lift the siege and give the conquistadores provisions. The Aztec leader replied that the people of Tenochtitlán no longer respected him and would not obey his commands.

The main square of the city was crowded with Aztecs at that time. Cortes grabbed Montezuma and took him to the roof of the building in which the Spaniards were staying, and commanded the Aztec leader to disperse the crowd. Unfortunately, when Montezuma tried to quiet the multitude, his people attacked him with arrows and stones. Several projectiles found their mark and Montezuma collapsed on the roof. He was taken inside where he died, slain by his own people.

Still under siege inside Tenochtitlán, the Spaniards attempted to flee. Their escape was discovered by the Aztecs, however, and the retreat became a disaster. The conquistadores suffered heavy casualties as they were attacked from all sides. They lost approximately 800 men in the battle of Tenochtitlán and subsquent encounters on their way to Tlaxcala. It was early July, 1520.

Although Cortes had suffered defeat, he had no intention of returning to Cuba. He was determined to regroup and return once more to Tenochtitlán. The Spaniards made preparations for the return. Their plan consisted of four phases: recruit as many Indian allies as possible; secure the mainland and drive the Aztecs into Tenochtitlán; lay siege to the city and take control of the lake; and, when the siege exacted its toll on the weakened and starved Aztecs, begin the final assault.

In order to control the lake, Cortes had Panfilo Narvaez's fleet dismantled. He employed thousands of Indians as porters and the ships' pieces were thus transported to Tlaxcala, then to Tenochtitlán, where they were reassembled in smaller versions of the originals. Bernal Diaz estimated that a line of porters eight miles long transported the pieces. All of Cortes's men were not convinced that they should return to the capital, but Cortes's determination prevailed once more.

Religion is yet another factor that must be taken into account when analyzing the conquest. To the Spanish, the world was governed by two forces: God and Satan. Catholicism had been triumphant against the Moors and against the spread of Islam. It certainly would sustain them against the heathens in the new lands.

The conquistadores had witnessed the results of human sacrifices, had seen the skull racks and viewed with revulsion the myriad idols adorning the native temples. They were shocked at the native practice of cannibalism and accused the Aztec priests of practicing sodomy. It was their Christian duty to eradicate these evil forces. The Spaniards never wavered in the belief that their god was the one and true god.

Contrary to the conquistadores, the Aztecs believed that the world was governed by the cosmic forces of destruction. Before being elected First Speaker, Montezuma had served as a priest. He was a dedicated adherent to the sacrificial-appeasement approach. The gods had to be mollified so that the world would not self-destruct.

Numerous allies were also an important aspect of Cortes's success. Because the Aztec state was parasitic, tribute was demanded of subjugated tribes. Tribute-paying tribes constantly sought the means to rid themselves of Aztec hegemony. A serious flaw in Aztec conquest was that they never developed any political infrastructure to solidify their victories. Tribute was the primary motivation for conquest. Tribute-paying tribes, initially hostile to the Spaniards, eventually sided with the conquistadores.

Cortes took full advantage of the enmity directed toward the Aztecs by the coastal Indians and, later on, by the Tlaxcalans. Indian allies were empoyed as spies, porters and warriors. When Cortes reentered the valley to begin operations against the Aztecs, he supposedly counted 100,000 Indians as allies.

Disease, unfortunately, was another ally of the conquistadores. The catastrophic consequences of the white man's diseases were first observed in the Caribbean islands. The island natives succumbed quickly to smallpox and, within a short time, entire island populations were exterminated. In time, measles, typhus and influenza also contributed to extensive demographic losses.

The Europeans had built up immunity to these diseases. The natives had not. Disease would kill more Indians than the Spaniards could ever dream of slaying. From a population of about 25 million in Central Mexico before discovery by the Europeans, the native population would be reduced to roughly one million by the mid-seventeenth century.

Smallpox infected the coastal Indians while Cortes was still in Tenochtitlán. News of a devastating sickness reached Montezuma. The reports were so dire that Montezuma outlawed trade with the af-

241

fected areas. It was only a matter of time before the inhabitants of Tenochtitlán suffered the same fate.

It has been said that if the Aztecs had pursued the Spaniards with a concentrated, combined effort when they retreated from Tenochtitlán, the conquest would not have occurred. The Aztecs, however, were suffering the ravages of a smallpox epidemic. They were preoccupied with their sick and dying as the disease raged through their city. Elated that they had driven the Spaniards from their city, the Aztecs were bewildered and demoralized by this deadly and invisible enemy.

The psychological impact of smallpox on the natives was dramatic. Why were the strangers not affected by the killing sickness? Only their people died. Were the gods of the conquistadores indeed more powerful than their gods? Had their gods forsaken them? The customary rituals, ceremonies and sacrifices were not appeasing the gods. Thus, disillusionment and doubt thwarted a concentrated effort by the Aztecs to rid their land of the conquistadores.

Tenochtitlán fell on 13 August, 1521. The siege, intense fighting and starvation had taken their toll on the inhabitants. Cuauhtemoc, the last Aztec leader, requested that Cortes allow his people to evacuate the city. According to Bernal Diaz, the evacuation of Tenochtitlán was a sorrowful sight:

> So yellow, thin, dirty, ... they were a pitiful sight to behold. Only the dead remained in the city ... and the ground was as though tilled where they had dug up roots to eat and even the bark had been ripped from the trees ... it is many ages since a people have suffered so greatly.

Although the Spaniards were outnumbered initially, they excelled in other areas. Military armaments, strategy, communications and intelligence, allies and command leadership were areas in which they were superior.

The Aztec religion proved detrimental to the inhabitants of Tenochtitlán because its practices embittered other Indian peoples. In addition, the legend of Quetzalcoatl stopped Montezuma from taking action immediately against the Spaniards. Finally, the lethal results of the white man's disease, smallpox, aided the final thrust against the Aztecs.

Each factor was of great consequence, and each was contingent on the other. It is conceivable that if the Europeans had not been dominant in one or two of these areas, the conquest possibly would not have taken place.

CHAPTER
TWENTY-NINE

Lieutenant Grant & the Missing Money

by John M. Taylor

Lt. Ulysses S. Grant was homesick. The war with Mexico was over, but the occupation lingered on. "Sam" Grant had not thought much of the war in the first place—he would later call it "one of the most unjust wars waged by a stronger against a weaker nation"—but as a professional Army officer he had done his duty. He had served with the armies of both Zachary Taylor and Winfield Scott. He had seen active service with the 4th Infantry Regiment, and had been brevetted for gallantry at Monterey.

The 25-year-old Grant, however, had never been seduced by the glory of war. Moreover, he was deperately lonesome for his fiancée, Julia Dent, to whom he had become engaged just before departing for Mexico. On New Year's day, 1848, Grant wrote from his camp near Mexico City, "It is now . . . strongly believed that peace will be established before many months. I hope it may be so, for it is scarcely supportable for me to be separated from you so long, my Dearest Julia."

Grant's friend James Longstreet stopped by to say farewell; his unit had been ordered home. But the 4th Regiment had no orders, and Lt. Grant stayed with the rest in his post as regimental quartermaster. The Illinoisan had no special aptitude for the housekeeping functions of his post, but he brought a certain imagination to his duties. When regimental funds became low, Grant organized a bakery, which not only provided bread for the regiment but sold to the chief commissary at a profit.

One of Grant's responsibilities was the safekeeping of government funds, however, and this was to prove his undoing. In June, as the 4th Regiment at last prepared to return to America, Grant became concerned for the safety of $1,000 in government funds—mostly silver dollars—in his custody. He had no safe, and the lock on his trunk was broken. He asked a fellow officer, Capt. John Gore, if he could place the money sack in Gore's trunk with its functioning lock. Gore was not enthusiastic, but eventually conceded the logic of Grant's request.

In Gore's words, he had the trunk "carefully guarded during the day, and placed in my tent during the night." The money was still in the trunk on 12 June when Maj. Gen. William J. Worth's division, including the 4th Regiment, participated in flag-lowering ceremonies in Mexico City. Four nights later, however, on the road to Jalapa, the trunk was stolen from Gore's tent while he and another officer were sleeping.

As Gore reconstructed the theft, the perpetrators carried the trunk some 600 yards to a mill race, broke it open, removed the money and threw the trunk into the stream. A search on the morning of 17 June revealed, in Gore's words, "many small articles, but no money."

Although the trunk belonged to Gore, the responsibility was Grant's; transfer of physical custody had not altered the iron fact that the Army held Grant accountable for all funds committed to his care. Grant promptly requested a board of inquiry, and Gen. Worth ordered one convened on 25 June. Its finding represented both good news and bad.

On one hand, the board found that "no blame can attach to Lt. U.S. Grant, that he took every means to secure the Money . . . and they exonerate him from all censure." On the other hand, the board's findings in no way altered the fact that Grant was accountable for the missing funds, which amounted to approximately one year's salary for an Army lieutenant.

• • •

Anyone who has ever taken on the IRS in a tax matter can sympathize with Grant's position. Indeed, IRS procedures, with their established channels for appeal, seem nothing short of enlightened by comparison with the unresponsive bureaucracy that confronted Grant. So hopeless was any appeal through Army or Treasury channels—the findings of the board of inquiry notwithstanding—that Grant did not even bother.

A letter from a Treasury Department auditor in 1852 noted that Grant's file contained no appeal for relief; the auditor added cheerfully that "the rule . . . in all such [appeals] is to disallow them, having no discretion to do otherwise." Grant's only hope was to find a Congressional sponsor for a private relief bill.

The debt resulting from Grant's Mexican misadventure was the first in a series of setbacks that were to dog him for more than a decade. The peacetime Army proved to be a succession of dreary frontier posts. Promotion was slow. Grant failed at several business ventures while still in uniform, and additionally gained a reputation as a drinker.

He was devoted to Julia, and when sent without her to an isolated post at Humboldt Bay, Calif., Grant's drinking contributed to a falling out with his commanding officer. The upshot was that Grant resigned from the Army in 1854, still liable for the money lost in Mexico.

The debt hung over him like a cloud. Although the government does not appear to have pressed for payment, Grant had no luck in obtaining relief through Congress. The first private bill on his behalf failed of passage in 1849. A similar bill was reintroduced in the next Congress by Rep. Jonathan Morris of Ohio, but appears not to have been reported out of committee.

All of this weighed upon Grant; in 1852 he wrote to Julia of his concern at not being able to travel to Washington to plead his case once more. "If I cannot go," he wrote, "I want father to write to our member of Congress and have one set of my papers, on the subject of the stolen money, saved. It is very important that they should not be lost."

A week later, in another letter to Julia, he was more cheerful:

I send you Capt. Calender's note by this letter. He has paid my tailor's bill so that I have not got a debt against me in the United States, that I know of, except my public debt, and that I shall go to Washington on Wednesday to try and have settled. I met [Edward] Marshall, member of Congress from California, who I knew very well in Mexico, and he promises to take the matter up as soon as he goes back to Washington.

If Mr. Marshall introduced yet another bill on Grant's behalf it failed of passage. One can only speculate as to how the matter might have ended had the Civil War not intervened, for by the time of Ft. Sumter Grant had been reduced to clerking in a leather goods store, and was probably less capable of raising $1,000 than he had been 13 years before.

In 1861, however, he began the meteoric rise that led to his becoming the senior general in the Army and, eventually, President of the United States. Soon, Grant would not have to worry about that missing $1,000.

A way station in Grant's rise was his capture of Ft. Donelson in February, 1862. To the Confederate request for an armistice, Grant replied that "no terms except an unconditional and immediate surrender" would be accepted. "Unconditional Surrender" Grant became a hero throughout the North.

A month after Ft. Donelson fell, Rep. William A. Richardson of Illinois introduced "An Act for the Relief of Lt. Ulysses S. Grant." It was reported out favorably by the Committee on Military Affairs in April, and passed by Congress on 17 June. One thousand dollars must have seemed a small price for a key rebel fort.

In his memoirs, Grant makes no mention of this painful episode, and who can blame him? Certain of his biographers, however, have manifested a defensive tone in discussing Grant's 13-year indebtedness. William C. Church, in a biography published in 1926, even embellished the facts a little: "Though he was not responsible for the loss, Grant, when he was able to do so, made it good to the Treasury."

But today it seems no more than fair that this service-incurred debt, which hung over the young Grant for so long, should finally have been resolved in his favor.

CHAPTER
THIRTY

Playing Taps for a Noble Instrument

by Ted Blankenship

N o doubt the last sound some of Maj. Gen. George Armstrong
Custer's men heard when they met their fate on that June
day in 1876 was the call of a bugle. After all, trumpets have
been as much a part of the military as weapons almost from the beginning. Although only the Sioux warriors who survived could have
told what really happened, it is reasonable to assume that bugles had
a part in the action because they were about the only way a commander could communicate with his troops in those days.

It had been that way for a long time. Roman legions marched to
trumpets and other instruments, and so did the ancient Greeks.

As recorded in the Book of Numbers, Moses was told to "make two
silver trumpets" and sound the alarm when he went to war. Joshua

had the sheep horns blown and the trumpets sounded before commanding the children to shout and bring the walls of Jericho "tumbling down."

Gideon used trumpets, too. He saved Israel from the Midianites, who, in one of their forays into Palestine, had murdered his brothers. He gathered 300 men and gave each of them a trumpet. They crept to the Midianite camp in the dark, and, on signal, blew all the trumpets at the same time. The terrified Midianites fled with Gideon behind them. He captured their two kings.

Col. James H. Wilson must have been a student of the Bible, for he used the same tactics 3,000 years later to rout Confederate troops in the Civil War. Col. Wilson brought 250 buglers together on a foggy day during the battle of Front Royal, Va., and they charged, all blowing their trumpets at the same time. There was a "swelling volume of sound" from all directions, and the Confederates broke and ran.

There was no problem rounding up 250 buglers then. Division had two, each troop had a couple and so did regimental headquarters. Col. Wilson had ten regiments in his division. They were all necessary then because almost everything was done at the sound of a bugle.

After reveille, the day's work began with stable call followed by calls for breakfast, sick, water, fatigue and drill. Mounted units then heard boots and saddles. After dinner call there were water, stable and, at about 5:45 P.M., attention, followed by assembly. The troops then fell in for retreat. There were even calls that signaled the start of school or church and warned when to wear overcoats.

There was a final roll call—then tattoo in the artillery or taps in the infantry. Taps has not always been the call signaling the end of the soldier's day—or his life. The last call was tattoo in the early days.

It originated in the 30 Years War, 1618–1648. It was sounded to stop the drinking of the troops every night. Originally the call was "tap to," which means "close the beer barrels." The provost hammered the bungs in and chalked a line across them to make sure they were not tampered with.

Tattoo is the longest call—28 measures—of which the first part is the same as the French call for lights out. It served the United States from the War of 1812, when the bugle first began to replace the fife and drum, until the Civil War.

It was replaced then because Maj. Gen. Daniel Butterfield considered tattoo too formal. In July of 1862, the Union Army was encamped at Harrison's Landing on the James River in Virginia. The troops had been through seven days of battle, and Richmond was still ahead.

Gen. Butterfield, who commanded a brigade in Maj. Gen. George

B. McClellan's Army of the Potomac, called his bugler, Otis Norton, to his tent. He whistled a tune, reading the notes from an envelope on which he had scribbled them. Bugler Norton listened, then blew them on his bugle. The two made a few changes, and the general ordered the new call substituted for tattoo that night in his brigade.

Those mournful sounds, strange then, but familiar today, became a hit in the brigade and then among nearby units. Commanders sent their buglers to Otis Norton to learn the call. Later, permission was given to substitute taps for the whole Army of the Potomac, and eventually throughout the U.S. military. It was so well received during the Civil War that even the South embraced it.

Confederate Lt. Gen. Thomas J. ("Stonewall") Jackson, returning from one of his frequent reconnaissances, was mistaken for the enemy and shot by his own picket. Surgeons amputated his left arm and he was on his way to recovery when he contracted pneumonia and died on 10 May, 1863.

As his body was lowered into the ground, gray-coated soldiers fired three volleys and the bugler blew taps—the call that ten months earlier a New York businessman turned soldier had scribbled on an envelope.

Those melancholy notes have pierced the air over many graves since then. And it has been the bugler's unpleasant task to blow them. The life of a bugler has never been easy. As always, buglers arose before the others, pulled extra duty at ceremonial occasions and, between musical stints, did other tasks.

In the Civil War, buglers and musicians helped surgeons with their grisly work. At other times they were stretcher bearers or fought beside the troops.

It was different after tanks and mechanized equipment began to replace horses, and whistles and hand signals superseded bugles for passing instructions to the troops.

The use of buglers continued into the Indian wars and through World War I, when horses were still important. They were used some in World War II, but other kinds of field communication began to take over.

The instrument itself had undergone changes over the years, but essentially it was a brass tube with a bell on one end and mouthpiece on the other. The tubing was wound around to shorten it and make a handle for easier carrying. Some were almost as big as a baritone horn and others as small as a cornet. Its name was changed to trumpet in 1923. Buglers since have been trumpeters, at least officially.

In 1943, the Army abandoned the traditional brass trumpet and

249

tried an olive-drab plastic model that some trumpeters insisted had a better tone. At least the mouthpiece did not stick to the lips on a cold day. Besides, it saved two pounds of brass for cartridges.

Bugles are still heard at military installations, but they usually are recorded and set to play automatically. Real ones are sometimes used on special occasions, but they are usually the kind with three valves rather than a "tube" with no keys.

No longer is there a trumpeter who can blow 67 different calls and play such ditties as "Rip Van Winkle," "Holy Joe," "Soap Suds Row," "The Colonel's Daughter," "No Slum Today" and "I've Got Three Years To Do This In."

About the Editor

L. James Binder, a native of Michigan, has been editor in chief of *Army* magazine since 1967. A newspaperman before coming to Washington, D.C., he has served in editorial positions with the Associated Press, the *Detroit News*, the *Pontiac Press* (Michigan), and the *Wayne Eagle* (Michigan). His work has appeared in various anthologies and newspapers, including the *New York Times* and the *National Observer*. During World War II, Mr. Binder saw action on a destroyer in the Pacific, and later held a commission in the Army Reserve. A graduate of Central Michigan University, he is married and the father of three sons.